THE REALITY CREATORS

An Epic Fairytale
About Life On Earth

Christopher Hall

Upon a great scene have descended people who've come running to help from the left and the right. No matter how they view the event and from what angle, they all care to be of service. This book is for them.

We are water drops that make up a watershed, a connected flow from the first drop wetting the soil to the millions more that make up a puddle and flow down a ditch to the river and out to the ocean that is all of us. Each little drop is spread out everywhere and is one with all the other drops. Together we float up into the sky, rain down upon the earth, support life, water trees, plants, and animals, and fill the seas in a never-ending cycle.

CONTENTS

THE REALITY CREATORS

CHRISTOPHER HALL

AUTHOR'S NOTE

I always thought arts and agriculture were my callings. I grew up on a farm in Vermont before making my way through an uptight boarding school, a lovely Quaker college, and three surreal years of grad school. These experiences led to my first career as a performing arts producer and designer. There, I began living a mission-driven life in San Diego; years later, I brought that mission to Oregon as a homesteader. Throughout, I have sought to cultivate compassionate social action in all my endeavors. To this purpose, my work has included producing dozens of critically acclaimed performances and festivals, participating in long-term urban redevelopment planning, homesteading, farming, fundraising for the arts, and starting up two farmers' markets. These days I'm engaging the public in water stewardship.

This book is one such endeavor, and I hope to inspire readers to act compassionately. Homesteading has offered me more than a decade to research and explore our society from a distant perch nestled in a rurally isolated and generationally impoverished region. I have approached my critique of society as I would a play script, and this book is the production of it.

I thank Gina LoPreste, who formed the mission to cultivate compassionate social action with me. She choreographed some of our generation's finest works of dance theatre, farms prodigiously, and periodically edited this book. I also thank Robert Hall Sr., who provided copy edits at an early stage, and Drs. John and Christine Gardiner for providing editing as well.

I am grateful for the cursory review in 2012 by a college

friend who said I had written an anti-intellectual treatise. This critique profoundly impacted me over the years as the book evolved. Mindful of his critique, I have explored the tension between a citizenry creating its own reality versus a minority creating it for them. I've also examined whether populism is anti-intellectual (it's not) and if discontent is an ironic trade-off for the comforts of civilization (it is).

Christopher Hall, January 2021

The world is a big place with seven billion inhabitants. Who cares if a wealthy minority of less than one percent wishes to go off on their own and do as they please, living their lives, however, wherever they want, lavished in such extraordinary luxury and opulence that none of the rest of the world's people could ever dream of such an existence?

(If none of us suffered for it, then perhaps none of us would care.)

INTRODUCTION

Reality Creators are oligarchs and plutocrats who own and manage the political economy in every nation on Earth. They are the ruling class. Generally speaking, they are less than one percent of the overall population. They run the private sectors in their capacity as corporate executives and board members and manage the public sectors as political donors, elected officials, theocrats, and high-level appointees. To varying degrees in different nations, the private and public sectors are either distinguished or indistinguishable based on which controls the other or whether there is seamless mutual coordination, respectively.

Together, Reality Creators also manage large swaths of the world through their foreign relations, using financial, diplomatic, colonial, and military means. *Manage, run,* and *control* are euphemisms for a panoply of activities, such as: struggle, fight, horse-trade, negotiate, back-stab, collude, cooperate, consent, equivocate, and in rare instances, conspire. A central tenet of this book is that Reality Creators manage their affairs out in the open, fighting among themselves for control over humanity, land, and resources to secure the peace and stability that wealth and power afford. They have no more inclination to hide their ideas and activities from us than do farmers from their goats.

Reality Creators' hirelings work in the upper echelons of media, military, religion, nonprofits, law (and its enforcement), insurance, think tanks, higher education, pharma, finance, and Big Ag. The most obsequious are lobbyists who surrender allegiance to any Reality Creators they can orbit, both public and private. Most of the hirelings go back and forth through the revolving door between the public and private sectors and across national borders. As such, they also manage public bureaucracies and elected officials' offices. These sycophants are among the wealthiest 10% of the population. They stridently defend their obsequiousness to prevent losing their class position by falling back into the lower ranks of society. The rest of us have virtually no agency to control the political economy or what else goes on in the world; rather, we are mostly participators. If the Reality Creators are the farm owners, then their hirelings are the farmhands, and we are the livestock. This is the real *Agricultural Revolution*.[1]

Reality Creators have contended for centuries that if we give up some of our rights to form their governments and corporations they head, then we shall get equal value in care and comfort from them in return. They call this agreement our *Social Contract*. It's a form of rent we pay, not unlike the deal Medieval peasants had with nobles when they traded in their livelihoods for security on the manor. I compare this arrangement to how my goats have appeared to consent to being fed, fenced-in, and milked on the homestead.

The term *Consent of the Governed* is an idea that has evolved throughout the ages, and it currently sets the parameters for our Social Contract, which is the "civilizing" force to which we consent. More specifically, we submit to two entities best understood as conjoined twins: corporations who provide us what we need in life in trade for the wealth we build for them, connected to governments who manage us with their laws in trade for the votes of political power we give them. It's called the corporate-government complex.

For those few who do well in the system, it's not a bad gig. But for the rest of us, it's not such a good deal because the terms and provisions of the Social Contract have never been as honest or just as we've been told they are. We build more wealth for the Reality Creators than we do for ourselves, and we are subject to their strict laws, rules, and regulations we do not write that benefit them financially more than us. We've lost more control over our lives than we bargained for, and this loss has bred widespread discontent and a predisposition by the populace to be on the defensive. Reality Creators have sought to mollify us by using their corporate media to obscure the irony that discontent is an unfortunate result of the trade-off for the comforts of civilization.[2]

But it's not just the media they use; everything comes into play. The Reality Creators have long since fabricated a fairytale world that has come to feel real and present. Nowadays, we experience and live each day in a virtual, dramatic reality. We participate in a fabricated reality we do not ourselves create. The Reality Creators create it. As a result, we lack the agency to control our lives. It's as if we are actors cast against our will into a fictional play written and directed by Reality Creators who do what they can to prevent us from exiting the stage and going out into the real world of our own making where we can see what's really going on and control our destinies.

This is due to the constant presence of our built environment that continues to ape Disney World architecture. It is also due to the constant stream of fantasia-like advertising on screens, billboards, and business signs; due to the perception that corporations are not only people, but are our friends, family, and emotional partners whom we bring home to live with as paternal suppliers of everything we need in life to survive; due to the persistent narratives in T.V. shows, streaming video content on the web, and movies, all of which are highly engineered to dramatically capture the senses and sensibilities of the populace to direct their acquiescent behavior; and due to the dramatic presentation of news and politics that fabricate the partisanship needed to drive us apart and corral us together.

All that is actually real is hidden behind this scenery. What is real appears unreal, if not impossible to perceive and believe, after so many decades of exposure to the Reality Creators' fictional drama. Generations of residents in the developed and developing worlds haven't lived in the real world for quite some time. Like dreamers, we can't know this until we wake up. This book has one goal: to wake up the populace.

Reality Creators are masters at gaslighting, a term derived from a play and then a 1944 movie, *Gaslight*. Gaslighting is now part of the lexicon psychologists use to describe an abusive act perpetrated by someone who seeks to control others by making them question their surroundings, history, and reality. Without irony, I hope to inspire readers to question their perception of reality and get out of the *Gaslight* of their lives. I call on readers to create reality together instead of obliviously participating in the reality created around them by a self-interested ruling class. This is the only way to push back against the gaslighting abuse described throughout this book.

The Reality Creators critiques the tiny minority of elite, powerful, smart, and wealthy establishment rulers and executives who are highly visible in all that they do. They own and manage the political economy at all levels (city, county, state, national, multinational – public and private) and prevent us from such ownership and management. Critics will say I am positing nothing new and that this activity has been going on for a very long time. They are correct; the time has come for the reality-fiction machine to stop.

Far from calling for a Kakistocracy (a society ruled by its least competent members) or an Ochlocracy (government by mob rule), both of which are simmering dangerously around the globe, I argue instead that we need to control the corporate-government complex more than be controlled by it.[3] We need to decentralize the management in a considerate and level-headed manner. Tearing it down or having it led by folks with few qualifications is unacceptable and disastrous. That said, it is unacceptable for Reality Creators to say that we can't have more agency than we have now.

Far from doing away with our social structure or democratic norms, I vigorously argue for more self-determination; we ought to have more agency in our daily lives. The term *The Tragedy of the Commons* refers to the anarchic behavior of the human herd to destroy the areas where they live and work because no one owns the land and assets; if they did own the land and if it was not held in common by society, the argument goes, then the owners would care for the land and assets, defend them, and protect them. This facile idea has been the reigning argument in favor of private ownership long before it was named in 1968. The details the argument leaves out include what to make of the concentration of ownership in a tiny minority ruling class; that is, what to do when the vast majority of the humans themselves become the over-grazing herd, and the land and assets are held in common by a small ruling class who has run amok over the world fighting among themselves for power and wealth.

Those very few who are established and ensconced in power must let go of their death grip on the political economy and stop fighting the rest of us when we seek greater agency in our lives. The form of social organizing that elevates the populace, the citizenry, is called *populism*. Populism isn't the storm of incompetent mobs we see inadvertently crashing through our social structure like a bull in a china shop; those are fringe fascists looking for despotic, totalitarian dictators to rule over them. The majority of the populace wants the exact opposite of that.

We must create a shared reality based on agreed-upon facts and cultivate compassion in and amongst ourselves to withstand the Reality Creators' efforts to divide and corral us as livestock. We need to create our reality instead of wantonly participating in the one created by the Reality Creators. In so doing, we'll be more likely to build communities from the ground up and replace the unilateral top-down control currently exerted upon us. Discontent is not necessarily the inevitable trade-off for the comforts of civilization; rather, it just seems that way under the Reality Creators' rule.

Too many of us mistake our rote participation in society for agency and don't know what we're missing. This is an acute example of living uncritically in the Reality Creators' fabricated dramatic world – an alternate reality where participation is seen as personal sovereignty. The only way for real democracy to function is when voters have the agency to control the government they elect. The only way for worker-consumers to live freely is when they have the agency to control the corporations needed for survival. Otherwise, they will remain hapless tools as wealth builders for the Reality Creators. Populism is the knowing, honest, and humble effort by the populace to control its destiny. We cannot resign ourselves to being helpless as my goats.[4]

This book reappropriates the term populism from the Reality Creators and their hirelings who defame it. Reality Creators intentionally mischaracterize populism to prevent us from effectively contesting their power. How? They inaccurately portray populism as if it were despotism, autocracy, totalitarianism, or a dictatorship. They deceitfully project fascism onto populists.[5] They falsely claim that democracy and governments are under attack by populists. They do not point to populists for evidence of their claims; instead, they point to self-aggrandizing malefactors. Reality Creators scurrilously ascribe to decent, peaceful populists the work of a few stupid, evil leaders and their angry mobs: for shame!

Reality Creators argue that populists view society in a black and white, *Us vs. Them* dichotomy. How dare they accuse us of the *divide and conquer* strategy they have long since perfected? Populists point out the vast economic inequality that exists today; the simple math is enough for the division between the people and minority elite to be revealed, all on its own. The Reality Creators complain that the populace unfairly denigrates the plutocrats, oligarchs, and their hirelings as "corrupt elites" and that we treat them as an undifferentiated monolith; meanwhile, they call us "the masses." The Reality Creators use sarcasm to belittle our legitimate critique of their rule and cynically suggest we are unfair to them – the gall.

Why are Reality Creators so afraid of the peaceful populace who just want more control and agency in their lives? Because ordinary members of the populace who want more control of the political economy threaten the Reality Creators' long-term neoliberal rule. That's what they're complaining about when they disparage us as unfit to lead ourselves.[6]

Similar to monarchs, Reality Creators don't want to share the power of the throne. To push back, they say we perpetrate terrible acts such as threatening democracy and wrecking *their* government. They deceitfully conflate us with bum-rush mobs and diabolism. For a recent example, the Reality Creators asserted their defamatory claims by calling the mob that attacked the U.S. Capitol populists. This is nonsense; those are not populists. They are fear-driven insurrectionists who pledge allegiance to a wannabe authoritarian-fascist who himself is a truly corrupt elitist.[7]

Reality Creators confer the term *populism* onto malefactors worldwide because it is a word people are still willing to hear in common parlance. Historically, Stalin, Hitler, Franco, Mussolini, Mao, Pol Pot, and others loom so heavily over the past that no one is willing to imagine their successors could be among us in the present or near future. Such terms as despot, autocrat, totalitarian, dictator, and fascist are unthinkable, whereas populism is unobjectionable.

Misrepresenting the term alienates populism from the citizenry and confounds the prospect of our self-determination. Simply put, ruining and defiling the word populism makes it hard for the populace to use. We need to take the word *populism* back. Since Reality Creators control the corporate media, correcting the record is extraordinarily difficult: the vast majority of images and ideas the populace confronts daily come from the most powerful corporate entities lacing the world in a tangled web of dramatic fiction that overwhelms all that we or the natural world have to offer.

The vast majority of citizens across the political spectrum – the real silent majority – just want more involvement in their government beyond voting for Reality Creators to rule over them. We want representatives, not overlords. We do not sufficiently control the governments we elect, nor the corporations for whom we work or from whom we shop. Ours is a struggle to regain control of our governments and livelihoods: this is what populism is, what the populace wants, and what the book argues.

We do not want despotism, autocracy, totalitarianism, dictatorship, and fascism. Indeed, many around the world have had enough of that already. Reality Creators say we threaten society when, in fact, it is the Reality Creators themselves who feel threatened. Their deceit on this matter is a bitter irony: they have used their corporations to control our governments by overwhelming our democracy through campaign financing and lobbying. We reject the gaslighting accusations that we are the very thing we want to escape and that they aren't already doing what they falsely accuse us of wanting to do.

Those who orbit the Reality Creators and provide them obsequious support represent the interests of corporate control of the government; they defame government control by ordinary people. They believe corporate persons should control the government instead of human persons. My argument for populism isn't *The People vs. The Government*; rather, it's the people versus the corporate sector for control of our government. Corporatism is the idea corporations should control the public sector; populism is the idea that people should. Just as mainstream political parties are founded on a bracing form of partisanship, the new realignment of political organizing should be human persons vs. corporate persons.

This book promotes populism from the standpoint that the vast majority of people are kind and decent, smart and disciplined, moral and compassionate.[8] We're not pure; we're poor (the top 20% own 86% of the nation's wealth in the U.S.). When we regard ourselves holding such virtues, we push back against the centuries-long effort to divide and conquer us, no matter our many differences. Our most courageous act is to stand together united by our virtues so we can one day become a countervailing power to the existing rulers who use us for our resource value. Believing that what we have in common is greater than what separates us is populism.

Those in power don't want populism because they would lose power. If we are to ever unite, it will be when we stop going after each other and focus our attention on those who divide us.

Therefore I must say that, as I hope for mercy, I can have no other notion of all the other governments that I see or know, than that they are a conspiracy of the rich, who, on pretence of managing the public, only pursue their private ends, and devise all the ways and arts they can find out; first, that they may, without danger, preserve all that they have so ill-acquired, and then, that they may engage the poor to toil and labour for them at as low rates as possible, and oppress them as much as they please; and if they can but prevail to get these contrivances established by the show of public authority, which is considered as the representative of the whole people, then they are accounted laws...

Thomas More, *Utopia*, 1516

"You are about to be told one more time that you are America's most valuable natural resource. Have you seen what they do to valuable natural resources?! Have you seen a strip mine? Have you seen a clear cut in the forest? Have you seen a polluted river? Don't ever let them call you a valuable natural resource! They're going to strip mine your soul. They're going to clear cut your best thoughts for the sake of profit unless you learn to resist, because the profit system follows the path of least resistance and following the path of least resistance is what makes the river crooked!"

Utah Phillips

PART ONE
What's Going On

"…people of various races, religions, nationalities, who, with all of their differences, have this in common: that they are seeking life, striving to improve the opportunities for its enjoyment, yearning for its enrichment, and, despite the innumerable disappointments which they have suffered in the past, willing to pay handsomely, in vast and patient effort for each tiny gain that they secure."

Scott Nearing, 1922, The Next Step: A Plan
for Economic World Federation.

"The first man who, having enclosed a piece of ground, bethought himself of saying 'This is mine', and found people simple enough to believe him, was the real founder of civil society. From how many crimes, wars, and murders, from how many horrors and misfortunes might not any one have saved mankind, by pulling up the stakes, or filling up the ditch, and crying to his fellows: Beware of listening to this impostor; you are undone if you once forget that the fruits of the earth belong to us all, and the earth itself to nobody.

Jean-Jacques Rousseau, 1754, On the Origin
of the Inequality of Mankind

Economic – Gives You Power
Uneconomic – Gives Others Power

E. F. Schumacher, 1973

CHAPTER ONE

Alpha & Omega

We're now alone on Earth, spinning around in a solar system that's a tiny speck in the galaxy. To some, it might feel as if our ancestors snuck off in the middle of the night like parents abandoning their kids at a forested campsite, and in the morning, we awoke to find ourselves forsaken. But more truthfully, we're the ones who snuck off in a fit of mischief. In the course of our cavalier rebellion, we abandoned their lifestyle and teachings in a great act of impetuosity. Now, eight billion of us are trying to get along on this rock in the solar system, sorting it out on our own. We can do better.

When the world wasn't global, our ancestors kept to themselves in smaller groups. They were self-reliant out of necessity. They were tough, principled, fearless, and competent. Regarding them as savages or indecent brutes is bigoted conjecture. We have a moral responsibility to regard them well. They may also have felt one with the natural world, looking up at the celestial bodies and the vast open space in between, needing few explanations for their direct experiences. They were one with the Earth and cosmos precisely because they did not understand scientific explanations that would have alienated them from everything around them. Even my son once said, "the more I learn, the less I wonder."

Our ancestors lived with a sense of wonder more than we do today. Theirs was a poetic view, whereas ours is a more prosaic view. They connected with the cosmos. We have explained it away, and that's how we came to be alone. This change occurred in various locations over a very long time, ebbing and flowing for tens of thousands of years; then, it picked up steam when technology and the division of labor began permitting some to have power over others in a strategic and political way. It most certainly intensified with colonialism, the Enlightenment of the seventeenth and eighteenth centuries, and the subsequent Industrial Revolution that further concentrated power and wealth into a tinier ruling minority.

Those with the most to lose had the most to fear, so they formed a paternal-political leadership to counteract the growing (evolving) sense of aloneness – that feeling of being lost in the wilderness to which we once belonged. It is not ironic that efforts to control the natural world made our existential problems worse as technology further separated us from Nature. The following example discusses the issue as it played out in the west.

Thomas Hobbes, a political philosopher central to the Enlightenment and the creation of *Social Contract Theory*, argued that our ancestors' lives were "solitary, poor, nasty, brutish, and short." He did not see the beauty in their lives. This discriminatory, ignorant, and irrational phobia persists today: people are terrified of how our ancestors lived before the so-called Neolithic Revolution. This fear is the driving force behind why we have abandoned our ancestors and why we cling to our fragile social structure and police state, feeling alone and scared.[1]

Hobbes and others pushed back against what they perceived was a natural tendency toward disarray; they called nature 'wild.' He and his peers argued that everyone needed to chip in their personal agency to form a government with leaders who would write laws to force us to get along, tamp down the wild, and wall off nature. We'd give up a large portion of our sovereignty to create a more civilized world, what some would call "a city on the hill" for its fortress-like dominance. Hobbes envisioned something else: a *Leviathan*, which is a biblical sea monster. His odd idea was that we'd populate the body and our leaders fill the head. Together, we would all get along under the authority of the beastly entity headed up by the leaders.

Since then, the explanation by Enlightenment thinkers is that we gave up parts of our hearts, minds, souls, spirits, and bodies – our very flesh – to animate the entity and provide the collateral for the terms of our Social Contract. This arrangement was to keep us functioning as organized and civilized labor-consumer-voters and end our nature-borne misery. It has not worked; misery is at an all-time high on our rock in the solar system, particularly for the bottom half of the world's population that is seven times as big as those who suffered mightily during the Middle Ages in Europe. Hobbes' metaphor is fitting given what the monster has done trashing the Earth and how it has digested us in its belly for our energy value over the past 370 years. Matt Taibbi's recent assertion evokes a related image: *"The world's most powerful investment bank is a great vampire squid wrapped around the face of humanity, relentlessly jamming its blood funnel into anything that smells like money."*

Under Hobbes' regime of state rule over individual sovereignty, the Reality Creators civilized humanity through the brute force of their enlightened knowledge. Under their leadership, we built a global world order of unprecedented wealth and power, mostly for their benefit. Along the way, we've increasingly lost personal agency, and our so-called rights have become increasingly alienated from us. The more rights we gave up to the beast they controlled, the more power they aggregated. As a result, we have become utterly reliant on the social, political, economic, and technological forces they manage. Each chapter of this book describes our reliance on these systems we do not control.

To describe the intensity of any Social Contract, one can draw a continuum with anarchy on the low end and communism on the high end. Somewhere in the middle are the capitalists who viciously attack either end of the scale: they found the *laissez-faire* sweet spot where they can express the exact kind of liberty needed to justify extracting our wealth with few regulations. In this middle position, we are, conversely, beholden to the precise amount of laws required to prevent us from pushing back. Capitalists are what Howard Richards calls *Middle-Wing Extremists*. When we stand up for ourselves and challenge the center position by going too far off to the left or right, we come under attack.

The Social Contract has become so binding that we're constrained; the liberté of thought has led to a lack of liberty. Sigmund Freud's final work, *Civilization and Its Discontents*, discusses how people bristle at the Social Contract. It has become clear that not only do we have an unfair, subordinate agreement with our government, but we also have lopsided agreements with the many corporations who provide us everything we need in life in trade for building their owners' wealth. Because Hobbes and other well-intentioned influencers thought we needed a powerful political-economic system to parent and nudge us along, we are ruled by corporate and political leaders who have abused the terms of our Social Contract.

When Reality Creators manufacture our consent, it's not just to play along with their casting, props, and scenery, all dressed up in their costumes to work, shop, and vote for them as their herd of livestock; it's also to consent to the racket in its entirety, including the unfair provisions of the Social Contract they have constantly rewritten without our consent. Their mission has been to gain our consent to give up consent, to vote away the power of our vote. As a result, not everyone is pleased with how our political economy functions because they do not believe the actions of the corporate-government complex are sufficiently justified.[2]

Nudging Us Along

Similar to us, early humans had to sort out *who got what*. The sorting out of *'who'* is a political process, and the *'got what'* is an economic process. Hence the term *political economy*. Getting essentials and holding onto them was hard. A sense of greed would have made it possible to survive, and a sense of love would have made it possible to get along. Their political economy functioned by way of ritual spirit derived from the cosmos imbued in the natural world around them. They didn't try to control the world; instead, they just lived in it. They didn't "other" the natural environment; they were part of it.

There are two models for how political economies work: one where the sorting out of "who gets what" is decentralized, such as theirs, and the other model, where there's a boss or minority in power calling the shots – that's us today. Recently, as our world has become more enlightened, engineered, and global, it has become bossier: our society has reached further around the Earth. A powerful minority intent on controlling everything runs the current version of the political economy right out in the open with little to hide. While many on Earth do not benefit from globalism, no nation on Earth is isolated from the effects of the dominant hegemonic forces of the western political economy. It feels like we cannot escape quantifying the price-value of everything any more than we can get off this rock.

Our political economy forces each to be alone from the other. We haven't a choice but to alienate each other through the process of competition because the social-contractual agreements with our governments and corporations are prejudiced against us, leaving us fighting over crumbs instead of breaking bread with each other. Greed has overcome love, and this imbalance is the most significant negative impact resulting from the Enlightenment. Who would have thought the *Liberty of Thought* would have a downside or that the open-minded ideas of the Enlightenment would be weaponized and applied to greed? Anyone who questions the Enlightenment is called anti-intellectual. Yet, it is the very height of intellectual liberty to question the authority and intent of those who would uncritically celebrate competition, atomize us, and force us to free ourselves from each other as the outstanding achievement of liberty.

To counteract the weaponization of the Enlightenment described throughout this book, consider this metaphor: we are water drops that make up a watershed, a connected flow from the first drop wetting the soil to the millions more that make up a puddle and flow down a ditch, into a creek, that flows to the river, and out into the ocean that is all of us. Each little drop is spread out everywhere and is one with all the other drops. Together we float up into the sky, rain down upon the Earth, support life, water trees, plants, and animals, and fill the seas in a never-ending cycle. Our ancestors are in the ancient forests, deep within the Earth, and at the bottom of the oceans. Our task is to reconnect with them and wonder again.

Each society, tribe, or community throughout time reflects on its circumstance and matures to the extent that its members connect with and grow from previous ancestors. Much of the problem discussed below is about how the Reality Creators further alienate us from our ancestors, nature, and ourselves by fabricating images, signs, and symbols that form a virtual reality that replaces our direct experience on Earth. The Reality Creators manufacture a virtual reality that has the effect of "othering" actual reality: now we live in their world, not ours, and we view actual reality as something untrustworthy.

First is the problem of volume: while there is some

independent media we produce that helps us see ourselves and find our way through the modern wilderness of existential threats, it's only a sliver of real information compared to the juggernaut of profit-driven corporate media that's designed to take up as much of our mental capacity as possible by luring us from our potential to lead independent lives. The plutocrats and oligarchs who own the profit-driven media seek to control us like farmers do their flocks. This assertion is a widely accepted fact; one of the countless examples can be found in the documentary, *The Social Dilemma.*

Second, let's consider the problems we face trying to produce our own stories. Of the media we control, there is a classic problem: in the present moment, we're simultaneously the creator, the subject, and the viewer of the stories we tell. As you can imagine, there's a significant conflict of interest between these three that we must address, and that adds a fourth party to the group, the evaluator. There is also a trade-off for getting self-reflective help now: many argue that contemporary media is the first draft of history, suggesting it's not well-written because the accounts lack critical distance.

Unlike historians, we struggle to stand outside of ourselves and see the world around us in the present. It has always been hard to be audience members for our actions because a conflict of interest bears down on us as the creator: we have a proclivity to spin our messages to our interests. Furthermore, seeing ourselves at the moment turns to narcissism if we aren't looking into the depths from where the surface has arisen.

But our contemporary problem is not only a lack of historical perspective. It's much worse: the Reality Creators who own and control a significant portion of the political economy manage the vast majority of the media for their benefit and thereby supplant the view we would otherwise have of ourselves with a fabricated virtual reality they create. They hijack our story through overwhelming brute force and insert their bogus narrative to interrupt and change the way we live, the way we treat each other, and how we feel about ourselves, all to profit off us.

Those who oversee the government and corporate sectors hire members from the creative class for this purpose. Richard Florida can tell you all about it in his sprawling work, *The Rise of the Creative Class*. If our political economy were a natural setting, then the creatives would be the hired landscapers. (I say this as a member of the creative class who has not yet sold out.) Consolidating media companies into five major corporations has made this possible and made it a lucrative draw for artists who want a good paycheck.

The owner-creator-publisher of the mass media content now sits high among the upper class and falsely depicts the subject to control the viewer. They are distanced like historians, not by time, but by their power, wealth, and class standing. And, because they are distanced, they can perfect their fabrications and test them through market research firms and focus groups. It's because we are all alive at the same moment that they affect us. It's a significant aspect of how the Reality Creators rule. Imagine if historians were alive during the time they wrote and had vast control of the economy and politics: history could hardly be believed; it would be written with a pen wielded like a weapon. So much of our current media is weaponized and used against us; this is the dark side of the Enlightenment.[3]

The adage that the winners write history explains why those who run the political economy own the media and control the social narrative. They fabricate a version of events that reflects their financial interest to shape our views on how to behave in a market-based society. The media is how they do the shaping. They don't want us connecting with our ancestors on our own because they think pre-modern people were brutish and lived uneconomically (for each other). They want us connecting with them, attached in a modern form of servitude. Great wealth is at stake since 70% of the U.S. gross domestic product relies on consumption from them; their profit accumulates by sluicing massive flows of excess capital from our daily lives toward them. The Reality Creators collect the spoils because they are always already the winners.

As a result, they don't tell us what's happening for real about life today inasmuch as they tell us a fictionalized storyline. This dramatic narrative exploits our tribal sensibilities and directs our production of goods and services and our consumptive behavior.[4] What we experience on T.V., social media, movies, and magazines affects us, and we live vicariously in these dramatic screen worlds. Not only do we have a hard time getting a decent contemporary perspective on our reality, as is usual for all societies, but much of our time is also taken up being at once lulled then aggravated to participate in an artificial narrative to work, shop, and waste, all to generate excess capital for those who already have excess capital. In his 1993 book, *The Virtual Community*, Howard Rheingold warns us about this, remarking that: "Attention is a limited resource, so pay attention to where you pay attention."

Programming 70 years of television, 30 years of the internet, and 20 years of smartphones has captured our sensibilities to such a degree we can assert without much hyperbole that our sensibilities aren't exclusively ours anymore. The automatons worried about by Kafka and the loss of humanity in humans by Orwell are no longer fiction. Yet, we live in a fictional world created around us the way artists create stage plays, and our virtual world has come to feel as real as the natural world.

To this extent, they have taken Shakespeare's claim "All the world's a stage" and have fabricated a parallel media world that runs alongside the real world. They are Reality Creators, and the effort is not so much to inform us as to conform us. Until recently, it used to be sufficient to control the land

and the people on it. But with land being such a limited and scarce resource (there'll never be more of it), they had to come up with a new invention. They created an alternate dramatic reality to augment the existing world and have thereby increased the portfolio of their "real estate" holdings. But it's not real property; in the strict sense of the term, it's virtual property.[5]

Unsurprisingly, they also refer to movies, books, and play scripts as property as they do land. They have added to the spatial mass of the Earth. They own this dramatic space, a new virtual reality in which we have become enclosed. They have utilized their prodigious financial resources to build up this artificial world around us like scenery and false walls. Disneyland is an absurd extreme example of what goes on every day in our quotidian lives: we live in a corporate fantasy world. Later on in this book, you may think of it as being put in a box, trapped in their managed market economy, or fenced in.

Historians will write that we were trapped in a fabricated reality we could not control. They will say this was special to our time that we didn't see about ourselves in the present moment. It was not that we couldn't get a good perspective on ourselves like any society has struggled to do; it's that the media frequently wheat-pasted over objective fact with subjective fiction, and we lived in these dramatic worlds. We didn't ask to be cast. It became increasingly difficult to see ourselves if not because of all the false garb,[6] then because they wrote their dramas into our quotidian lives. We could not escape their market-based stories any more than we could escape ourselves. This is what the conflict of interest looked like between the creator-subject-viewer media when we tried to sort it all out.

Subsequently, we didn't see that the corporate media messages directed toward us appealed to our wants and desires, so we were swept up into the thrall of their narrative plot lines. We became confused and thought the media was trying to hold up a true mirror. The chimera we saw seemed real after a while because we became accustomed to the persistent dramatic imagery. The creative class constructed fictional content and passed it off as real mirror images, and this led to our time being called "The Mendacene," named after the word mendacity.

To one degree or another, people mistook subjective reality for objective reality. When they got access to the internet, they held up their cheap broken mirrors that garbled all of this into white noise and social distortion. It's precisely these errors that caused our modern existential crisis described in detail throughout these pages.

Historians will complain that many of the research notes from our time could not be trusted or verified because they were deliberate gross misrepresentations of fact generated by corporate-directed advertising and entertainment media that sought to control our behaviors for financial gain.[7] In too many instances, they will conclude that what actually happened was never told to us, and what was told, never really happened. Upon discovering the few independent professional news reports and archeological finds in sedimentary layers, however, they will be able to confirm that these media fabrications were manufactured to control our emotions and behaviors to direct the flow of our wealth to the capital resources of a small minority of oligarchs and plutocrats who owned and managed the political economy.

They will unearth all the ephemeral crap we bought, and they will pick through the waste of our lives. Historians and archeologists will explain how we did not see the Reality Creators conflate our economic system with democracy and drag ethical notions of freedom, liberty, justice, and equality into the imperative of social responsibility that implored us to work, shop, waste, and fight for the right to enrich them.

Historians will say that too much of the media created varying degrees of fictional reality more than real reality and that it made quite a muddle of things for them to sort out about what happened on the Earth at this time.

They will say we had an even harder time trying to sort it out ourselves in the present moment because the media did not tell us they were misleading us. We frequently lost track that we were living in such a dramatic reality. Hundreds of millions of people in the developed world, perhaps much more in the developing nations, lived daily without questioning the big picture of their lives: what were we all wasting for? It was as if we were in a dream state but didn't know we were dreaming.

That is our contemporary period, and this book is about waking up, gaining control of the narrative, and getting back to what's real. It is not too late to regain control over our lives because there are still independent, professional media outlets that strive to be heard among the din of advertisements, infotainment fantasy, and internet crackpots. When removed from this mind-altering substance that has our society in the grips of a hallucination, withdrawals are not unbearable despite extraordinary screen-addiction rates.

Despite the doom and gloom about what the historians may write, we still have a chance to change their future historical narrative. We, too, can create reality by ignoring the media's fantasy, by telling our own true stories, and by living our own real lives. We can change the history they would otherwise write, and that is our task: to go back in time to the actual reality that we are in now and change the way historians will write about us in the future. We need to go back to the present that is real.

We see our modern era in the fine-grain detail created by the never-ending media streams of advertising, T.V. shows, movies, social media, radio, the internet of everything, news, and editorial reports. We learn about our lives through books, magazines, performances, artwork, scholarly papers, scientific and technological progress, religions, education, and music. Too much of this comes to us as we stare down at our phones or into other screens. We look at the world in which we live through a device, or as philosophers said back in the old days, we see reality through a veil: it's a version of the world, but not the world itself. (Indeed, it is now the case that the object itself is also veiled.) If we are to be true to ourselves, we need to control the world we see with greater sovereignty and agency, and that starts right here at our feet.

Before the modern era, our experience with the world was much more earthy, direct, and tactile relative to our lack of technology. Even more recently, in the vast expanse of rural areas where people lived before WWI, there were few media outlets besides religion, word-of-mouth, rarified libraries for the literate, and scraps of newsprint. In the cities, the media told details about society that were accessible to the educated class. For the most part, the circumstance of the lives of those in the past was hyper-local. It was right there at their feet. They could feel it, see it, and hear it for themselves: it was their objective reality. No one had to tell them what was going on in the world; they were already there, right in the middle of it.

Today, if we want to know the weather, we look it up on our phones instead of looking out the window or even going outside. The modern era saturates us with interpretations of our reality, rich and poor alike, rural and urban. The myriad ways we learn about ourselves today are through the subjective lenses controlled by experts who zoom in with their point of view and focus their devices on us to shape messages that are suggestive in ways that benefit them at our expense, literally.

Despite the preponderance of misrepresentations about our lives produced by those with a financial interest in our human resources (coupled with how hard it is to escape these loaded messages), there is hope. When we see, feel, and hear for ourselves, our experience does not always align with what they tell us. This is becoming an increasing source of tension in society today; however, we can resolve the tension by sorting through our reality as evaluators. It is an expression of our power and agency when we express this quality.

Too frequently, corporate media experts lull us into thinking that we should not trust what we see, hear, and feel for ourselves and convey that our objective reality cannot be as genuine or exciting as their subjective reality. We should push back against such manipulation. Of course, there needs to be a balance of learning from our own experience and others because we live in a global, high-tech, connected modern world that conducts a lot of international trade.

Learning about the world beyond our own direct experience is always essential. Yet we must do it with a critical eye since too much of the media is untrustworthy and corrupts what is real. In our modern era, too much of the focus is on learning from the media owners who manage our political economy for their benefit. Too few of us can afford beautiful and enlightening liberal arts educations that teach us to think analytically, synthesize responses to those analyses, and, therein, question the corporate media and political machinations.

The disjunction between what we see in the media and what we would otherwise experience for real is greater today than ever before. Consider how we live in neighborhoods with a mix of people who share various political and religious views and our kids who run around inside each others' homes as if they live in them all. When we turn to the media, we're told about issues that divide us; we see ads that patronize us and insult our intelligence; we're told we don't emulate our neighbors' purchases enough; we see politicians for whom we voted telling us our neighbors are our enemies: we are flat out lied to.

We endure the incongruence between what we hear, see, and feel for real and what we are told by those who financially benefit from producing a false narrative of who we are and what our life is like. We have become so inured to the gross misrepresentations of our lives in the media that we take these false portrayals for granted and don't always see them as betrayals of our conscience, spirit, and character. While we see frothing mouths from the left and right on T.V., we stand politely in line to vote and hold the door open for each other in public. We share meals. We root for the same teams. We work together. And we shop together. Our great American tradition is getting together around holidays knowing there will be friends and family members with different opinions. We love each other, we argue, and we get along: this is what makes us great.

Opposites still attract no matter what they tell us. What we have in common matters more than anything else. Common decency still exists, no matter what they tell us. We are kind, gentle, and caring people. The story that lies ahead is about how we are not free from an overwhelming force that creates the reality of our lives, preventing us from creating our own reality.

That overwhelming pressure and force smothering us is the political economy: it is the alpha and omega of society. It shouldn't be, but it is. This source of power controls how we live from day to day. Each chapter of this book explains what the owners and managers of the political economy have done and are doing to us so that you can become empowered to create your reality, tell your own stories, and trust in yourself to cultivate a life of your own making.

"Formerly there were those who said: You believe things that are incomprehensible, inconsistent, impossible because we have commanded you to believe them; go then and do what is unjust because we command it. Such people show admirable reasoning. **Truly, whoever can make you believe absurdities can make you commit atrocities.** *If the God-given understanding of your mind does not resist a demand to believe what is impossible, then you will not resist a demand to do wrong to that God-given sense of justice in your heart. As soon as one faculty of your soul has been dominated, other faculties will follow as well. And from this derives all those crimes of religion which have overrun the world."*

Voltaire, "Questions sur les miracles" (1765)

"Dividing the American people has been my main contribution to the national political scene since assuming [the Vice Presidency]... So that there can be no misunderstanding about my feelings on this subject, I not only plead guilty to this charge, but am somewhat flattered by it."

Vice President Spiro Agnew one month before
the 1972 Presidential election

"The supranational sovereignty of an intellectual elite and world bankers is surely preferable to the national auto-determination practiced in past centuries.

For more than a century, ideological extremists at either end of the political spectrum have seized upon well-publicized incidents to attack the Rockefeller family for the inordinate influence they claim we wield over American political and economic institutions. Some even believe we are part of a secret cabal working against the best interests of the United States, characterizing my family and me as 'internationalists' and of conspiring with others around the world to build a more integrated global political and economic structure – one world, if you will. If that's the charge, I stand guilty, and I am proud of it."

David Rockefeller, Memoirs, 2003

CHAPTER TWO

Reality Creators

There aren't many works on how our political economy negatively impacts people.[1] For members of a society to comprehend how their political economy functions and what it does to them, they need greater exposure to the subject. A small fraction of the media saturation telling us what to buy and consume would be more than sufficient. This book concerns people in the developed and developing worlds directly and indirectly concerns people in the undeveloped world insofar as they are impacted by the former two.

The political economy is the corporate-government complex that sorts out where everything comes from that we need to live and delineates who gets more or less of that stuff. Those who can control the political economy get more of that stuff, are fabulously wealthy, and do what they can to remain that way. No one wants to fall backward in the class structure, especially those who have the most to lose. The people who own and control our political economy are Reality Creators, and they want to retain the power to shape our society and the way we live our lives.

We need to create our reality as well by imagining what's happening to us. We must go beyond the thrall of media and assert what's real in our lives. Only then will we overcome our station as participating humans and become creators. To the extent that creativity separates humans from other animals, it has also been what separates us from the Reality Creators.

Being told fabricated narratives by those who create our reality must be met with the force of our own creative capacities. This requires first coming to accept certain truths we have not been able to discern among the overwhelming blather of the media world, the dramatic world, the mad world we live in today.

Here's one such truth. We have a common existential problem that is so ubiquitous we take it for granted or don't notice it: we rely on large corporate entities to exist day in and day out for all that we need to survive, both directly and indirectly. A big "So what?" you might think. There is no current alternative to living our lives now, which is the greatest constriction to our liberty today in the developed world.

But what about small businesses? Do they not rise up and overcome? There are a substantial number of them, right? Aren't they independent? Yes, small businesses are us, the commoners, left to navigate the market system at our own risk. Far from overcoming, many small businesses are overwhelmed. Large corporations supply small businesses with goods and services and set the prices, political rules, and regulations they must follow. Where do small businesses get their wholesale goods and services from? How are supplies and energy delivered to them? Who controls the burdensome regulations they must follow?

Small businesses struggle under the system run by the owners and managers of the political economy the same as individual persons do. Small businesses don't plan and control the political economy with politicians as big businesses do; instead, they are subject to unfairly manipulated market forces that are hardly wild or free. Today, many economists believe the free-market is a relic of the past, a neoclassical fairytale we keep hearing about in the media. A so-called free-market is an impossible ideal in the face of such significant influence and power wrought by those who financially benefit from manipulating it.

Our social structure, as such, binds us into rote, ongoing participation. The political economy owners don't see it as a problem; they see it as their income, a secure receivable account since we all must participate. They provide us our goods, services, and jobs; we work and shop, and they profit from both activities, coming and going. When they make money, they make it from us. Their wealth has not ever come from anywhere else.

This racket is possible because they also control our government, passing laws to ensure that our day-to-day survival enriches them efficiently and without interruption. We do not control the government we elect; we never have. The terms of our Social Contract have been breached. The private and public sector elite work seamlessly together to run a big farm, with us being their livestock who have no real say in the matter. Perhaps you think this is hyperbole or disrespectful. I argue it is not, no matter how cynical it appears. Throughout the ages, we have been compared to animals, particularly livestock. Instead of being abused as animals, we should take that reference back into our hands and own it; take back the power of that analogy. We are, indeed, animals. St. Francis of Assisi would approve.

When the farmer sells a side of goat at the farmers' market, does he go back to the homestead and pay the surviving goats the money? No, he keeps it for himself. The money flows to the capital interest of the farm and the farmer, not to the workers who produce the meat. My goats wouldn't know what to do with dollar bills; they'd try to eat them, increasing the value of their flesh to no avail. The wealthy owners of the corporations and their siblings in government think we don't know what to do with money. They think we'll waste it on ourselves no better than if we were buying bread to feed the pigeons resulting in fat birds like the famous scene from Mary Poppins.

Reality Creators hire us to work for them and then they sell to us back what we need to live at the end of the day after we spent eight hours providing all those services and building all those goods. They believe it is wasteful to direct any more capital toward us than necessary to show up to work the next day and shop. They want all the excess capital for themselves. As a farmer, I take the least amount of money from selling the side of goat at the farmers' market to buy hay for the goats to eat, and I keep the rest of the capital for myself.

I spent time growing up on a farm as a kid and spent my recent past homesteading. These two experiences book-end the two-decade stretch of my life in between as a city-dweller. I have always lived like others, and upon reflection, I realize that rural homestead farming is not much different than suburban and urban life. A friend said to me, "Chris, we just play farm." What he meant is that no matter how close to the Earth we get, no matter how deep we dig our fingers into the dirt, we're never further away from modern life than anyone else. Our political economy is inescapable like a fenced-in pen, and its reaches are worldwide.

The Family

Before going any further, I want to dispel a conventional notion that politicians are necessarily independent people who periodically do favors for corporate leaders who return those political favors through all manner of campaign financing and perks. Indeed, most politicians and wealthy private interests are part of one extended and enmeshed community who work together seamlessly on their respective duties within the political economy. Some switch back and forth between public and private sector positions in what has been called the revolving door. In many cases, it's an open breezeway, and as they continue to renovate, it's becoming an open arena.

What appears to us as inappropriate favors are the gifts they exchange, just as any family shares gifts. We fixate on these tokens thinking erroneously they matter to the big picture. These mean virtually nothing in the scope of the global political economy they manage. To them, petty corruption is like getting a penalty for putting their hands on a soccer ball. When it comes to a quid pro quo, it's not gifts or petty corruption that counts; rather, it's seamlessly working together to run the political economy, mostly by competing against each other, but also less frequently, by working alongside each other when it suits them.

Occasionally, we see government agencies coming down on corporations and corporations standing up to government intrusion into their businesses here and there. In these specific occurrences, it appears as if we live in a system of checks and balances. Teddy Roosevelt did smash the monopolies a century ago. But this apparent righteous judicious activity is a tiny fraction of all that goes on. It represents minor turf battles between the operators. Generally, we see politicians and corporate leaders working and squabbling together to manage us while we dutifully go to work for them, shop from them, and then cast our votes for them. We shall not overcome through such participation. There are ordinary people like us who have managed to get into various positions within the political economy. However, we've been unable to compete for power in a manner that has a persistent material effect on our society. We'd notice the result by now if there were one.

The U.S. government is a public sector corporation,[2] not unlike private sector corporations. It competes to be the biggest, most successful corporate entity in the world. In their own way, all other nations want similar success as do multinational corporations who compete as peers. For example, Apple is larger than 80% of all nations. Microsoft, Amazon, Alphabet (Google), and others are right in the mix. Most nations get their power from citizens who vote their support; others get their popular support by authoritarian means. All nations have a monopoly on taxing their people and forcing them to war. The private sector corporations operate slightly differently; they charge money for goods and services for profit. They, too, get citizens to vote, but with dollars instead of ballots.

To fully appreciate the notion of the Reality Creators,[3] we need to see them at the individual level and in the aggregate, where we zoom in and then zoom out to see the whole. They comprise a gestalt; the Reality Creators' overall effect as a group is greater than the mere sum of what its members would do individually. When we look at the individual members, we will see well-intentioned humans who believe in democracy, corporate governance, equality of the law, justice, freedom, liberty, apple pie, and baseball games. They will appear kind, generous, and willing to help serve on soup kitchen lines. They will dress down and attend state fairs.

The corporate executives will talk about bringing good things to life, doing no evil, and doing god's work. They will say we deserve a break today, that we can have it our way, or offer us trays of cake. They will want to connect us to our friends. They will provide us goods and services we need, and we will appreciate them for that. We'll identify with their brands, wear their images and logos, and feel a sense of pride when others see us making such smart, discriminating, and enlightened choices. We will have countless bumper stickers and window decals advertising corporations and politicians. We'll view them as we do sports teams with which we identify: we'll cheer them on in large parades and public rallies, copying the media's dramatic soft drink ads we see in which a protester hands a riot cop a cola.

A gestalt is a whole or unified entity that did not exist until its parts came to be glued together, so we don't see the parts anymore and only see the whole. A gestalt feels like magic to this degree. It's the sound of music when you can't hear the individual parts. And so it is with the Reality Creators:

individually, they are decent, hardworking elite leaders who proclaim great ethical notions and aspirational visions for our society. But, taken as a whole, the cohort is an oppressive, controlling mass lording over our lives for the sole purpose of extracting our excess wealth of body, mind, and spirit. It is precisely the competition between them fighting over us that makes their rule impossibly difficult to abide by. And it is the mass, this uncontrollable whole, that goes up against the free-market economy and just sits on it.

Most Reality Creators do not see themselves contributing to such a powerful, all-consuming entity because they are lost in the wilderness of the whole that is bigger than themselves. Tell them it is so, and they will vigorously deny it because they may not even know they are part of the whole. The prescient are aware and simply lie convincingly. The nature of the corporate-government complex is that no one is in singular control; it is its own being, fluid, dynamic, amorphous, and suffocating. No one member is responsible for what it does: they are only culpable together as a single unit.

There is no countervailing power to rule over the Reality Creators and reel them in, control their impulses, and force a moral code and ethical system onto them. As a whole, they cannot police themselves any more than an army can defeat itself and still be an army. We, the people ironically called *the masses*, are not capable of prevailing over the power gestalt. We are atomized, splintered, distributed against one another: we are not ourselves a political gestalt and cannot, therefore, be a countervailing power. We are not part of a whole greater than ourselves, but rather are ourselves apart from everything else. The Reality Creators keep us apart from each other to prevent us from forming into a countervailing power. This is the most significant breach of the terms of our Social Contract.

Importantly, we should note that there are few meaningful and substantial differences between the red and blue clans (political parties) as they otherwise promote in their media. They are distinguished only by the particular methods they use in farming. This is a controversial statement because we can plainly see what many consider significant differences: down the river, one kind of farmer likes to push for more milking and less hay, while the other farmer up-stream thinks a bit more cud-chewing time and petting will make the farm run more smoothly. Despite these differences, we can tell what unites them by what they do not fight over: one way or another, they are going to run the farm and milk the goats. In the U.S., this debate has been settled since May 9, 1865, the end of the Civil War.

The differences we see among these teams are mostly the wedge issues they argue about on how to manage the various aspects of the political economy. While these wedge issues are important and attract all of our attention, we ignore the more important and consequential fight among themselves over the wealth we build for them. We get wrapped up in the details of their show-boating wedge issues arguing taxation, immigration, healthcare, climate change, abortion, guns, interest rates, CEO pay, trade deals, tariffs, growth, and war. Strategically, these issues are meant to never get resolved. We struggle to step back and look at the big picture: their fight over the wealth we create for them and how that negatively impacts us. If we had more agency controlling the government we elect, not only would we keep more of the value we create, we would also seek to resolve the wedge issues instead of constantly making them worse. The wedge issues were never as bad as they have become in the past 50 years.

The most striking example is how we get swept up in their arguments over climate change while we go about using their wasteful out-dated technology just so they can profit from our labor and consumption functions in the short-term. One side denies there is sufficient scientific evidence to prove the climate is changing. Some admit there is change but no evidence that humans are the cause. Most claim the evidence is overwhelming and irrefutable that humans have caused the climate to change beyond a point of no return. Of this majority, many say they'd rather just adapt to climate change than try to reverse it. We stand on the sidelines picking sides for whom to believe since we don't conduct the research ourselves; meanwhile, they go about fighting among themselves for the spoils of how to capitalize on this critical problem. The blues want to make money retooling the global energy production sector, while the reds want to stampede to the melting Arctic Circle for the effervescent energy resources coming up from the thawing permafrost. We lack agency in this debate, evidenced by how nothing has substantially changed since it started. Yet, we are 99% of the population contributing to the issue.

With this in mind, it doesn't matter who has the upper hand in the political economy at any given moment. Our collective experience has not ever been substantially better or worse in a persistent way. No matter whose hue is in control among the factions of politicians and executives, half of us will always cheer them on while others will complain; meanwhile, they go about extracting our wealth with impunity. The fallout is our lack of agency to shape the world we live in by any other than inadvertent means or under the direction and control of a very small minority, the Reality Creators.

The lack of consensus on support for our political and corporate rulers belies partisan arguments that our overall experience is substantially and persistently better under the control of one or the other political paradigm. Our experience is deeply compromised under both. Today, no one is happy about any of it. Because the prominent wedge issues preoccupy and divide us, the critical concern related to their fight over accumulating our wealth continues apace. This is the core problem we face today. If we could get them to stop fighting over us, the world would be a better place for all because we could have a better chance at meaningfully addressing the wedge issues. Instead of being preoccupied with the nature of the *wedge*, we could find common ground by focusing on what we have in common more than what separates us. The only way out is for us to become creators of our reality together.

To frame the big picture about our lack of personal and civic agency are the words of Walter Lippmann, one of the most important political writers of the twentieth century: "The public must be put in its place…so that each of us may live free of the trampling and the roar of a bewildered herd." And this: the herd must be ruled by "a specialized class whose interests reach beyond the locality."[4] In this statement, "each of us" refers to the Reality Creators, and we are the herd they need to manage. By putting us in our place, Lippmann means dividing us up and preventing us from moving like a giant mass. On the public sector side, they manage us by writing laws. On the private sector side, they feed and entertain us, inspire us to hand riot police refreshments, show up to work on time, and shop 'til we drop. Social Contract, indeed.

The Goats and the Deer

There are two circumstances that corporations have developed over the past couple of centuries that have inadvertently abridged our agency more than at any time in the past: we are reliant on the amazing technology they have developed and on the extreme division of labor they have mastered to run their systems efficiently. No one believes the owners and managers of the political economy originally envisioned that these circumstances would play into their favor as structural controls over the worker-consumers. But since events evolved over the years as they have with less self-reliance and greater specialization, the Reality Creators eventually took note and began to use technology and our division of labor to herd us more productively.

First, we rely on the successful functioning of modern technology to survive throughout the day. Our survival requires electricity and petroleum. Who can think of anything they do in which technology didn't come between their body and the Earth? What items don't travel on tractor-trailer trucks or in shipping containers? What services don't rely upon industrial energy sources? Look around at all aspects of your life and note the things you made by hand directly from the Earth compared to those items you purchased from a store. Even backyard garden vegetables have products such as seeds, soil, hand tools, well pumps, fuel, fertilizer, trips to the store, and many other industrial goods and services.[5] Penned up, my goats require similar technology to survive. They would die without water and feed, and their lives would be miserable without shelter: they do not live freely like the deer who stare at them through the fence.

The second concern is far from new and has been vexing us for a long time. In our political economy, we rely upon an extreme division of labor where others do necessary activities that create the goods and services we need to live. The parts others contribute are so specific that no one person has possession of the whole process. Instead of working on a project from start to finish, items come to us made by others, and we assemble them. Or the items are ready to use and consume. A person assembling a structure from industrial building materials and using modern power tools relies on an extraordinarily long stream of complex processes the carpenter, electrician, plumber, and equipment operator never see.

Far too many people around the world unanimously celebrate the atomization of labor without question. If there ever was too much of a good thing, it's our extreme division of labor and the world-wide unanimous consent of how useful it is. A reasonable division of labor makes for a great diverse culture, but our extreme division is the height of reckless codependency. We are so enmeshed that we believe self-reliance is getting a job from a boss who rents us for eight hours per day and then shopping from him to buy those things back. Without high modern technology working near-perfectly, our extreme division of labor would be impossible.

How can you tell when there has been too much of a division of labor? When it becomes apparent that we lack real-world living-on-Earth skills and are competent at only one or a few tasks that technology has yet to usurp. Another metric is how much technology does for us to the extent we couldn't survive without it. The more skills we lose to technology and the division of labor, the more dependent and fragile our lives and society become.

All this is made more worrisome because we depend upon the few less-than-one-percent Reality Creators to manage this technology and the extreme division of labor. Since they own and control the political economy, they are responsible for keeping it going in ways we cannot: no one ever blames the livestock for why the farm failed. The ruling class will keep the political economy up and running so long as the excess capital keeps flowing towards them, so long as the farm is profitable. They own the corporations that hire us, that tell us what to buy, and sell us what we need to survive. They own the banks and the monetary system that bale and deliver the hay. They control the political system that manages us and oversees the necessary resource wars and global trade. And they know we're hooked on it all. Our social structure is fragile, and criticizing its complexity has been met with much derisive criticism. We have an existential problem because we can't readily address how the political economy negatively impacts our existence.

The essential core of our freedom is limited, but an alternative to this system's structure could come at significant risk to our welfare. What if the goats can't live like the deer? In this book, expect to be alerted to this problem, but not so much about solving it right off the bat. (Chapter nine offers a longer discussion on this topic.) It would be ironic to argue that any one person has a solution to a problem that stems from too few persons in leadership positions. What you will hear is this: be your own creator; create your truth; believe in what's there at your feet; tell your stories; reject *ad hominem* attacks from those who say you can't or shouldn't create your reality because you're too uninformed, too incompetent, or can't be trusted to know what's right for yourself and others. Together we can support each other in this effort to live with greater agency. We need to be the creators of our social structure, the builders of our own house. We have lost the skills that our ancestors worked hard to preserve for us so we could hand them down through the generations. Now what we have to offer is artificial intelligence, robotics, and fabricated media narratives that misrepresent reality, all set in the context of a wasting world.

Until recently, our ancestors depended on the rains and the vagaries of the natural world to find shelter, food, and security. They succeeded despite how hard life was. Since the Industrial Revolution, we now rely upon artificial systems to provide all that we need in life to live. The trade-off for a comparatively easy life is a proportionate lack of control over it. These modern systems are fragile, not just because their continued operation is still dependent upon the unpredictable natural world, but more importantly because hardly anyone knows how to do much more than their one specific day-job, an occasional hobby, how to drive, and how to shop. The conventionally wise cheer an ever-increasing division of labor and deride those who are jacks of all trades for being masters of none. This sarcastic criticism is as dangerous as it is ignorant.

I do not like the idea of the "push the one red button" specialized job no matter how detailed, intellectual, and challenging it is. Nor have I liked that I must shop for all I need in life after leaning on the button all day long. It isn't that I don't like work or shopping, although I admit to having felt caged by the modern workplace and awkward pushing my little wheeled prison-box around in front of me at department stores. I feel trapped. Where can I get all I need if not from the company store? I can't get it from the natural world as it was for a long time in previous generations. Now my essential supplies must come from the owners' modern stores.

To the skeptics, recall, small businesses get their raw and wholesale goods from big corporations, as they do their energy supplies. They are subject to punishing political regulations imposed upon them by the lobbyists working for such corporations. They are subject to fiscal and monetary policies they do not control. They provide services that require the support of infrastructure well beyond their means. Small businesses are us; too often, we're regulated out of business or swallowed up in the course of industry consolidation.

If we can't get what we need or want from a store – any store – we cannot get it, no matter what "it" is. This is the core problem of people who work but still struggle financially through life. Never before in history has this been the case for such a large general population, except, of course, for slaves, serfs, and oppressed subjects of dictators. Adherents to conventional wisdom don't want to talk about the drawbacks of the Industrial Revolution, our modern social structure, and technology. Too much is going unsaid: we'll never hear about this in their media, so it's up to us to become the evaluators and promote our perspective.

Sages say, "write about what you know." Well, I was born into this world "as it is." Working my days to buy processed food, fuel, and toilet paper has been a big part of my life, like millions of others in the developed world. Several generations have passed, and now we don't know how to get by on our own anymore. We lack the living-on-Earth skills and have begun to hand these skills to intelligent machines owned by an extreme minority. Who owns the livestock, the hired hands for eight hours per day, and the robots? We need to shed our participating shells and inhabit our selves ourselves.

Throughout these pages, I have been cavalier about issues that people take seriously: their position, condition, and station in life. No one likes being called a dependent farm animal, a psychopathic boss, or Bigfoot. Nor do they appreciate being told that working a full-time job they struggled to get to buy shelter, processed food, and toilet paper is not freedom. We live in a world built around us that has limited choices. *Choice Architecture* is an Orwellian term that describes how we are given a box in which to make decisions – Orwellian because the box is the ultimate control we cannot escape.

Please understand I have tried not to make these circumstances personal. Still, I can see how impossible it is not to experience pain when describing normal social behaviors and activities with such apparent disdain: we work, we pay, we pollute. We do not control our lives beyond the simple boxes we are put in, whether playpens, school boxes, work boxes, home boxes, shop boxes, prison boxes, or the boxes created by the streets that look like fences. We don't control the production of goods and services upon which we rely. Frighteningly, it appears that the political and economic systems are *Too Big To Control*, even for the few bosses.

In this book, I relate our history, our present moment, and our future from the perspective of the losing end by describing present daily life as a constant state of loss and the future as a landscape made up of all that we have lost and have yet to lose. In this story, we'll learn about a great fraud: how our lives came into debt through the development of an extreme, unsustainable division of labor where we each owe the other our part of the whole to a fault, how our lives have become indebted to the work done for us by technology to a fault, and how we are in arrears to the minority owners who view our labor as their capital, a debt they force us to pay off five days per week.[6] By all accounts, the Reality Creators have defaulted on the provisions of the Social Contract and prejudiced our standing by belligerently forcing us into their debt.

We are all part of a giant co-dependent society, and that's exciting, awesome, terrifying, and down-right unsustainable. Without it, we wouldn't have rock 'n roll or rocket science. Nor would we have nuclear weapons, toasters, a changing climate, and extreme economic inequality. Telling my version of our story is the least I could do, as many others have done in the past.

From the earliest times, grandma sat with the kids around the campfire and told them stories, and through the ages, these stories evolved with the times. However, one thing has never changed and has been the same throughout all generations. It is the germ at the center of the seed of all these stories: here is the story of *The Reality Creators*.

Reality Creators

Reality Creators have been around since the beginning of civilization.[7] They're the folks who came up with the Social Contract and set the terms of the agreement. They are in charge of everything, except, perhaps, at which department store we choose to push around our shopping cart, which political team we root for, or which red button we'd like to press all day. The Reality Creators shape the media that directs and informs these meager choices of ours.

Here's what a Bush political strategist said to Ron Suskind during an interview in 2004:

> That's not the way the world really works anymore," he continued. "We're an empire now, and when we act, we create our own reality. And while you're studying that reality judiciously, as you will we'll act again, creating

other new realities, which you can study too, and that's how things will sort out. We're history's actors...and you, all of you, will be left to just study what we do.[8]

Among the Reality Creators, there are many different personalities, each with considerable power to control. In this cohort are competing interests and power-plays: kin, friends, and colleagues will behave in ways that look like sibling rivalry. Some are sworn enemies, others are warring clans, and all will shift alliances as they please.

Reality Creators are not uniform. They are creative and competitive in their effort to run the private and public sectors. The world is a big place, and there are many competing factions among them, yet they're all working toward the same goal: personal wealth and power by controlling the land and the people on it. Just because they are all after the same goal does not mean they are necessarily conspiring together; indeed, they are competing with each other. Each, in their own way, fights over the spoils and argues how to go about running the political economy.

This racket was going on in Europe for a thousand years among the kings, lords, dukes, nobles, and their in-laws: they were all upper-class scrambling for the power and wealth that comes from land allotments and the peasants that go with them. Shakespeare's history plays and tragedies are not about history and tragedy as much as they are about the infighting among the Reality Creators over labor and land use policies.

In 1922, in his work, *The Next Step: A Plan for Economic World Federation*, Scott Nearing put it this way:

"Whether the object of the contest be trade, markets, investment opportunities or resources, the result is the same —rivalry, antagonism, bitterness, hatred, conflict. Probably it is fair to say that these economic rivalries constitute the largest single force now operating to keep people apart and to continue the economic desolation and chaos under which the world is suffering."[9]

One symbolic example of this struggle is the Ivy League rivalry, especially when they play their football games, which symbolize the elite's fight to control the lands and labor of the people who watch their struggle and then visit such strife upon each other in the stands. Buying tickets to watch grown men fight over the ball is a participatory activity similar to how we vote and purchase against our interests and then watch what happens. Pretty much everything the Reality Creators do is right out in the open: there is no conspiracy of a secret cabal; on the contrary, they build stadiums, lazy-boy chairs, and run the media to put it all out there right in front of us just how they want us to see it. Watching governments and corporations go up against each other is no different than watching football games with cheering citizens and brand lovers cheering from the stands. They all fight over political and economic power that is ours to start with.

But what about the activities we know that are protected by intellectual property laws and are classified as secret by the government? Why is there a constant effort to cast sunlight on so many activities that are not apparent or are over our heads? What is it about the gulf of awareness, the intellectual distance, that exists between the populace and the Reality Creators that's arguably the same relationship as that between the farmer and the goats? The important distinction to make is that the Reality Creators are out of the closet about being the owners and managers of the political economy. They are not a secret faction or a cabal as many mistakenly allege. But they do exist on a higher plane and operate in ways we do not perceive: some of their work is simply incomprehensible to us.

Their ideas are often way over our heads in the flies, or beneath the boards, under our feet. Put another way, we have no idea what is said inside the football huddle or the signs at first base. There is little effort made by the Reality Creators to hide them because we can't see or hear what's being said. Because we are always playing catch up trying to figure out what they are doing, we never quite get ahead of what's happening to us. We experience their presentation of reality and react to their fabricated world without much agency to create it ourselves. The goats see what the farmer is up to; his actions impact their lives, but they can do little about it.

Reality Creators manage the populace in the same way that George Orwell put it. The pigs, sheep, and cows, the chickens, horses, and dogs usually have no idea what the farmers are up to, what they think about the animals' lives, and what the long-range strategic plans on the farm are. For example, when the smart pigs get their chance at wielding power and running the farm operations, they exercise authority over the lesser animals by similar means. Farmers have always been intellectually distant from their flocks.

The reason to cast sunlight on what's going on is to have more agency in our lives. In the new "Reality-Based Community," where working people chase down the Reality Creators, trying to expose these activities using hard evidence alone, it is always after a long term of discovery that they gain any traction. Evaluation is expensive and hard to conduct. The creative plans that the Reality Creators execute at all levels seem to be a few steps ahead of us, including the best researchers. There are some strategies and game plans we will never discover. There needs to be equal parts art and science that we engage, fathoming the ways and means of the Reality Creators. We need to wonder what's going on while we sort through all the hard data. As Jessamyn West said: "Fiction reveals truths that reality obscures."

The Reality Creators sit around and come up with ideas that are creative as the day is long. For example, their exotic financial bets use fiction as collateral. They creatively write and pass laws. They make up legal decisions in the courts as they please. They are endlessly inventive at making goods and services, then artfully directing us on what and how much of their stuff to buy. Their excuses for war, peace, and trade change repeatedly. They come up with reality as playwrights do. They are selling out at the box office, with most of us buying their fabrications in the mainstream media. A fundamental assertion of this book is that it takes too long to realize what is happening to us, and it's good when we figure some of it out. But we need to get ahead of them. We need to more effectively distinguish how their dramatic subjective reality becomes our daily objective reality.

Professorial and journalistic allies in the greater-than 99% tattletale on what they figure out the Reality Creators are up to, though it's not clear what they miss. At times their data-based research about what they discover is so shocking it can sound fictional. We write them off. As Mark Twain is misquoted to have said, "It's easier to fool people than to convince them that they have been fooled." (Not ironically, it's almost impossible to correct the record on this quote.)

Seeing what's going on is hard when the political economy's machinery is not apparent or when the media obscures it. Even our smartest allies in academics, politics, and independent journalism cannot figure all of it out through their reverse engineering of this reality. What can we do? We can imagine what they do to us while also studying hard professional evidence.

Hard facts are the highest moral good, but we've all heard the cliché before: if you sense it's going on, others have already thought the same and put it into practice; we find out about it after the fact. To stay abreast, we need to imagine what's going on to get to the truth; only then can we preempt what is happening to us. The Reality Creators use artistic alchemy to turn their subjective ideas into objective facts. We can only see what they are up to by conducting the same creative process. Understanding what is going on is the precursor to being able to change what we want about our lives.

The people who will complain about this call to action are the neoliberals described in detail in chapter six. These Reality Creators have invented a term so stultifying that its name causes the average person to spiral into despair even before the meaning begins to sink in: *availability heuristic*. It means that what we think of is what first comes to mind. They claim that what comes to our minds is the wrong answer because we lack the elite knowledge and academic position to comprehend what is correct. They are scolds. They view us as intellectually limited as a farmer does goats. Malcolm Gladwell argues against this, saying that we should trust our intuition more in his book, *Blink: The Power of Thinking Without Thinking*. He argues that the world would be a much better place if we trusted our instincts more.[10]

The availability heuristic indictment is that non-elites, "the masses," make the wrong choices; ergo, we can't possibly become our agents, our creators. They say we need their help to live, that they need to 'nudge' us along the right route because what we come up with on our own is wrong, shallow, and cannot be trusted or used to forge a decent life for ourselves. They have about as much respect for us as they do our ancestors they call brutish. Of course, they denigrate us to streamline their control over us as their wealth creators, and the 'nudge' is their version of a riding crop. The debasement of our representative government relies upon this patronizing idea that we cannot effectively make the best choices for ourselves. The same applies to the shepherd, his crook, and the flock. Too much of the media relies upon the notion that we continuously need to be told and shown everything with hooks, crooks, crops, and dramatic appeal. It is as condescending and disrespectful of an idea to control the herd since the days Walter Lippmann sought to raise the alarms about corralling us.

To be fair, it's true that humans think by way of the quickest and easiest recollection that comes to mind because the obvious answer is often there waiting on deck. Another heuristic, *Occam's Razor* suggests that the simplest answer is often the right answer by way of minimizing extraneous data.

Our thinking is not anti-intellectual or facile as the neoliberals will accuse. Sure, we will be wrong from time to time in what we think. Gladwell has numerous examples of bigotry and other problems arising from the use of intuition and gut reactions. But the availability heuristic, in this case, Occam's Razor, is not always wrong, and that it is right often enough to be useful and applicable to the cause of gaining control of our lives. Frankly, it is quite revolutionary for us to push back and say that we trust ourselves. It should be noted that falling for absurd and dangerous conspiracy theories is pitiful; however, Reality Creators create mendacious narratives and use fabrications to manage our political economy, and that is deplorable. Their mass media manufactures consent (a term coined by Walter Lippmann and made famous by Edward S. Herman and Noam Chomsky). Who are the Reality Creators to lecture us about whether or not we can be trusted to trust ourselves?

Grandma knew that we couldn't control what had already happened. We were left to the telling of it. The Hopi Nation has this saying: "The one who tells the stories rules the world." The Reality Creators already know this; that's why they control so much media. We need to tell our stories so one day we can rule our world together. If we are to fight back and gain traction in our lives and become more self-reliant like our ancestors, we must be willing to discover our Truths and stick to them regardless of what the Reality Creators or their underlings force upon us.

What is going on in our lives is the Reality Creators' providence until we take charge. This book seeks to inspire folks to live and think outside the boxes the Reality Creators construct and become more independent. We were taught to read between the lines in literature, using our creative imaginations to comprehend what was going on in prose and poetics. We should also read between the lines of reality, both real and virtual. Through such introspection, we can carefully figure out what's going on in our lives right now.

Today it seems like facts are as real as fiction and that fiction is as realistic as facts, and that's as real as it gets in our postmodern world where truth is now in the eye of the beholder. Relativism is a huge problem because we must share a common understanding of reality; we can't survive in a world full of alternate facts. The Reality Creators have sown chaos by calling into question whether or not we can trust ourselves. They tell us not to discriminate against lies and falsehoods, which they claim have every right to exist alongside inarguable truths and hard data. They intentionally conflate the real and the dramatic to confound us.

Finding your truth is not the same as blatantly lying. We must stand for our shared objective reality and distinguish it from the Reality Creators' imposing subjective reality. We must maintain our dignity and integrity when we stand up for ourselves; otherwise, we are no better than those who gaslight us with their lies.

We need to become our agents, act on our behalf, and create our reality together.[11] We need to control the debate, tell the stories from our perspective, frame the ideas and issues as we please, and stop blindly accepting the version of events and opinions from the Reality Creators who gaslight us. Perhaps if the goats knew what the farmer was up to, they wouldn't just stand there.

"I'll be long gone before some smart person ever figures out what happened inside this Oval Office."

President George W. Bush, in an interview with the Jerusalem Post, Washington, D.C., May 12, 2008

"Artists use lies to tell the truth."

Alan Moore

"We didn't rely on somebody else to build what we built."

Sanford Weill, former CEO and Emperor of CitiGroup trying to deflect the fact that the people of the world built his wealth.

"I owe the public nothing."

J.P. Morgan

"It may be that we are puppets-puppets controlled by the strings of society. But at least we are puppets with perception, with awareness. And perhaps our awareness is the first step to our liberation."

Stanley Milgram, Social Psychologist who pioneered studies in obedience.

"None are more hopelessly enslaved than those who falsely believe they are free."

Johann Wolfgang von Goethe

CHAPTER THREE

People Vote, They Don't Lobby; Corporations Lobby, They Don't Vote

We belong to the largest human population ever, yet we're managed by a tiny minority who own and control much of the political economy that envelopes the Earth. Even those in undeveloped nations cannot escape the control of the minority. In the developed and developing nations, we live in a high-tech modern world fueled by extraordinary energy resources driving a global marketplace casting about too much waste onto the Earth and into the air and seas. We can nuke the planet. Tomorrow life will be worse because we have reached the limit to how bright our future can get.

The claim of a brighter future tomorrow is dramatic marketing and false advertising by the Reality Creators to keep us in their thrall for as long as possible. Certainly, flora and fauna on Earth aren't seeing it. Believing the brighter-future dogma is a social disease resulting from poor education and a dearth of independent media. Assertions that the Reality Creators have not mismanaged the political economy are blatant lies told by the very people who created the disaster and are capable of promoting that false message in their media. For them to say that we can benefit from the political economy as it is currently structured to solve our long-term growth, resource, and waste problems is the logic of the addict: just a little more of what has got us down will raise us up.

The plutocrats and oligarchs claim to steer society for the benefit of the human race, but that has not been the result. Hobbes' metaphor of a Leviathan has begun to feel real because the corporate-government complex is more a monster than a benevolent parent. Soon we will have sentient artificial intelligence that will make the point quite literal. Reality Creators say they're selflessly doing god's work, but the aggregate facts bear out otherwise. They work to benefit themselves no matter the negative impacts on the rest of us. As addicts, they cannot stop because they refuse to admit the problem. The terms of our Social Contract have become deplorable and constricting. We are boxed into a tight space: we'll shop for all that we need in life until we drop and waste against our will because we too are now addicted.

Our culture is like a thin film of plastic stretched out over the natural world, keeping us from contacting it. We conflate the developed world with the real world. We've begun to think the plastic film and all that is staged upon it is real. We can't get by without the proper functioning of the sprawling, global, free-trade, high-modern technological system that has recently evolved to take care of all our day-to-day needs. For us, our developed world is a Nanny World taking care of our needs day in and day out. It's a mistake to think we take care of ourselves. Sure we brush our teeth, but where do the brush, paste, water, sink, and bathroom all come from, and who owns the manufacturing and sales assets?

We have made a deal per the terms of our Social Contract: in trade for an easy lifestyle with the luxuries kings and queens of the past could never have foreseen, we have given up much of our sovereignty and can't do much of anything besides taking the test, pressing the button, going to the box to get our stuff, and retiring. Technology has invented the toaster and the addiction to it. Luxury and competence are inversely related, and our relentless pursuit of the former has got us lacking the latter.

Lacking self-reliance is ubiquitous across the developed world. Who do you know who does not live off the Reality Creators' rent-seeking corporations? They either make it, or truck it, fuel it, or feed it. You name it; they do it for us. It is a blip in time that has passed since we lost the skills to care for ourselves in such a manner. Soon enough, there will be a preponderance of robots, computer algorithms, and automated systems doing the work of the corporations. Too many of us will be standing by, no longer working as their hired hands and livestock. In the documentary, *Capital in the 21st Century*, by Ian Pemberton on the subject of Thomas Picketty's 2013 book by the same name, Ian Bremmer states:

> At the end of the nineteenth century, horses were critical for industrialization, and then they weren't. Because you have all these industrial processes that are much more efficient than horses are. And, for all of the technophiles that are saying technology has always created more jobs, and so it will continue to...I say technology has always created more jobs as long as you had things that human beings could do. But when technology starts actually getting at the basic functionality of the human being, then human beings start becoming the equivalent of horses.[1]

Homeless people are as close as anyone gets in our society today to be free from relying on the corporations and their power brokers, yet even while most don't work for them, they push around welded shopping carts full of corporate stuff. If that's not ironic enough, we see terrorists wearing Nike t-shirts and driving around Ford pick-up trucks out to destroy our political economy they call "The Great Satan."

In our modern life, we don't have the living skills our ancestors developed over the millennia because the development of technology in the last 200 took over most of those jobs. We lost control of our lives when we lost the ability to work for ourselves, and now we are losing work altogether. Automated systems are becoming better at working like indentured servants than humans. We are at risk of having nowhere to go and nothing to do, living locked up in cities and suburbs and stranded out on rural hinterlands. To be clear, the historical claim that 'we'll always find other good-paying work to do when we're displaced from our jobs' is coming to an end. In the past, automation and technology increased human productivity, whereas today, they do not; they remove the human from productivity.

We cannot survive without the fragile and complex supply chains that make up our society. Indeed, the more complex our society becomes, the weaker it is. It is not hyperbole to say those chains have bound us to the system we depend upon, nor is it an exaggeration to say that those chains will now begin to lock us out of it. We are not able to live outside the box. We have to live inside the box unless we want to live under a bridge. We're virtually incarcerated inside the box, and now it looks like we might get locked out of it. This feeling is a useful measure of how close we are to approaching certain societal limits. Our myopic media keeps all of this out of focus.

It is incorrect to say that we collectively provide for ourselves when we work for or rely upon large corporate entities because we do not control the workplace and we do not set the prices for all we purchase. Furthermore, big business rules over our small businesses. The Reality Creators permit a few employee-owned big corporations, but like unions, they have been reduced to symbolism because there is way too much wealth to lose by sharing it with "the masses."

The corporate workplaces exist primarily to build the bosses' wealth, and secondarily, bale the hay to feed us. Unionizing the large-scale modern industrial workplace to set the terms of our labor is such a struggle because the corporate workplace is the Reality Creators' homestead. We can't tell them what to do on their farm any more than the goats can tell the farmer what to do. The robots will never complain about pay and work conditions. Hence, corporations work furiously to make them affordable replacements for human labor.

Neither we nor the robots can take over the workplace because the nature of a modern technological corporation requires an economy-of-scale with a CEO-led dictatorship from the top. John Kenneth Galbraith called it the 'technostructure,' the organizational pyramid of executives, managers, and engineers acting as one unified force for capital accumulation. If we could gain control of and run the corporations, we would have by now; we've tried mightily and not been able to make it work. Instead, we work for them to shop from them, and that is all they mean to us, and that is all we mean to them. Corporations are legal fictions, and they are the lead actors in the political economy drama.

The Reality Creators sneer that we are too stupid and lazy to be successful; however, they make it impossible for us to pull ourselves up by our bootstraps because they retain all the wealth, resources, and political power by which to do so. As a result, we are forced to rely on the few job creators for employment on their terms in their jobs, building their wealth: stupid and lazy, indeed. Too many people are dependent on the few for economic growth[2] and political leadership.

The destructive irony is that we may have built it, but we don't own it until we buy it back from them on their terms. The owners come in between ourselves and sever the connection between the work we do for them and ownership of the subsequent goods and services that result from it. They legally rent our very selves for eight hours per day. They own us and control us, and then we pay that rent income right back to them to gather up all the stuff we made for them during those eight hours to survive another day to work for them. Our problem is that we don't own ourselves; we are owned. The fact people like this system is why we're called sheeple, a term first used in 1945 by W.R. Anderson.

Our situation is the textbook definition of a protection racket: we agree to pay them with our labor on their terms; otherwise, we starve and suffer exposure under a bridge. There is no other option for hundreds of millions of people. Relatively few can ever start their own businesses, and a protection racket such as this functions on extortion, where there is no other option.

To make corporations profitable for the few owners accumulating the excess capital that flows from all of our daily activities, they have to break a cardinal rule of Nature: *Cheap, Fast, and Good; Pick Two*. If it's cheap and fast, it's not good. If it's fast and good, it's not cheap. If it's good and cheap, it's not fast. Reality Creators break this rule to make their stuff cheap, fast, and good. To pull off this crime against Nature, someone has got to pay. Guess who it always is? You and me.

This structure breaks workers' backs and crushes consumers' spirits – respectively, the left and right sides of each one of us. Many have tried to change this structure over the past 150 years, but it may be the case that if we succeed, we may go without the goods and services we rely upon each day. Why? Because we've over-extended ourselves with an extraordinary population density requiring massive resource flows extracted from the Earth's ecology to fuel the human economy, and there may be no turning back without extreme suffering. This circumstance of our society has us in a bind.

Reality Creators dominate the free market economy; in so doing, they make it their manipulated market economy. They have monetized every aspect of our lives to extract the wealth of our work, our consumption, and even our love for each other. Individually, they would never see themselves acting in such a way, or at least admit to it. The overall effect consists of individual struggles for success in a competitive field fighting over us. The following discussion explores how Reality Creators control the public sector as they do the private sector and why they use our government to manage us.

A Human Resources Department

The Founding Fathers never envisioned the U.S. government as a parent to take care of us as babies. Theoretically, we're supposed to take care of ourselves; however, the Reality Creators' corporations have taken over the effort because they realized they could profit off the service. They are the nanny sector, and our political economy is one big childcare business. The Reality Creators repurposed the U.S. government over the past 200 years to write and enforce laws to make the private sector function as a wealth-building apparatus to funnel capital to those who rule the private sector. By constitutional design, the U.S. government is not a powerful top-down dictatorship. It is supposed to be a tool of the people, a republic designed to assist the private sector.

Unfortunately, the public sector's inherent weakness has been exploited by the few Reality Creators who have amassed enough power to control the U.S. government ahead of the rest of us. The U.S. government is a republic with representatives ostensibly governing on behalf of the citizenry; however, too many of those politicians work on behalf of the wealthy corporate interests who have taken near full control of it with little effort. The U.S. government is powerful to the extent that we vote to give it credibility to lord over us. The more we vote, the more credibility we give the government that rules over us.

The Reality Creators use governments across the world as their Human Resources Departments to control us with governmental laws analogous to corporate HR policies. The public sector is a giant, multi-tiered human resources management division functioning under private sector control. Hobbes' notion of a Social Contract has failed.

Taking control of governments is colonialism. The Reality Creators colonize us so we can serve their wealth creation. As in the past 500 years, when kings wrote laws to permit privateers to colonize the New World for profit, colonizing is going on today within our nation (discussed at length in chapter five). The United States population has become so large that we have taken on the same kind of burdens that colonized people in the undeveloped world have known about elsewhere. For example, in the nineteenth century, when colonialism was in full swing, the combined population of the Americas and Europe was close to the same as the entire U.S. population today. Today, domestic colonization is now going on within the United States borders. Many U.S. citizens now suffer the same plight as traditionally colonized people.[3] Corporate colonialism conducted overseas has come home to roost here in the U.S. and it will worsen as globalism wanes as discussed in chapter 6.

When it comes time to complain, we should first point our fingers at the source of all that is everything in our lives: the Reality Creators' all-powerful corporations, and second, at the patsy, weak U.S. government that we elect, but they control. We should not loathe or blame the public sector, the Nanny State itself. Instead, we should despise that the Reality Creators took control of the U.S. government from us and use it against us. Now we can't help but vote against our interests when there is an election because our votes put them in power over us. It's not the government that is to blame; it's just a tool. Instead, it's the influential Reality Creators who control the government to whom we should direct our resentment. If someone hits you with a hammer, blame the person, not the hammer. Populism is the movement to take control of the hammer. The government is not inherently bad; the Reality Creators who control it are to blame for how it treats us. This is a critically important distinction to make.

Because the Reality Creators use city, county, state, and federal governments as tools to manage us, they have a delicate public relations issue to handle. When times are bad for the economy, they want us to blame the government, deflecting criticism from themselves in the private sector. They play good cop – bad cop, with their corporations being the good cop that provides us with the stuff we need in life and our government being the bad cop that takes it all away. They call it our government when they portray it as the bad cop; otherwise, control of the public sector belongs entirely to them.

Since the Reality Creators control both the public and private sectors, they have built a corporate-government complex that is greater than the mere sum of its parts. This totality is what makes the populace go along with whatever the corporate-government complex does because there is no other option; it is everything, and they control it all. It is the dominant hegemony: food and fuel are at the store. This totality is a defining principle of fascism, where the corporate-state axis is paramount above all else. What choice do people have if the corporate-government complex permits or prohibits whatever it wants, decides when it's going to war, or that it's going to bail itself out printing money as it pleases? What control do we have over all the Reality Creators' laws written to manage us and favor them? What can we do about the ratio of money that flows to their capital investments relative to what flows to us?

Imagine if you were a Reality Creator and had control of an enormous government apparatus with power over millions of citizens that derives its credibility from those citizens when they choose to vote. Imagine they thought they were choosing you to represent their interests each time they voted, but instead, they chose to put you in political control over them to do as you please. Imagine if you used the governments' great power to manage these people in ways that increased the efficiency by which you could direct the flow of their capital resources toward your upper-class tribe.

Imagine if you looked down at 335 million U.S. citizens, or the rest of the world for that matter, and saw an enormous pool of human resources and wondered: "Hmm, how can we sluice the wealth off their backs, as much as they'll tolerate, forever into the future? How much of their capital do you think we can direct away from them and pool into our accounts?" The answer to these questions is in the economic reality we see today. Any legislation passed to comfort the citizenry is what I do when I pet my goat for a bit before milking.

To help put our situation into perspective, here's a story by Clarence Gillis, a Canadian miner, labor advocate for miners, and politician, retold in 1944 by Tommy Douglas, on the occasion of his inauguration as the Premier of Saskatchewan, Canada. Instead of farmers and goats, he talks about cats and mice:[4]

> This is the story of a place called Mouseland. Mouseland was a place where all the little mice lived and played, were born and died. And they lived much the same as you and I do.
>
> They even had a parliament. And every four years they had an election. Used to walk to the polls and cast their ballots. Some of them even got a ride to the polls. And got a ride for the next four years afterwards, too. Just like you and me. And every time on election day all the little mice used to go to the ballot box and they used to elect a government. A government made up of big, fat, black cats.
>
> Now if you think it strange that mice should elect a government of cats, look at the history of Canada for the last 90 years and maybe you'll see they weren't any stupider than us.
>
> Now I'm not saying anything against the cats. They conducted their government with dignity. They passed

good laws - that is, laws that were good for cats. But the laws that were good for cats weren't very good for mice. One of the laws said that mouse holes had to be big enough so a cat could get his paw in. Another law said that mice could only run at certain speeds so a cat could get his breakfast without too much effort.

All the laws were good laws. For cats. But, oh, they were hard on mice. And life was getting harder and harder. And when the mice couldn't put up with it anymore, they decided that something had to be done. So they went en masse to the polls. They voted the black cats out. They put in white cats.

Now the white cats had put up a terrific campaign. They said, "All Mouseland needs is more vision." They said, "The trouble with Mouseland is the round mouse holes. If you put us in we'll make square mouse holes." And they did. And the square mouse holes were twice as big as the round ones, and now a cat could get both paws in.

And life was tougher than ever.

And when they couldn't take that anymore, they voted the white cats out and black ones in again. Then they went back to white cats. Then to black cats. They even tried half black and half white cats. And they called that a coalition. They even got one government made up of cats with spots on them: They were cats that tried to make a noise like a mouse but ate like a cat.

You see, my friends, the trouble wasn't with the colour of the cat. The trouble was that they were cats. And because they were cats, they naturally looked after cats instead of mice.

When we vote, we elect cats into power regardless of their red or blue color. We have been voting against our interests in electing cats for too long, and it's become unsustainable.

We fail to recognize that we mice have more in common with each other than we do with the cats, no matter how obvious and glaring our superficial ethnic, political, and geographic differences are. The various colored cats will always declare that all mice are equally tasty, no matter their color.

We don't hold the cats accountable for our struggle because we can't win against the cats. We go after each other instead, fighting over the limited resources they leave behind for us. While they fight amongst themselves over the vast sums of capital we create, so too do we fight over the pitiful remainder they let us keep to feed and house ourselves.

There is a term called *last place aversion*; no one wants to be in last place. No matter how far down the scale we may be, we can always blame others for competing with us for resources. People blame others who belong to different ethnic groups or are equal to or poorer than them. They say that others are not worthy of the same benefits they receive. Yes, this is the ugly side of our competitive society at the bottom of the ladder, and it's not by accident. The Reality Creators argue wedge issues, such as "Billy got this...Sally got that," to keep us gnashing our teeth at each other instead of at them. To believe that this characterization is a cynical and unrealistic view of our society is just more evidence of their media plan working.

We vote based on diverse economic, social, moral, and racial issues that affect our place in line. We are countless splintered individuals because these wedge issues drive us apart. It's quite chaotic, but the magic of their voting system brings great order to this mess. When all the votes are counted, the Reality Creators aggregate this disorder into one of two outcomes. Necessarily, those outcomes are not accurate distillations of the mess of splintered voters whose lives they've shattered. Instead, it's a sweeping up off the floor of all those splintered lives into two piles, which then get thrown away into the dumpster they set on fire; meanwhile, the owners and managers of the political economy go ahead and do whatever they want. It doesn't matter who gets elected so long as the Reality Creators win. This is why many citizens don't vote; it's not that their vote doesn't count. Rather, they know their vote empowers the Reality Creators and not themselves.

For those of us who still show up to the polls, we want the feeling that we are empowering ourselves, no matter how divorced from reality our feelings are. To have personal agency, we align ourselves with the red or blue team we identify with, based on the morals for which those teams fight regarding the wedge issues at play.

Back to the sports metaphor, we are like the audience at a football game between the elite football teams: we are not the players; we just root for the team we believe in. They do all the playing, creating reality on the field, and we put on our colored jerseys and root for the reality we like better. Because it is a zero-sum game, one team has to win over the other. The watchers have no power over the game. It does not matter who wins; that is arbitrary. What matters is that the players control the action. We just go along with the outcome. The team players differ in how they play the game; however, they have a common cause to get the ball, score points, and get us to pay for the tickets.

To the Reality Creators, it doesn't matter who wins or loses. It matters that the people come out, watch their game, and yell epithets at each other when one team necessarily wins and the other loses.

Vote For the Lobbyist

We don't run for statewide or federal office because we are too busy trying to make ends meet. Can you imagine running for office? Usually, all we get is a chance to vote for insiders who have bubbled up to the top of the candidate pack. Voters want to be on the winning team, and we aren't ever on the winning team unless we pick one with the winning candidate. To nudge us, Reality Creators spend money, saying: "Vote for the Winner!" So long as voters feel like they won and other voters feel like they lost, citizens will always believe that what mattered was who won or lost. Indeed, the only outcome that has ever mattered is that a Reality Creator won.

Corporate interests fund candidates and splash their faces all over the media to be as recognizable as one of your best friends: come election day, you hope you're on the winning team voting for your new friend. The rare populist politicians who are not on the corporate dole will inspire the mice people; however, given the historical facts, how long do they ever hold power, and how many bills do they bring to the floor that get passed into law?

When Reality Creators get into political office, it's smooth sailing forward. On the rare occasion, when mice-people vote one of their honest pip-squeaks into office, that politician will experience isolation and attacks when they engage the political process. Like us, he or she will get blown off: recall Dennis Kucinich on the left and Ron Paul on the right when they were in Congress. The only thing these two men ever had in common is that human persons supported them instead of corporate persons.

We can't lobby because there is no difference between the corporate boss and the political boss; they are the same. They are siblings belonging to the same family, and they only talk to each other. Of course, there are rare exceptions. However, the rule is that we don't have the power to control the government we elect because politicians often ignore our voice messages and e-mails. They will not meet with us one-on-one except in rare circumstances, and when they do, they smile warmly, shine us on, and ignore our requests. Politicians hold town halls and street-corner gatherings, but these events are less about addressing community interests than they are about planning for the next election cycle. The farmer spends time with the goats, but he's not going to hang out with them except when kids are born; otherwise, it's to count them, sort them, manage them, milk them, and decide which get sold, which get pregnant and which get slaughtered.

The result is that citizens hardly ever try to lobby their elected officials compared to the massive and colossal effort done by the corporations. Reality Creators aggregate corporate lobbying into an efficient process that is big enough to control the entire government from top to bottom. They want to make sure none of us cut into their turf. Unlike individual voters, Reality Creators organize to become greater than the sum of their parts. They also prevent us from trying to organize. They benefit by their unified stance against the voters who are split into many pieces: red, blue, black, white, boy, girl, north, south, east, and west, gay, straight, trans, educated, abled, and not.

Over the years, there have been changes. Now the way lobbying works is that politicians don't write bills as much as they receive them in final draft form from their confidant lobbyists working for corporations. Corporations retain the best lawyers because they can afford to pay more than anyone else, and they provide a service to the political staffers who do not have the same resources in their offices. The American Legislative Exchange Council (ALEC) is one example at the state level. The lobbying work done on K Street in D.C. at the federal level is another example. We believe our elected representatives spend all day long creating and negotiating legislation on our behalf, but that is not true. Politicians spend much of their time socializing with their elite peers and working together daily.[5] It is said politicians in Congress spend more than half of their time fundraising, but that is just a way of spinning the private discussions and socializing with corporate lobbyists about what needs to get done and how to pay for it.

Let's also consider what has been called the revolving door phenomenon. We know some Reality Creators like the political scene for the power ruling over a nation confers, and others prefer the corporate scene for the money. It's a matter of how they like their power: political or economic; fame or fortune. (It's well known throughout history that wealthy families are loathed to talk about their wealth, and ones that do are considered the rude Nouveau Riche; generally, they do not like fame.) One might be inclined to think the power of a multinational corporation concentrating hundreds of millions and billions of dollars into the accounts of their owners and managers would always be preferable to the political power made available by national governments with supranational power, but that is not so. Political power over nations, particularly developed nations, affords the managers strength to control whole regions of the world, enact wars, and dominate monetary systems, food, natural resources, and minds by means of propaganda that motivates millions to do what they would not have thought for themselves to do. It's one thing to rake in extraordinary wealth, producing and selling goods and services people need to survive. It's quite another to receive the political support of tens and hundreds of millions of those same people to go about ruling over them and pressuring other nations with your military garrisoned on their lands.

For some Reality Creators, working for the government can be seen as tithing, giving back to their plutocratic community. For the lifers in the political realm, you can bet they get their dues paid since the private sector pays salaries and bonuses more than the best and brightest would make in government. Despite the glory of political power, it's a pretty bad pay cut to go do government work. In part, this explains why the revolving door and the open breezeway are so busy: somebody's got to run the government, so they take turns.

No wonder people loathe our democratically elected government: it's a bad cop.[6]

"I see in the near future a crisis approaching that unnerves me and causes me to tremble for the safety of my country... corporations have been enthroned and an era of corruption in high places will follow, and the money power of the country will endeavor to prolong its reign by working upon the prejudices of the people until all wealth is aggregated in a few hands and the Republic is destroyed."

Abraham Lincoln, Nov. 21, 1864

CHAPTER FOUR

When the Reality Creators Make Money, They Make It From Us

There are two levels in our society: an upper world the Reality Creators inhabit at the colonial farmhouse and a lower world at the barnyard where the work is done managing us. My goats don't think of themselves as being managed; they take their circumstance for granted, if for no other reason than because they were born into it, and that's all they know. Animals on a farm pay rent with their labor, excretions, and their lives. They live in stalls and stay within boundaries. It's unlikely that their situation stands out to them as exceptional or odd. Borders between nations are like fences between the stock pens[1]. No matter where folks reside on the Earth, the Reality Creators will manage them like farmers manage their flocks.

Another way to perceive this social structure is to view the Reality Creators like Greek gods who are shaped like humans but exist on a higher plane, expressing omnipotence and omniscience. While these gods are occasionally petty and vengeful, "doing gods' work," they are benevolent overseers of the best interests of humanity. They have a sense of Noblesse Oblige, a sense of responsibility for us, based on a concern for our long-term welfare.

In the modern era, the Reality Creators have their interests in mind: owning the land and the people on it like a farm. They don't think they owe us anything more than what's required to keep us working for them and consuming their goods and services that we must buy to survive. It was J.P. Morgan who said, "I owe the public nothing," after decades of sluicing the wealth off of our backs. Reality Creators believe our wealth is theirs, and some are indignant that they even have to go out and collect it from us. Adam Smith, who believed in the inherent goodness of those in power, would be devastated by the "Greed is Good" motto of our contemporary era.

Why are the Reality Creators entitled and self-absorbed? Are they selfish by nature, nurture, or both? Does such self-centered behavior come from a monarchical birthright or exposure to all the luxuries that power affords? For all his greatness, Zeus did not wield financial weapons. This is a considerable difference between him and the drone-striking Reality Creators of today who have that monetary power.

Watching kids play Monopoly can help explain some of the personality changes money-power has on people. Kids experience radical changes to their personalities when deposing others. The rules require that they win by making others lose, which makes them more important than others. Kids cry when times are bad for them on the board and laugh with demonic pleasure when the plays turn in their favor. They game the game by cheesing rolls of the dice, stealing property cards and money from the bank, and by deliberately miscounting spaces and then claiming ignorance when caught. It is not a far stretch to say that poorly regulated capitalism, writ large, has this nurtured effect on people, fomenting the desire to act in self-serving ways despite the rules of the game and the feelings or welfare of others.

In her article for *CFA Magazine*, Sherree DeCovny explains that:

> Studies conducted by Canadian forensic psychologist Robert Hare indicate that about 1 percent of the general population can be categorized as psychopathic, but the

prevalence rate in the financial services industry is 10 percent. And Christopher Bayer believes, based on his experience, that the rate is higher.[2]

Are persons who lack empathy and can't feel for others attracted to the financial sector, or are they made that way on the job? Does it matter how they got ill? No, what matters is that they are ill, and there is not, nor will there ever be, a program that could help them: Scrooge is a fictional character, and his redemption is a fairytale. To be more charitable, we could say that Reality Creators lose control of their better instincts when they compete in the political economy. They get lost in the wilderness of the gestalt that makes their aggregate behavior rapacious and damaging to the people of the world and the Earth.

All this reminds me of a story about the Monopoly attitude: Hank had a lovely Kombucha mother mushroom in a jar that made him an endless supply of Kombucha tea, a great healthy drink. He peeled off the mother's layers and passed them out to a few people he knew who had heard of the tea before and were curious. One such person, Matt, knew much about the mushroom colony and had been looking to find a mother. Hank thought about the infinity of the mother and how he had helped spread her daughters out to start new infinities, and this pleased him morally.

Some time went by, and Hank lost his mother. She had died while he was on vacation, so Hank went to Matt and asked him if he would peel off a layer of his mother he'd given him months before since his had died recently. Matt stared at Hank and said, "that will be $25, please." Hank stood back and thought, "did he just say he's going to charge me? Am I dreaming?" Reading his mind, Matt said, "Hell yes, this is the American Dream! Mothers forever, but you gotta pay for yours." Hank complained he'd given away his mother for free, "...how dare you charge me for yours?" "Hey, don't take it personally; it's just business, Hank."

That's it; it's just business, they say. And it has been decreed by the rules of the game that Matt is free to be as rich as he can be off mothers, an endless supply of mushroom layers anyone can profit from if they bother. But some people don't want to profit off mothers, like Hank. "But that's fine," says Matt, "don't sell yours, all the better for me."

It's True: Work Will Set You Free

Ever since the Enlightenment helped spark the creative ideas of capitalism and the Industrial Revolution, economies have increased momentum. Capitalism has utilized colonialism, slavery, artificial machines, wage slavery, natural resources extraction, and "interest" in investments to provide the capacity for economic growth and the concentration of wealth into accounts of the few who possess large amounts of capital. Capitalism has also used the enlightened ideas of freedom, liberty, equality, and justice to defend extraordinary class inequality: liberty to accumulate unlimited wealth, freedom from government regulations, and justice from the hordes surging at the gates clamoring for help.

The history of the Reality Creators goes back much further than the Enlightenment and the Industrial Revolution. Reality Creators have been lording over and ruling the populace, accumulating power and wealth for themselves since the beginning of human agricultural activity 12,000 years ago. The over-arching single-minded mission of all the Reality Creators has always been to force us to be dependent upon them, to be in a constant state of debt to them, from generation to generation. Reality Creators are of the cruel opinion that we must pay back our *Original Sin* for trespassing on the land they own, having been born into their world. We are morally required to pay our rent-debt to build their wealth, thereby enduring a lifetime of poverty as penance. For us, birth is the crime, and life is the time. This is really what the Social Contract looks like.

This obligation is a baseless and false reality fabricated out of whole cloth by the Reality Creators. In his *Debt, The First 5,000 Years*, David Graeber eloquently describes why "primordial debt" is a mythical fantasy that inadvertently has justified the oppression of the populace. We can see elements of such thought throughout regions around the world.[3] Even today, we look up at tall buildings, whole cities, even the apartments we live in, and think this is a world in which we must pay rent to owners to survive.

Throughout the ages, Reality Creators have always been willing to change tactics as needed to maintain a strict focus on their strategic mission to lord over us to build their wealth for them. Not ironically, the poor represent a great amount of wealth potential, and the bosses will not let that go to waste, benefitting us unnecessarily. Reality Creators have always thought of us as another livestock species, the hired hand, and they think paying us is as odd as a farmer paying goats.

In agricultural and industrial societies, there is a pattern of control that runs throughout all the ages across the entire world. For one example, when the Roman Empire fell, the slaves and the poor had no protection because they had never known any different life than slavery and poverty. Terrorism ravaged their lives. To survive, the former slaves traded in their freedom for security and became Medieval peasants. They appealed to the landed bosses who had security forces for protection. In return, the poor had to work building value for the wealthy landowner. It was their Social Contract.

This Medieval peasant lifestyle in Europe went on for hundreds of years. The peasants lived in extreme poverty; their overlords taxed them to the degree that their lives were almost unbearable. If they didn't die from the evil of such privation, marauders frequently raided their villages and killed them.

Their overlords took their food and supplies as taxes, paid as a protection racket to fight off the marauders, but the peasants didn't even get that service much of the time. Then, in the eleventh century, the idea of feudalism came about in northern Europe, where a strict, hierarchal array formed when the King of France had to look over both France and Britain at the same time. He had conquered Britain in 1066 in *The Battle of Hastings* and had to rule both nations.

To lord over two countries at once, the king had to put lords in control of large areas in Britain as his proxies and then sub-lords in charge of smaller areas within the main lords' charge. This parceling out the land brought about modern ownership of property and greater ownership of the peasants' lives since they came with the land. This transition is when the peasants became known as feudal serfs. It didn't take long before they burned out from the brutal and cooped-up feudal lifestyle: it was too much like being a lamb or a goat. While their livelihood was one rung up the ladder above being a slave, it was still an indentured lifestyle. Ironically, this frustration coincided with the lords kicking the serfs off the land to graze sheep instead. No doubt the serfs took offense at the irony of being replaced by sheep. To the lords, they were all animals. For a time and from an agrarian sense, the sheep were more valuable than the serfs.

By 1500, the peasants' revolts and the *Black Death* forced a change in how the Reality Creators managed the political economy. Being smart, resourceful, and always willing to adjust tactics, the Reality Creators came up with the idea of ameliorating the revolting serfs' complaints. They did this by commuting the serfs' labor to wages: "you work for us and herd the sheep, and we'll pay you...Heck, you can go into debt, rent from us and run the farm."

Commuting the labor of the poor to wages had the psychological effect of once again removing them from feeling like farm animals because their compensation was not a stall-like shed, hay, grain, or wheat. Instead, they accepted an abstract form of wealth (coins) that, if accumulated, would make them rich like the nobles who were free to do what they wanted. Feeling a potential for freedom was an experience that they never had, not as a slave nor as an oppressed peasant. They had always associated freedom with nobility, the wealthy upper-class rulers. Attaining freedom by accumulating wages was a compelling idea: *work would set you free.*

Capitalism is the accumulation of excess wealth by a small percent of society who use that excess to make investments. Not all investments are suitable, however, and the bad ones strongly correlate with unrestrained self-interest. Capitalist banking is the cotton gin of finance. The notion of working for money to attain freedom was born. Men thought that this was great: get a job working for the wealthy landowners; borrow their money to run the farm themselves; accumulate their money; build up excess reserves, and soon, be rich like them.

But the scheme hasn't worked out so well because the Reality Creators have fought hard to accumulate profit by getting that money back from us. We have always lost the struggle to direct the cash flow our way; those who argue this is not the case are Reality Creators and their hirelings. At any given point in time, there's only so much money to go around the economy. The Reality Creators have never wanted us to get more than the minimum income they believe is necessary for them to profit at the fastest rate.

When we work for Reality Creators, they pay us as little as possible, which is always much less than the economic value of the work we do for them. When we rent or borrow, they come out ahead. We fail to get financially ahead and attain the freedom we have dreamt of because the wealth we build for them is more valuable than what we earn. As time has gone by, the money has trickled away from us. Nothing has ever changed in centuries of the so-called Social contract agreements.

Reality Creators invented capitalism to make it easier to accumulate wealth from people. They commuted our labor to currency in the transition from feudalism to capitalism. Then they rigged the game of Monopoly to get back as much of our hard-won currency as possible. Coins and bills have been used as batteries to store the value of our labor. Once they figured out a way to turn our physical and mental energy into matter using coins, they stopped at nothing to get their hands back on our cash they paid us. Whenever the Reality Creators have made money, they have made it from us.

In this model, the owners profit by underpaying wages in compensation for our labor; then they profit more by overcharging us for the goods and services we made while at work. They lobbied this system into laws to prevent us from ever getting much of the money they print or enter into ledgers. Accumulation such as this is the kind of profit farmers make from their stock animals. Sure, the goats get fed and housed, but only minimally, and never do they profit. Slow and steady wins the race, and over time, with great patience, they have skimmed off much wealth from us.

Say a company pays you $400 per week for 40 hours, but in reality, you believe you're worth $15 per hour; at least that's what it takes to scrape by, which is $600 per week. In these terms, the company profits off you $200 per week by not paying you a fair wage. Then you go home to live your life and become a consumer living paycheck to paycheck, spending all that $400 back to the companies by paying for goods and services you need to survive that aren't found on the homestead anymore. You buy food, shelter, health care, transportation, entertainment, and education. However, the actual costs for these goods and services are over-priced and are worth about $300, so the company profits $100 off you when you shop.

The company profits a total of $300 per worker-consumer per week, a figure they can project on their spreadsheets. But this is only one part of their profits they make from us: the $400 the bosses spent on the labor of the worker in the form of weekly wages comes right back to the company when the consumer spends that $400 buying all the goods and services they need to live. At the end of the week, we're broke, and all we have to show for our work is the trash from the expendable goods and services we consumed just to live long enough to go back to work the next week. We've been facetiously told that "you can have it your way," as the consumer on the right, or "you deserve a break today," as the laborer on the left, in the same tone as Marie Antoinette said, "...let them eat cake."

Forty percent of Americans could not pay an unexpected $400 bill. We own little in this world. Much of what we do own, we immediately consume. The rest of our property breaks prematurely or is mortgaged and owned by banks. Since countless corporations provide the goods and services we need to live, they are undifferentiated and fungible: one is the same as the other with a singular mission to profit off us. Working for Walmart and shopping at Home Depot is not unlike working and shopping at the same place, the Reality Creators' manor, *The Company Store*.

Life goes something like this:

> Come over to my house and grow carrots for me; I got the land, seed, and water. Make sure you thin them and weed them well. Don't let them dry out while they're germinating. I'll make sure there are long enough beds to cultivate so that you're busy through harvest. I'll pay you in carrots all season long from stores leftover from last year's carrot harvest. I'll only give you as many carrots as you need to eat to be strong enough to come back to work each day.

After harvest, I notice that you have farmed for me ten times as many carrots as you could eat all year long, and that's considering all you ever eat are carrots. Since I'm a benevolent farmer and want you to show up to work next year, I'll let you have some carrots to tide you over until next spring. Bye. Now I have 90% of all the carrots you grew for me. I'm going to save a few for next season's wages, sell off the rest, pay off my overhead, and then I'll be rich! Thanks for the help, Mr. Rabbit. One day I'll have you over for hasenpfeffer dinner!

Why We Work For Others and Not Ourselves

The Enlightenment and the Industrial Revolution increased food production, which resulted in a population boom from one to seven billion. There were brilliant Reality Creators who knew all along that building the herd would build their wealth, so they watched this process evolve naturally, and at times, did what they could to nudge it along.

As the population herd grew, the Reality Creators had to bale more money to pay us for extracting and adding value to natural resources we need to live. This inflated the monetary supply, which became even more money for the Reality Creators to get their hands on. To nudge this process along, they created big central banks such as the Bank of England in 1694 and the U.S. Federal Reserve Bank in 1913. They practiced fractional reserve banking (described below) and eventually got off the limiting gold standard that had put a ceiling on how much money they could print. Now they could create new money as needed by writing it down into their ledgers, saying monetary growth was good because we'd all love to have some of it.

The enlightened idea of money-creation is one of the greatest inventions of all time because it accelerates economic growth.

Banks lend out more money than they have on hand, simulating up to a ten-fold increase in funds available to promote capital growth. Except for a few occasions, cancer being one, there have not been successful complaints lodged against the idea of growth, whether the expansion was in population, Gross Domestic Product, resource extraction and waste, or an increase in wealth inequality. This is not to say there haven't been a great many such complaints; it's that they have not ever amounted to much.

Notably, Reality Creators have no more use for the money they print than a farmer does the hay they bale. The farmer must filter the hay through the goats to produce milk and meat in the same way corporations and their owners filter money through humans to produce all the goods we make and the services we provide. What good are paper bills and ledger numbers if they don't become tangible goods and services like rings, yachts, vacations, armies, and fancy dinners?

Ah, but there's more to it than that. We want money for ourselves to survive. There's a strong demand for it, and that increases the value of money all on its own. We also want to be rich, so money becomes even more valuable. However, because the Reality Creators write laws that siphon away this valuable currency after we have made it worth something, they accumulate most of it while making sure we only get enough to survive. Now, more than feeding us, the hay-money can make us dance, jump through hoops, and do all manner of tricks because we become desperate for the dwindling supply of cash that trickles away from us. Because this charade goes on, we get tired; they get rich and economic inequality increases.

The more we dance, the wealthier they get. When we have dancing babies, they keep baling more money as needed to enter it into circulation. Our desperation for money and their desire for money keep the circulation going. This tension fuels our economy and drives us apart from each other into a disparate class structure made robust by the tension.

Here's a wonkish explanation: if Reality Creators printed as much money as possible to be indefinitely rich, it wouldn't do them any good until they spent the money by filtering it through us. The problem is, too much money would enter circulation. A vast supply of dollars would fall out of helicopters everywhere. We'd all get so much of it we'd run up the price of a pack of gum to $100, and their vast investments and savings accounts would become devalued. However, by filtering less money through us, they keep a lid on inflation. They maintain the value of their wealth and they get all the luxuries we make for them.

To put this into perspective, imagine there is a world-pile of money fixed in size at any given point in time, except that our labor, used for extracting and adding value to the world's natural resources, increases that pile once the goods are made available to the market for consumption. To pay for the additional activity transforming the ecology into the economy, Reality Creators periodically increase the money supply by fiat. The pile of cash ten years ago is less than the current world-pile of money. A yet-to-be monetized rock in the mountain a decade ago is now a steel spring in a car and a beer can. Rare earth elements dug up from residents' backyards in undeveloped nations are now in our 'i-God' devices.

The raw materials from natural resources that we dig, drill, and carve out of the Earth, plus our labor making the products shine, put value into the money Reality Creators print so the money is not just worthless green paper when they pay us for all that work. Then, once we secure the value of that money, the Reality Creators seek to get it back from us. This is how we build financial wealth for the bosses. They get our wealth by profiting from the goods and services we buy back from them after working all day making those very things for their companies.

Because we keep expanding our population and desires, they need to whip out more cash to pay us our pitiful wages. We put the value into the currency day in and day out, and they work like the dickens to get the valued cash back from us once we've enriched it. We take the green paper and give it value by working and shopping just as my goats eat the hay and give it value in the form of milk and meat.

People have been doing what they can to get their hands on as much as possible from that pile of money for a long time, but only a few rake it in. Inequality, while the norm throughout history, has become much worse in recent decades. Individuals can't effectively compete against big corporations to get the money back out from the world pile of wealth they built. Most people can only own a sewing machine or a car, much less a sewing factory or car dealership. Those few who do own large assets use those assets to acquire more assets; make a profit on 100 sewing machine girls to fund the next purchase of 250 sewing machine girls and boys. Same with other consumer items or services, including financial assets accumulating interest.

Ordinary people who are not born into money have to rely on the American Dream to own factories and become wealthy. Given the low success rate of dreamers, few have become rich. Why can't more who dream succeed? Why can't more have factories and big businesses? Why can't everyone be rich and use heavy equipment to bulldoze the pile of cash into dump trucks, reach out with steam shovels and dig in for gold?

The short answer is that we're too busy adding to the pile to have time to dig out of it, and even on a good day, we use trowels and our bare hands to dig into the pile. The longer, more detailed answer is that if everyone had the same amount of money, no one would be rich. Wealth only exists when there is inequality. The greater the disparity, the greater the relative wealth for the few. This is why the bosses are always pressing the capitalism button so damn hard. No other economic system in history is as useful as capitalism at concentrating wealth; it's an amazing engineering feat.

With the actual game of Monopoly, each player begins with the same amount of money. That is pure communism, with enforced rules of equality: *yuck, no one likes that*. No one is wealthier than the next; no one is rich or poor. By rolling the dice, inequality arises, which is the entire point of the game. The end is the opposite setup compared to the start, where one has gained all the land, assets, and money, and the rest have nothing: *yuck, no one likes that either, except the one winner*.

In reality, however, a tiny minority has already started the game with significantly more cash, and they roll more (loaded) dice more often. Those who own and control the game of life also possess political power to make these unfair rules into law. Why do we play the Reality Creators' game in real life when we know we're going to lose? Because we cannot live without the corporate systems we've come to rely upon to survive, we agree it's easier to live within the rigged system, so we play the game of Monopoly, knowing it's a losing proposition.

While we acquire just enough income for ourselves to make it back to work the next day, Reality Creators increase the relative financial distance between them and us. For some to be rich necessarily requires many others to experience poverty. So long as those who are rich use their wealth to maintain and secure their economic status, there will always be poor. This is a fundamental structural element of our society, and it requires a great deal of work on the part of the Reality Creators to maintain it.

We're too occupied working to build the Reality Creators' wealth to build our own wealth. The only time people work for themselves is when there is not a split between the laborer and consumer: your pay for chopping the wood is your consumption of heat in the winter. We haven't got the time, skills, or, in some cases, the desire to live life on the Earth on our terms. The simple shopping, driving, and workplace skills are pretty much all we know. These skills are useful so long as the bosses' pay is good and the cash is not more useful for starting a fire in the woodstove. American Dream life skills work as long as the empire lasts by tautological fiat: "We're great; therefore, our money is great." Or, wait, is it the other way around?

Only a few can realize the American Dream; otherwise, there'd be too many sewing factories, car dealerships, and banks. The people of the Earth can only consume so much. A majority cannot succeed and strike it rich with their moneymaking enterprises and still have enough buyers for their goods and services. In the game of capitalism, like the game of Monopoly, extreme inequality develops. A few people own the means of production and control the supply of money. Because money creates power only when some have it and others don't, it follows that the American Dream is not about widespread prosperity. It's about those few who win the lottery or who dream about a series of good dice rolls at the casino: for most people, the dream does not materialize because the house always wins.

Creating Wealth Through Fractional Reserve Banking

If all this would seem enough to satiate the Reality Creators' appetite for wealth, then life would be better than how we live today. But, there is still much more they do to manipulate our political economy that makes life difficult for so many. Throughout the recent past, voodoo financial innovation has prevented the American Dream from becoming a reality for those who've been told their only option has been to dream. This innovation has enabled a handful of individuals to concentrate more wealth than millions of other people could gather for themselves combined.

It's common knowledge that the top 26 wealthiest people on Earth possess the same wealth as the poorer half of the world's population. The plutocrats' peers and hirelings wrote laws to permit this reality; the poor did not. Among examples are the laws permitting fractional reserve banking the wealthy invented hundreds of years ago. These laws spawned many new practices in the contemporary period that will also be discussed in this chapter.

Fractional reserve banking means reserving the smallest possible fraction of cash in the bank that the law will allow without collapsing and needing to be bailed out by the Central Bank. This risky business is based on the idea that not all the banks' customers will want all their cash back or liquefied at the same time, such as when the Great Depression occurred in 1929. The governments bailed out banks when the fiction failed again in the Great Recession of 2008.

The Reality Creators invented fractional reserve banking to speed up our ability to transform the ecology into the economy so they could make more money at a faster clip. On the surface and despite the devastating ecological waste generated by such high production levels, fractional reserve banking is supposed to be universally good. But it is not. The benefits always accrue in proportion to the amount of financial wealth people already have. Those who possess a lot of capital benefit much more than those with little or none at all. It's as if they start the game of Monopoly with many orders of magnitude more wealth.

Banks are not content to loan out money and only show it on the borrowers' accounts. Rather, they retain that value on their books as well, even though they don't actually have it for real. Bankers collaborated with their peers in government over generations to write laws allowing this fiction to become a reality. This is an example of creating reality out of thin air.

Banks loan out money but do not subtract the value of it from their ledgers or electronic vaults. They multiply the cash reserves they store in their banks by ten times or more by merely pretending to retain what they have loaned out. Multiplying money allows economies to expand at inflated rates. This is fractional reserve banking; it increases the overall affluence of advanced societies, benefitting those who own a lot of capital considerably more than those with little or none. There is an inverse correlation between how low a reserve fraction is and how much more wealthy the Reality Creators are than the average median income in a given society.

With fractional reserve banking, it's as if the banks are in debt to the customers they gave loans to because the banks are simultaneously borrowing the money from the customer in an alternate fictional reality to keep the holographic cash on their books. But, when a bank customer defaults on a loan or when there's a bank run, then that means the bank has to borrow real funds from another bank (who keeps the value on their books too) or be bailed out by the central bank that just prints it out of thin air; obviously, they can't get it from the customer. So, in reality, banks are going into debt to each other every time they make a loan to a third party. Banks are always in a state of debt to each other, and when one bank fails, a chain reaction precipitates throughout the system. Yes, it's the law because they wrote it that way. If you want to loan out more money than you own, then all you have to do is get a bank charter.

For example, banks originate loans ten times the value held in their electronic vaults. Banks create new money each time they make a loan to a person by copying the dollar amount from their computer hard drives and pasting it into that person's account, located on the same hard drives. What the person receives is brand new electronic money. It is a copy/ paste, not cut/ paste. In the old days, banks used pencils, paper, and erasers in ledger books, but it was still the same shell game.

Say a bank has $10,000 in reserve; they'll make ten $900 loans at 5% interest and keep the original ghost-value on their books. The ten borrowers then spend their $900 loans, which end up in various other banks as new principal cash, who then use that money to underwrite their own new loans in the same way, making 5% interest on each.

This practice goes on from bank to bank until each 10% reserve dwindles the loanable principal amount to the point when there finally is nothing left to loan. At that point, the total amount of newly created money in the economy is $90,000; added to the original $10,000, the new total in the economy is $100,000. Banks also charge us 5% interest on the $90,000 for the cost of borrowing the money at each bank. Eventually, the first bank gets paid back the ten $900 loans it originated, but the value of those loans is multiplied throughout the economy and lives on in other banks.

Since all banks are connected, they continuously receive deposits and make loans, passing this newly created money between each other. Therefore, the aggregate effect is that all the banks have loaned out ten times more than they have in reserve at any given point. When there's a bank run, and everybody wants their money back at once, it's hard to distinguish fractional reserve banking from a Ponzi Scheme except that the big central bank, the Federal Reserve, bails them out.

While we all get to invest our loans and make a small increment of profit off them if we're lucky, the bankers do much more business making 5% interest on nine times the original amount and don't require luck to become more wealthy than the rest of us. Not a bad gig if you can get it.

With fractional reserve banking, Reality Creators photocopy money. But, banks go over the legal limit of photocopying our money all the time, and so they have to take out loans from each other to cover how much cash they're supposed to have in their reserves. They imposed this limit on themselves. They know this is a risky business and need self-governance to mitigate their greed and prevent the entire system from crashing more often than it already does.

What is so shocking is that 85% of all loans are solely between banks, whereas the remaining 15% of loans are to people and businesses who do real work. Banks go over their legal reserve limit on purpose. Banks package and repackage dollars back and forth by loaning to and borrowing from each other. And they profit by making interest along the way. This is called the *Interbank Lending Market*, justified by the shocking claim that they need to cover their over-leveraged balance sheets by swapping money back and forth, enriching themselves by earning interest from each other.

For example, during the day, Bank A has purposely loaned too much money relative to what it has in its reserves, so it gets a loan that night from Bank B to cover the expense. Now Bank B has loaned too much to A and has to get a loan from Bank C the next morning, who now needs to get a loan from Bank A, and so on. This is a revolving scheme, where each loan is newly created money to cover the last. If it were ever to stop, the whole racket would collapse and need to be bailed out as it did in 2008.

To make as much money as possible, banks over-leverage themselves and run on the edges of risk. This is perfectly legal, but it sounds like racketeering:

> ...a service that is fraudulently offered to solve a problem, such as for a problem that does not actually exist, will not be affected, or would not otherwise exist... Particularly, the potential problem may be caused by the same party that offers to solve it, although that fact may be concealed, with the specific intent to engender continual patronage for this party.[4]

The Reality Creators resort to another form of financial innovation when their schemes fall apart, and the photocopier breaks: they fire up the printing press at the Central Bank and hand out the money directly to the next biggest banks. The Federal Reserve Bank (FED) is a U.S. private bank, not a public bank. It works on behalf of the U.S. Government to print money as it sees fit when the other banks need loans or have a severe liquidity crisis and over-leverage themselves to the point of going under. A liquidity crisis is when banks don't have enough of our money in their reserves, can't loan each other money as usual, and need the FED to bail them out and print a special new type of cash for survival. This particular cash, 1s and 0s entered into their electronic ledgers, is called *Central Bank Money*. This is different from the regular electronic money smaller banks create when they use the photocopier to make loans, which is called *Commercial Bank Money*.

For example, in 2008, banks realized they were significantly over-leveraged and didn't have enough of our money from bogus mortgages they shouldn't have originated, so they had to get bailed out by the FED. The bailouts prevented bank and corporate failures that the "ABC-XYZ" swap and derivative investors bet on. Investors borrow excess capital from banks and use those loans of newly created money to fund their casino-style bets that those banks and other corporations will or will not fail. If they bet right, then the banks lose the bets and fall to their knees. Should the bank failures have been allowed to happen in 2008, like dominoes, one bet after another would have been lost, causing hundreds of trillions of dollars in bets on such failures to come due.

The Reality Creators thought printing up just a few trillion dollars to prevent the bank and financial house failures was far better than allowing them to occur. This prevented triggering hundreds of trillions in holographic money to come due through failed bets placed by the Reality Creators against each other. Why were there more dollars in these holographic markets than exists in our economy? Because banks funded these bets with loans that were newly photocopied money. If too many bets were to come due, there'd have been a stampede on the banks with investors seeking their winnings. It would have been as if the banks were galactic-scale casinos, and the collapses would have dwarfed the value of the entire world's financial resources.

We backed off the edge of a bottomless pit. Now, however, the banks know they can play their game of Monopoly risk-free, betting they will get bailed out with taxpayer money to save us all from the next alphabet-soup abyss. This betting goes beyond manipulating the game rules; it's rewriting the rules as in Calvin Ball, making up a new game of economic roulette, however often necessary.

Since U.S. dollars are not backed and limited by any real value such as gold, but by the fiat promise of the U.S. government to pay them back, the FED has created the new money at will and loaned as much as it wanted to banks at near-zero interest, almost for free. The sole factor limiting them from printing infinite money was their fear of inflating the money supply, making their currency worth less, thereby countering the benefits of printing it in the first place. They printed precisely as much as they thought would get the job done.

But where did it all go? Where's all the money they printed? Reality Creators make and preserve the value of their money by hiding it. Reality Creators bury their treasure in tax havens to keep it from us. It is claimed by Nicholas Shaxson in his *Treasure Islands: Tax Havens and the Men Who Stole the World*,[5] that half of the world's wealth is hidden to evade taxes in home countries. Because the money builds up, excess profits are taken out of the system and buried on Shaxson's "treasure islands," pirate style. They hide their cash to prevent it from entering the economy where we could get a hold of it. Otherwise, the cash would swirl around in such great quantities that the oversupply would devalue the currency. This would force the Reality Creators to get a haircut on the value of their holdings while we pay $100 for a pack of gum or loaf of bread. Reality Creators came up with ways of preventing their money from trickling down to us, all the while lying to us that their financial game plan includes such leakage.

We do not control the governments we elect. We would live in a more equitable world if banks were not allowed to redline the economic engine at full tilt, over-leverage their balance sheets, and squeeze every possible bit of wealth out of our bank accounts they bank on. Transforming the ecology into the economy as fast as technology will allow has its limits. We all suffer from the negative impacts in the short-term through economic inequality. Eventually, we will suffer in the long-term, too, due to the change in the climate.

Historians will say that fractional reserve banking increased the rate of economic growth in the short term. They'll observe that greed burned out the ecology to such an extent that we sacrificed the long-term prospects for humanity. They will also say that the media cheered this resource extraction, consumption, and waste process as a moral imperative, creating in people's minds the patriotic notion that living with abandon was ethically justified if not spiritually divine. Historians will say that we partied in the short-term and left the hangovers for future generations. This assumes that there will be historians; it's also possible that it may just be archeologists who are digging around.

"When asked once, "How much money is enough money?" He replied, "Just a little bit more.""

"He" is John D. Rockefeller

"There are two ways to conquer and enslave a nation. One is by the sword. The other is by debt."

John Adams

CHAPTER FIVE

Real Fiction

Corporations want as much money as possible, just like everyone else who considers themselves people. However, human persons can't compete against corporate persons who possess resources across nations and act over many generations. It's like ordinary people going up against monarchies that last generations by accumulating land and wealth. It's not possible, and often it's dangerous to try. The American Dream fails to deliver for so many people because few can be a giant, and the small people always lose. *David and Goliath* is a unique story. That's why we keep retelling the same old tale and use the title to refer to the rare underdog.[1]

The following discussion is about how the Reality Creators preserved their monarchies by transforming them into corporations. In the U.S., the Founding Fathers and their successors established corporations in the decades following the Revolutionary War, which would be an irony if it weren't so blatantly duplicitous and hypocritical. The transformation came to a head in the second half of the nineteenth century after a spurious U.S. Supreme Court statement in 1886. Reality Creators wrote laws and hijacked the Fourteenth Amendment to the U.S. Constitution to ensconce corporations as persons and build a corporatist state: a government of, by, and for corporate persons far more than it is for human persons. Theirs is a long, slow coup that has not been successfully contested.

Since the beginning of European colonialism in the sixteenth century, the Reality Creators' companies have always been set up to make money for the managers and investors, using the goods and services we make, and they own, as ways to run their system of wealth creation. Delivering profits to owners and shareholders is their original, primary, and sole purpose, and it has grown more purposed since. Except for non-profits that were first permitted in the twentieth century and have missions unrelated to profit, every other venture fills a niche in our lives for the express purpose of making money. Here's how profit-based corporations got their start.

During traditional monarchies, kings and queens had issues raising money because taxation was limited to what the poor could offer, which was too little for their tastes. The problem the aristocracy had, a problem for all times, was that the poor could not build as much wealth as the bosses wanted because they always wanted "just a little bit more."

One alternative to raising money was fighting wars pillaging each others' kingdoms and colonies. But it cost too much to get the goods since warring is never cheap. So they came up with the idea of legal pirating, which is to say, the kings decided to legalize certain types of piracy, creating a mercenary force of private businessmen. This alternative was more like private sector bullying than military officers warring. They called their legal piracy *privateering* and distinguished it from all other types of piracy.

Kings and Queens sanctioned privateering as a financial and ethical alternative to war. By doing so, they conferred justice and morality onto the practice. It was among the first public-private partnerships of the modern era. Indeed, privateers were lawless as the modern-day Somali Pirates, who are widely renowned as unregulated pure capitalists. Privateers raised their own money for ships and crews to go out onto the open sea and pirate other ships and lands to bring back treasure and imported goods to the king. This arrangement was the beginning of joint-stock companies in the modern period and the beginning of colonization.[2]

Colonization was the first iteration of globalization efforts by the Reality Creators. They saw human and natural resources all over the world, ready for exploitation. These private-sector-funded operations functioned under a revokable charter from the monarch. Privateers forcefully boarded boats and landed on the shores of indigenous peoples. They looted and took what they wanted with or without trade agreements. The native people and captains of plundered ships from other nations could not hold the privateers personally accountable for their misdeeds. Privateers traveled to places all over the globe and traded goods with the native people they came across. To say it was trading is a stretch because they frequently took advantage of the natives by maiming and killing them and destroying their villages. The trading was more like stealing because the privateers had an elective mandate to pay for their acquisitions.

The Massachusetts Bay Company, the Dutch East India Company, the Hudson Bay Company, and many others were all chartered to rake in income from around the globe for monarchies, privateers, and their investors.[3] When an indigenous person or captain of another ship asked what authority did Sir Francis Drake have to take their natural resources and cargo (after years of being an unaccountable buccaneer), he responded by holding up a charter in a language they could not read from Queen Elizabeth, whom they'd never heard of before. This violent power, justified by the monarch, gave the privateers license and immunity to act with impunity and not be held liable for their actions. Anything the privateers did was not their fault any more than, say, a soldier was held responsible for acts of war declared by the same king. Drake, Pizarro, Columbus, and others like them would kill those who got in their way. The Reality Creators wrote Maritime Law to justify their actions, not to limit them.

The ethics of profit-taking began to change with the Enlightenment of the eighteenth century and the struggles of the Seven Years War (1756 – 1763), the American Revolution (1765 – 1783), the French Revolution (1789 – 1799), and the Industrial Revolution (1760 – 1840). These events led up to the European abolishment of privateering in 1856 and the U.S. abolition of slavery following the American Civil War in 1865. Back in the day, privateers could always skim off the top of the spoils they were collecting for the king and investors, tip themselves with a treasure chest here and a bucket of jewels there, and bury it. With a new set of national governments emerging, especially with official state-run republics and democracy in America, there were weaker kings and failing monarchies. For private businessmen, tipping themselves became even easier. In the monarch's all-powerful place was a new government entity they could control by writing laws, becoming elected officials, or bribing them. Making money for themselves became the private businessmen's central goal since paying back their collected spoils to the new government was no longer seen as their mission but as a tax. The Reality Creators changed their profit-taking tactics because their desire for money and power did not lessen; if anything, it strengthened. They became the new power base, the new bosses, the Robber Barons of the nineteenth century.

In the U.S. and parts of Europe, the enlightened ethics of having inalienable rights such as justice, liberty, freedom, and equality made the premise of traditional privateering impossible to continue out in the open since it was brazen stealing and killing. The power base could no longer easily get away with blatant acts of violent oppression in the service of their wealth accumulation except for when it came to slaughtering Native-Americans and imprisoning and lynching African-Americans.

So the Reality Creators found a more subtle way to make money while still getting away with the spoils; they created a consumer-based society run by corporations. Sheldon Wolin calls the transition the result of *Inverted Totalitarianism*, where we trade in our rights for a sweet treat. The shift is from using the stick to motivate people to the carrot. In this case, the treat is consumerism, the 70% chunk of our GDP that results from buying up all the goods and services from the Reality Creators we previously made for them while at work.

Reality Creators conflate shopping with having inalienable rights to the extent that now we *shop 'til we drop*. But, we shop for their goods and services, whether directly from their corporations or from our small businesses who rely on large corporations. Our subjugation to the Reality Creators continues because, in this scenario, we effectively buy our rights from them: life (food, health, security), liberty (shelter, transportation, banking), and the pursuit of happiness (education, entertainment, vacations). When we don't have much money, they say *we can have it our way* for $1.99 or give us a public defender: you get what you pay for.

Reality Creators alienate us from our rights because they rule over our Social Contract for their benefit, not ours. They constantly change and constrict the terms and provisions for their benefit. Rather than being inalienable, we enjoy our rights in direct proportion to how much wealth we possess. The Reality Creators view rights like they view money and believe that there's only so much to go around. They view rights as precious natural resources, and like wealth, they want to concentrate rights unto themselves: freedom isn't free; only the Reality Creators can afford it. This attitude runs counter to the entire political philosophy of the U.S. and other democratic republics that explicitly call for spreading out rights among the populace. Like love, there is not supposed to be a limit to the proliferation of human rights.

To perpetrate Inverted Totalitarianism, the Reality Creators had to establish corporatism, a government of, by, and for corporations. And, the proliferation of corporations in society required a "genetic modification," where corporations became persons so the U.S. Constitution could protect them. As a result, corporate lawyers were able to successfully argue that the Fourteenth Amendment could defend the rights of corporate persons. The U.S. Supreme Court and European courts engineered this legal fiction. Here's how.

The Reality Creators came up with the idea of creating fictional corporate persons similar to the fictional money creation described in chapter four. While considering their options, sipping gin at the country club, one of them might have very well said: 'If we can't get a king to write up a charter and justify our actions to limit our liability for all we do in the course of privateering, then let's get the new government we established to write laws allowing us to modify joint-stock companies and put the burden of liability onto those entities. We shall call them corporations.'

Their idea sounds ridiculous because it is arbitrary and fictitious, but that's how the transition occurred to modern-day business incorporation. Reality Creators sat around and came up with the notion of shifting blame onto a corporation. If Drake were alive today, he would not point to a charter sanctioned by his queen. He'd point to a charter approved by the new government that he'd control. That charter would say that Drake isn't liable for actions he'd take while clocked in on the job; rather, it'd be the government-chartered corporation who did it. All of this fiction was in the pursuit of riches, the same as before.

It is ludicrous to say a corporation can accept liability for the actions of humans. Only people can accept liability because we are thinking, feeling, sapient beings with the capacity for reflection and premeditation. A rock cannot be held liable for hitting you, but the rock thrower can. The pig is not responsible for making you sick; the butcher is. The dog may be put to sleep for biting people, but the dog's owner is held accountable: euthanasia is not punishment; rather, it prevents future attacks. The NRA claims that guns don't kill people, people with guns kill people, and people have to want to load the gun, pull the trigger, and shoot up a school full of kids, which a rock, pig, or dog cannot do. Ironically, they argue that weapon manufacturers cannot be held responsible for these acts of terrorism. This glaring inconsistency demonstrates the artifice of their corporate personhood fabrication that otherwise claims responsibility in general day-to-day business when it suits them.

Since it is preposterous to permit our representatives in Congress to write outrageous laws saying a corporation is a person who can accept liability on behalf of the humans who run them, the Reality Creators had to come up with another legal solution. Instead of regular law-making in Congress, they went to the world of law created at the U.S. Supreme Court, where black-robed judges with lifetime appointments create federal case law. It's the kind of law that arises through court decisions at all judicial levels responding to lawsuits against the laws that start as bills in the federal legislature, statehouses, counties, and cities. Judicial case law results from judges tweaking the laws written by the Reality Creator politicians. Sometimes this benefits the populace; more often, it benefits the Reality Creators. When Reality Creators can't get what they want in the first draft passing their legislation, they tweak it with great patience in the courts until it's to their liking. (It's very difficult for common people to control *Common Law* briefly described below.)

Reality Creators call our judicial system *Common Law*, an innocuous sounding name. It says that judges can keep tweaking laws based on complaints they get, and most of the time, whose complaints do you believe they hear the loudest? Elected politicians pass whatever laws they can get away with without us freaking out, but of course, the laws are never severe enough nor tailored just right to suit their needs. So, they perfect their laws in their courts. This is how they continually revise the terms and provisions of the Social Contract. When we try to engage the courts in this process, the law appears to side with us by happenstance: the decision benefits the Reality Creators primarily, and us, secondarily. Other times case law appears to benefit us is when the Reality Creators deem it necessary for a little leniency to keep the farm running efficiently; to them, mercy is just another cost of doing business. Every decision I ever made farming my goats was to benefit me; when they enjoyed the fruits of my decisions, it was purely incidental to the farmer-based goal.

Corporate personhood became law over time, during which Reality Creators wrote numerous books. Corporate personhood is a key development inspired by Enlightenment philosophers. Chief among the published books were William Blackstone's *Commentaries of the Law of England* in 1765 and Stewart Kyd's *Treatise on the Law of Corporations* in 1793, works considered complementary to Adam Smith's *The Wealth of Nations* in 1776. The first two are legal treatises that envisioned corporations. The third is an economic treatise that honed capitalism. Together they and other writers (Locke, Hume, etc.) represent the birth of our modern political economy, not coincidentally at the time of the United States' founding and the writing of the *Declaration of Independence* in 1776. Blackstone called corporations artificial persons. Kyd said they are "a collection of many individuals united into one body, under a special denomination, having perpetual succession under an artificial form, and vested, by the policy of the law, with the capacity of acting, in several respects, as an individual." Smith laid out a system on how people accumulate wealth in commercial economies.

Then in 1819, Supreme Court Chief Justice John Marshall said:

"A corporation is an artificial being, invisible, intangible, and existing only in contemplation of the law." (Notably, Smith was not a fan of *joint-stock companies*, which would later come into common parlance as *corporations*. But that didn't matter since there was considerable pressure elsewhere on the matter.)

All this movement made obtaining the privilege of incorporation easier to get because the changes increased the sovereignty of private corporate charters and made them more person-like.[4] After the Civil War, the states passed the Reconstruction Amendments to the U.S. Constitution. Shockingly, the Fourteenth Amendment extending constitutional rights to former slaves was later construed by the Reality Creators to extend constitutional rights to corporations.

The Reality Creators claimed their corporations needed the same constitutional protections as former slaves. But how in the world could they argue the U.S. government could constitutionally protect corporations like human beings? It's preposterous. They never whipped corporations, bound them in shackles, or stole their children. In the words of Mark Twain: "The only difference between reality and fiction is that fiction has to be credible." Maybe, here, Twain was wrong.

U.S. Supreme Court justices cemented corporate personhood in a famous 1886 court case called *Santa Clara County v. Southern Pacific Railroad Company*. It was shady because they weren't presented a court case on the merits of the idea. Rather, the idea evolved politically for years before they came out during this particular court session and said it was so, right from the start of the argument. The in-house court reporter told of a discussion among the justices during the court session, in which they said: "corporations are persons within the meaning of the Fourteenth Amendment to the Constitution of the United States."[5] The court decision paved the way for corporations to legally accept the liabilities of the real flesh and blood humans who own and manage the corporations.

The court reporter went on to explain that: "Before argument, Mr. Chief Justice Waite said: 'The court does not wish to hear argument on the question whether the provision in the Fourteenth Amendment to the Constitution, which forbids a State to deny to any person within its jurisdiction the equal protection of the laws, applies to these corporations. We are all of the opinion that it does.'"[6]

The way it went down was absurd. The justices made a huge earth-shaking assumption that came out of thin air with dubious fictional legal presumptions and precedents from the likes of Blackstone, Kyd, lifetime-appointed judges, and from the spurious claims made in 1886 by the attorney in that court case. The justices agreed with the lawyer from the railroad company, and we all got railroaded. No one could stop them, and since then, no one has. The Reality Creators who made up this fiction and refined it over the years evolved the name from "joint-stock company" to "corporation." The Latin word for *body* is *corpus*. The attorney for the railroad corporation presented the idea to the Supreme Court justices that a corporation is a person, *a priori*, and the judges agreed with him as if it was always divinely ordained.[7]

The U.S. Supreme Court classified corporations as persons in 1886 by fiat, acting as if they were taxonomists. Since then, further case law decisions have solidified that fictitious invention.[8] The courts have used the Fourteenth Amendment to benefit corporate persons by orders of magnitude over human persons in court decisions.[9] People did not riot in the streets because the news was kept silent, which is perhaps the best example of what the red and blue teams agree upon. To this day, people still do not understand what a coup this activist judicial decision has had on their lives. Corporate persons are widely regarded as sociopaths who act in self-centered and narcissistic ways, which is why Google sought from the start to promote its brand "Don't Be Evil" to set itself apart from other corporations.[10]

This judicial activity has been the basis for all manner of corporate law, which is the realm of defending corporations' actions as if they were constitutionally protected U.S. citizens. As many have said, "I'll believe a corporation is a person when Texas executes one."

Back when kings made decrees, people went along with them. Today when the reality-creating justices make up narratives, we too go along with them. Fractional reserve banking and corporate personhood are fictional, mission-critical cornerstones of our political economy that the red and blue teams agree upon. You will never hear them argue about these structural issues in the news, nor how these fabrications breach numerous provisions of the Social Contract we have with them.

Artificial Law Made to Order

Let's move on to corporate-influenced politicians who also make up narratives out of thin air in legislative bodies and call them laws once they've agreed to the storylines. Politicians can't make unreasonable claims the way judges can in the courts. When they try, the claims never make it out of committee. The reason is that politicians are much more exposed to the citizenry than judges are. But the scope of laws our elected legislators pass is so extensive, the breadth of the legalities covering us more than equals the fewer precedent-setting judgments handed down from the court bench. Elected officials and appointed staff in cities, counties, statehouses, and the federal government pass laws that they and lobbyists make up out of whole cloth. As in judicial case law, much of the legislation is creative writing, pulp fiction to benefit corporate persons more than human persons.

Long ago, ancestral Reality Creators structured a new way to get along together and began enforcing fictional laws they made up artificially. This is now called the development of civilization. The laws that seemed to be fair were like the ones that said, "Don't kill your brother, Cain." Ancestral Reality Creators changed the natural way of life by creating laws and interrupting the wild manner in which life had previously been lived. For better and worse, this has occurred for the past 12,000 years. When the Reality Creators gamed the system, it was always worse for those who lost.[11]

Despite the pervasiveness of our modern civilization, the wild is not entirely gone. A while back, Bambi the cat came running around the corner of the greenhouse with a smug look on her face exclaiming: "I have currency! I caught it! It's mine!" She ran off with a fat green bug in her mouth that I worried was a praying mantis, so I followed. She stopped around the side of the greenhouse to get away from me. When I appeared around the corner, she took off again, across the garden and into the rocks and trees. But I did see it resembled a fat and juicy tomato worm more than a mantis. I felt better about that since killing a mantis is like killing a hawk. I felt a sense of guilt; the cat did not.

The cat found this calorie-based currency in the same way people generations ago found theirs: hunting and gathering nature's currency that grows and runs all over the place. The cat pounced on the bug. It took cunning and skill, perhaps less than it takes to catch a bird. Still, work was involved. Once the rush of catching the prey was over, the cat started to protect its rights to the prey it worked hard to catch. The cat knew others would similarly work hard to catch the same prey; however, they would spend their energies struggling to get it out of the mouth of the original owner of the prey. The cat bolted each time I got near to look at her catch, worried I would take it from her. If it had been a praying mantis, I would have spent time trying to catch the cat and free the bug to assuage my bleeding heart.

Many animals have the instinct to protect possessions for which they have worked, which any reasonable human can understand. Animals look upon caught prey as still in play until they eat it because they don't have made-up laws. But people have made up rules to govern what is or is not in play to mitigate theft and crime, or in many cases, to enable theft and crime.

Because cats don't have such rules, they have to play by natural law. To civilized people, this seems cruel and unusual: another cat bullies the one with the prey and gets it from her; that is how it goes. Perhaps she fights to get it back. Either way, there are no artificial laws to control their behavior unless humans such as myself get involved. In that case, I'm another animal. Anarchy or natural law says: whoever ends up with the bug gets the bug with no remorse or guilt, and it stays in play until torn apart and eaten. Laws that people write short-circuit this process through strict enforcement. Among humans, a police officer is supposed to stop a purse snatcher who considers the lady's purse as still in play, and a bank regulator is supposed to do their job.

The way you can tell if a law is real is whether it requires enforcement. Natural law needs no enforcement; artificial laws require constant enforcement and the alleging of guilt. Gravity, entropy, evolution, the four seasons, predation, and love need no enforcement. But what about the laws the Reality Creators make up? They need constant enforcement by a massive, tiered policing system comprised of boots on the ground, investigators, regulators, an extensive court system, and office workers crunching all the paperwork. We have well over one million officers and 800,000 National Guard troops in our nation keeping order. While we like our homes to be safe, the Reality Creators manage "public safety" so we can show up to work each day and efficiently funnel our capital their way, uninterrupted. Public safety officers enforce the Social Contract. The National Guard will keep the peace and put down large-scale civil disobedience should the police prove incapable of controlling a rebelling citizenry who revolt against unfair provisions of the Social Contract.

Reality Creators know public safety expenses are a necessary cost of doing business in the course of pitting us against each other, keeping us divided and disempowered. To be fair and sympathetic, the cops on the beat are subject to the same problems we experience: they are us. We should remember the claim by Robber Barron, Jay Gould, in 1891 that he "could hire one-half of the farmers to shoot the other half to death."

Reality Creators believe we need "America's Finest" police force in every U.S. city. For many years they stamped that slogan on patrol cars across the nation. It was an absurd impossibility that each city could have the finest force, yet that's what they believed they needed. Understandably, we need the police to stop daily violence and mobs; for that, we are grateful. This, however, does not excuse the awful times of widespread injustice, racial profiling, and inequality by which authorities enforce their laws. Nor does it address the reason why we're so frequently at each others' throats.

What about the largest military of all time? What does that say about efforts to maintain an empire? The U.S. military is equal in size to the next ten largest militaries in the world combined. Are U.S. laws that unnatural? Does the U.S. need to garrison troops in 150 countries to ensure their corporations can operate without any problems? Yes, they do, and we're the ones they put on the front lines.

Consider the struggle Gandhi had gaining independence for India by wresting control from the British elite rulers. While the colonizers had enough enforcement to control the

fractious Indian people,
they could thwart Gandhi's every move. Until WWII, Britain had enough force to rule the colony and string along the people with promises of one day being free. But, when the war broke out in Europe, there wasn't enough British force to spare ruling the people in India and fighting off Hitler at the same time. The British gave up full enforcement of their laws over Indians because they no longer had enough power to colonize India, put up with Gandhi's relentless pressure, and fight WWII. It didn't take the British long to figure out that Hitler was worse than Gandhi. The British Empire collapsed as a result of WWII. There was little justice in the Social Contract the British rulers forced onto India. Rather, they conducted a colonial invasion and occupation in which the Indians had little say. The British abrogated the Indians' rights and did not confer to them anything resembling security, stability, peace, and justice in trade for the exploitation of their natural and human resources.

Civilizing acts have equal opposite uncivilized reactions. Killing off the Native-Americans, taking their sacred lands, and creating an economy supported by free African labor civilized the wealthy colonizers. The atrocities done to the poorer sections of the world's people have always been a counterpoint to the civilizing done to benefit the upper-crust tier. Take note of how the U.S. became civilized under the new democratic laws that permitted the sickening and slaughter of tens of millions of Native-Americans and the enslavement of Africans. Today, neoliberal corporate-driven globalism uses the same playbook with a little less stick, installing petty dictators and wrecking undeveloped nations.

Enforcement of artificial laws creates negative effects on certain people to the degree that those laws are intended to create positive effects for those who write them. Laws saying "Don't Steal Bread" mean that people who would otherwise buy the bread, but can't afford to, go hungry instead. Anatole

France said: "In its majestic equality, the law forbids rich and poor alike to sleep under bridges, beg in the streets, and steal loaves of bread." Similarly, in 2010, the U.S. Supreme Court decided that the law permits rich and poor alike to contribute as much money as they can afford to fund political candidate elections. *Let them write checks.*

Fabricated laws written to benefit one class of people usually hurt others, either by accident or predetermined intent. It appears that laws protect one against another, and all too often, we're the folks who are pitted against the law. We are not all equal under the law; we never have been.

In his work, *Civilization and its Discontents*, Freud argued that feelings of guilt make civilizing humans possible. This civilizing process limited the liberties of those humans, perturbing them. This explains the notion that breaking laws is a guilty act. In the wild, cats don't feel guilty for their hunting. Only people can allege guilt when they break artificial laws. The laws that people like the best are the ones that benefit everyone, such as the Ten Commandments. Since these laws appear natural, hence inalienable, maybe even supernatural, folks like them more than the fake laws that only help corporate interests.[12]

The most artificial laws are the ones for which the corporate industries lobby. We are not unanimous in our consent that those of us who break these laws are guilty. The people who consent unanimously to these laws are the Reality Creators who stand to benefit from their enforcement; they are also the folks who had a hand in writing them. They engineer these laws to benefit corporate persons and disadvantage human persons. Ironically, those who write these laws are the guilty parties because they have to breach common decency to invent these laws and see to it they get enforced. They choose to hurt the majority of others for their sole minority benefit to profit and maintain their plutocratic status.

When we complain about being civilized by their fake laws, there's not much we can do about our discontent. Not just because they influence and control the courts, a nearly insurmountable burden, but also because multiple corporations contract with lobbyists to represent entire industries, making them *Too Big To Sue*. It's hard, if not impossible, to sue a whole industry compared to individual corporations.

Most people don't ever read the bazillions of special interest bills and riders (earmarks) that lobbyists push for at the city, county, state, and federal level. U.S. citizens and others around the globe have a gigantic world full of laws we are obliged to follow that benefit the Reality Creators who wrote them. We are all made more dependent by the laws passed on behalf of the few corporate beneficiaries who have a hand writing them because we are all the subjects of those laws limiting our liberty, freedom, justice, and equality. Of course, most of us agree that certain artificial laws are needed since we all live in a civilization of one type or another. The point is, we don't make them up, our overlords do, and that's a problem for us. Reality Creators use the government as their own HR department to manage us as a form of domestic colonization. They don't care what we look like; to them, we're all equally tasty.

"The first truth is that the liberty of a democracy is not safe if the people tolerate the growth of private power to a point where it becomes stronger than their democratic state itself. That, in essence, is fascism, ownership of government by an individual, by a group, or by any other controlling private power."

Franklin Delano Roosevelt

"Fascism should more appropriately be called Corporatism because it is a merger of state and corporate power."

Misattributed to Benito Mussolini

"I'm talking about the real owners now... the real owners. The big wealthy business interests that control things and make all the important decisions. Forget the politicians. The politicians are put there to give you the idea that you have freedom of choice. You don't. You have no choice. You have owners. They own you. They own everything. They own all the important land. They own and control the corporations. They've long since bought and paid for the Senate, the Congress, the state houses, the city halls. They got the judges in their back pockets and they own all the big media companies, so they control just about all of the news and information you get to hear. They got you by the balls. They spend billions of dollars every year lobbying. Lobbying to get what they want. Well, we know what they want. They want more for themselves and less for everybody else."

George Carlin – 2005

PART TWO

Why It's A Problem

"The real menace of our Republic is the invisible government which like a giant octopus sprawls its slimy legs over our cities, states and nation. At the head is a small group of banking houses... This little coterie...runs our government for their own selfish ends. It operates under cover of a self-created screen...seizes...our executive officers... legislative bodies...schools... courts...newspapers and every agency created for the public protection."

John F. Hylan, Mayor of New York, 1918-1925

"The world's most powerful investment bank is a great vampire squid wrapped around the face of humanity, relentlessly jamming its blood funnel into anything that smells like money."

Matt Taibbi, 2009

CHAPTER SIX

Why Reality Creators

Cannot Be Trusted

Reality Creators have too much going on. Their herd has increased by seven times since the Industrial Revolution, and it has started getting out of hand. It shouldn't be unexpected they'd eventually lose their grip on the vast power they wield because doing God's work is too much for any small set of humans to control. The work requires so much power that they cannot manage it properly. There are too few Reality Creators with too much responsibility. Call it the Atlas Age. They're shrugging along with way too much weight on their shoulders.

Reality Creators cannot carry the whole Earth. We can trace many of our problems back to the fact that they try. Sure, they have us constantly increasing productivity doing all the real work, but imagine a farmer with too many plows in the ground, a smith with too many irons in the fire, a cook with too many pots on too many stoves, or a banker with too many loans; it's just too much.

It isn't that they are jerks, aren't any fun to party with, or aren't exceptionally strong and smart. It's that they can't control their accumulated power in a manner that benefits all of us. They use their power to benefit themselves. Because we are susceptible to their whims, we are at greater, accumulated risk. Our risk accumulates in direct proportion to how their wealth accumulates. When they run up the price of oil and food, start a war, or drive our economy into the ground to increase the relative financial distance between them and us, they are not ignorant, incompetent fools; rather, they are the wealth-accumulating Reality Creators. They can't help but misuse their power to benefit themselves at our expense because they are mere parts subsumed into the larger whole described in chapter one. They are the Leviathan; we are its prey; that's why we're in its belly.

Power and control are not synonymous as they appear.[1] Lord Acton suggested that power corrupts humans.[2] It is helpful to see the gray area on a variable scale: as power increases, control over it decreases. With little power, control is easy; with absolute power, infinite control is required. Lacking sufficient control over power allows things to get out of hand. It's hard for a child to have the ability to control a walk-behind trencher or manage the power of a backhoe or muscle car. Likewise, it's a struggle for even the elite among us to control the vast power of big multinational corporations, militaries, colonies, governments, and supranational organizations. The power overwhelms them, and they get knocked about by the machinery, or they become corrupted. Capitalism permits only the successful people to rev up the economic engine to the red line and burn it out like a 16-year-old given the keys to a Porsche.

Power over huge populations, billions, is a new phenomenon, less than a few hundred years old in our civilized world, reaching back thousands of years. We are familiar with walking a few miles per hour, and having power over small families and tribes, if not just ourselves. Before the modern era, we lived the slow life. We didn't have fast food, mass weaponry, and global financial markets looming over hundreds of millions of people. Today, a few companies lord their food over much of the world in a manner that profits the powerful who seek "rent" from those of us who get hungry three times a day. The Industrial Revolution created these systems, and humans haven't evolved to keep up with the increase in power. If our biological evolution had been able to keep up with our recent technological concentration of power, perhaps the Reality Creators' expression of reasonable control would be to reject excess power.

For a long time before the Industrial Revolution, control was haphazard because power was haphazard and uneven. When the Industrial Revolution increased power during the nineteenth century, billions of horse-power-watts were created and burnt up daily. As the power became mechanized, the control became centralized and strategic. The few who held the reins of that power at the time became the future titans of industry and government. The Industrial Revolution machinery transferred power directly to the CEO Robber Barons' pockets because they could reach customers worldwide. This great power provided the capacity to mechanize society, produce dependent wage slaves, increase control over the government, and build a colonial empire at home and abroad. The idea we live under the terms of a just and moderate Social Contract is a fantasy.

If the Reality Creators had enough control over their power, they would act more compassionately, more out of a sense of community than competition. Theirs would be an ethical system prioritizing control over power, concluding that having greater control is more important than having greater power. For example, the Reality Creators should promote the idea that it's a moral imperative to check in with the Joneses, see if they have food to eat, fresh water to drink, and see if they are healthy, warm, and dry. But they don't. They promote competition with the Joneses, keeping up with their purchases, and kicking or ignoring them when they are down to get ahead. They want us to covet thy neighbor financially.

Reality Creators want us to stop at nothing to compete for

money because that makes their immense and inevitable wealth accumulation morally aspirational and virtuous for those of us who won't ever get it. They want us to resent those we view as unworthy of public support. When there are others next to us playing their position in King of the Hill, we make sure to take them down with us as we're kicked about. This makes it easy for the Reality Creators to stay on top and not slip below their class position; they have us beating on each other doing much of the dirty work for them. Noblesse Oblige be damned. The Reality Creators haven't ever cared for us in the way they have cared for themselves except when considering how our welfare benefitted them.

For example, the Reality Creators have decided in the developed world nations that if they want to extract as much wealth as possible, they've got to stop wasting it on the populace. Why would the farmer want to pay any more than necessary to feed the goats and chickens? What's it to them if they have lower-class workers or middle-class workers? More or less profit, that's what. And why waste that profit on us? In Mary Poppins, the dad takes his kids to see his workplace at the bank and make their first deposits in interest-bearing accounts. However, on the walk to the bank, the boy spends his tuppence on a bag of bread to feed the birds. This charity upset the bank owner because he sees what a waste of money feeding the pigeons is, exclaiming to the young boy: "Feed the birds and what have you got? Fat birds!"

Although Henry Ford thought it necessary for his workers to be paid well enough to afford his cars, the globalization of labor has since diminished his argument: the U.S. is only 5% of the world's population, and in the past couple generations, the offshoring of labor has split the worker from the consumer. The term for this phenomenon is *Labor Cost Arbitrage*; it essentially means having poor workers in one part of the world build products for wealthier consumers in another part. Once again, however, times are changing. Since the early

2000s, globalization is shifting, and the physical distance between the laborer who builds for the consumer is shrinking because poor people are now becoming commonplace in wealthy nations and because a small minority of rich people are beginning to filter up in the class structure in poor nations. The Labor Cost Arbitrage no longer holds people across borders; now, the disaffected workers are across town.[3] The bottom line is that the absolute number of employed hired-hands becoming useless birds is increasing, and they're subsisting closer by. It is darkly ironic that Ford contributed to making the horse into a pet.

In the course of determining how to continue motivating the populace to desire consumer goods they cannot afford (to keep currencies desirable and maintain their values), the Reality Creators have taken two actions. They have said buying something for $1.99 is *having it your way,* and they have since learned to apply the "it's the getting, not the having" principle to the economy: wanting something has more force of desire than having it. Their media pushes the desire button hard constantly, and when we look around for what we can afford to buy, we satiate ourselves on cheap crap. The Reality Creators always seek to siphon as much excess capital from our labor-consumer function as possible, and they have figured out that we don't have to spend huge, absolute amounts of money to profit off of us; rather, they just need to keep us wanting more money while increasing the relative distance between us through extreme inequality.

The most significant result of this charade has been that middle-class members have lost disposable income over the past couple of generations and have had difficulty covering the cost of living, even on two incomes. According to the RAND Corporation, the ruling class wrote laws that effectively breached the terms of our Social Contract and sucked $50 trillion from the middle and lowers classes over 45 years beginning in 1975.[4] Today, the third income producer in the middle-class family is named "debt."

Pathological Neos

The following discussion profiles the Reality Creators' political and economic psychology. It explains why they can't be trusted as good-faith parties to our Social Contract.

Of all Reality Creators, the most spooky political stooges are neoconservatives and neoliberals. They are not ordinary, decent conservatives and liberals from among the general population; rather, they are among the owner-managers of the political economy, which includes their cohort of hirelings, sycophants, and enablers. There's a range of visibility neocons and neolibs have in the media. The general rule of thumb is the spookier and less visible the operative, the better and smarter the neo. The best go unnoticed, while the "honest" ones are out front and center telling everyone their plans to take over the world.

The neoliberals are the shadiest dissemblers, whereas the neocons are less obsessed with hiding their activities. Neocons enjoy the bad press they get, whereas the neolibs always disdain all exposure, which is why their public personas are distinct from their private personas. To varying degrees, the interventionist people involved in or around the corporate-government complex are neocons or neolibs.

The neos we don't know about are stealthy; they're few in number. They act in ways we haven't yet imagined and wouldn't even recognize if they conducted those actions in plain sight. As for the activities we could discern, they ensure secrecy pervades our corporate sector, government agencies, political offices, public safety apparatuses, and, of course, our military. Their secrecy simulates a higher-order of sapience we do not possess, creating an intellectual distance, not unlike the gulf between farmers and their livestock. They correlate our relative level of sapience with our class standing: they're the real homo sapiens; we are inferior. It would not be surprising if they were found to classify us using the Linnaean system.

All neos recognize the power of the poor because that's the source of the Reality Creators' wealth. They fear the proletariat to the degree they desire its resource-rich value. To neos, risk management balances the destructive forces of a rebelling mass with the creative forces of a servile and productive proletariat.

There are a few distinguishing characteristics between neoconservatives and neoliberals. In one, the cons want to take over the world to protect and enrich themselves, whereas the libs want to take over the world to save it for everyone, regardless of whether many have to die and the rest suffer for the cause. As cats, neoliberals see no other option but to catch all the mice to save them, whereas the neocon kitties believe they must catch all the mice before the mice catch them. Neoliberals are the folks who taught the neocons during the Vietnam War that they had to destroy the town of Ben Tre in order to save it. A great neoliberal institution of our time is the U.S. Forest Service that burns down the forest to save it. Perhaps Howard Zinn said it best: "The notion of American exceptionalism—that the United States alone has the right, whether by divine sanction or moral obligation, to bring civilization, or democracy, or liberty to the rest of the world, by violence if necessary—is not new."[5] "The Beatings Will Continue Until Morale Improves," goes the old saying.

In another distinction, the libs believe that "a class of wise and virtuous people ought to rule over the common herd"[6] whereas the cons think corporate persons ought to be doing the job. One way or the other, the neos are both going to rule over us. The neolibs believe they can use the government to manage the populace. They know the government is a darn handy tool in their accumulation of our wealth. Neocons, however, don't regard the government as such a safe tool. They read their history and see how the populace could temporarily gain control of the government and upend the rulers' paradigm of power.

Neocons don't trust the government and believe it's safer to do away with it, except for the security part that protects them and their <1% status. Less government to them is less to get in their way ruling the world: the up-front costs and overhead managing the populace is much lower. Instead of draining the government of its life force, instead of reducing government like old-fashioned conservatives, neocons want to kill it off for good, homeland security and defense excepted. They want to cut taxes for themselves and run up war deficits to cripple the government and force defunding the 'discretionary' domestic spending allocated on our behalf. "Shrink it down to the size where we can drown it in the bathtub," Grover Norquist said.

Because neoliberals are an undefined bunch, much of this discussion seeks to contribute to the effort by many others to understand them.[7] As mentioned, neoconservatives have nothing to hide; they personify "What You See Is What You Get." Neoliberals outnumber neoconservatives many times over. Neoliberals used to be quite different from who they are today. Like many political terms, economic terms have changed in meaning over time. For a political example: how different are today's Republicans from the party of Lincoln, and how different are today's Democrats from the Jim Crow era? Many a KKK member was a Democrat.

Here's a brief discussion on neoliberals. In 1920s Europe, the inter-war period in Germany was a time of great suffering due to the ravages of WWI and the subsequent punishing sanctions enforced by the victors. Bleeding hearts in Germany wanted to find an easier, softer way to manage the economy than how classical *economic liberalism* of the nineteenth century functioned, so they formed *neoliberalism.* Economic liberalism was laissez-fair, unregulated capitalism. Here, the term *liberal* meant liberty to do whatever one pleased with few restraints, rules, and regulations. It is not to be confused with contemporary left-wing liberal politics, which promote market controls. Rather, Reality Creators could act with unrestrained liberty no matter the negative consequences on others. The system was nearly indistinguishable from piracy. Indeed, we called the Reality Creators of the nineteenth century Robber Barons.

Economic liberals fought back against this new idea of neoliberalism because it was too soft. Proposals cut into their profits with stiff regulations that helped the poor and middle-class, and made them look bad in comparison. So, Economic liberals shamelessly took over the term *neoliberal* to launder their image and use it to provide them political cover while they were busy taking over governments, installing political puppet dictators, and instituting rapacious monetary policies. By the middle of the twentieth century, economic liberalism had morphed into neoliberalism to cover up their nefarious activities. That's why neoliberals are secretive and despised today and why they do not act like modern-day, peace-loving liberals. Regular old liberals are the folks who prefer sharing, community support, and helping those who are disenfranchised.

For the last 70 years, the economic liberals' foreign policy has directed the take over of countries by installing dictators who permit U.S. and European corporations to colonize their people. Installing the Shah of Iran in 1953 on behalf of British Petroleum is one example. Installing Augusto Pinochet of Chile to stop his predecessor from favoring his people over U.S. global interests and geopolitics is another blatant example of the kind of leaders neos installed on behalf of the multinational corporations. Numerous African nations got the same treatment. A subset of these neoliberals are called *Economic Hitmen*, a term described later in this chapter.

Neocons, on the other hand, pretty much never bothered to launder their image. They care little about what we think of them. They are antsy, mission-driven crusaders wanting to rule the world. The difference between old fashioned conservatives and neocons is that the former has always been content to set themselves up with a nice cup of lemonade, sit in the swing chair on their porch with a shotgun on their lap, isolated, happy, and content. Neocons are way too jumpy for that. They drink rocket sodas, get up off their porch, chuck aside the shotgun for heavy weapons, and seek out the evildoers before they strike. More than preemptive strikes, these hawks prefer preventive strikes, ones that have good, long lead times. When 'the other' is fomenting evil, neocons hit them at the earliest stage possible.

The best neocons are clairaudient and can hear when their enemies call, even when the rest of us hear nothing. They know when danger is far off, long before it's within earshot. They think sitting around waiting for trouble is paranoid and reactive at best, ambushed at worst and that confronting issues is better than waiting for them to arise.

In wanting to have it all, neos instigate events. For example, beyond recognizing the danger from afar, neos create it when it suits them; they create reality. They start with a small concern of their own, similar to how they see trouble far off on the horizon. But then their little idea grows bigger as it gets closer, and it becomes more fleshed out. This is how neocons ginned up the second Iraq war and how neolibs rigged the Great Recession. Both events grew and grew as if they were distant threats looming closer and closer.

Here are three examples of the Reality Creators at their best worst:

1) Leading up to 2008, people over-extended themselves in their mortgages because the Reality Creators encouraged

people who could not afford house loans to go into debt way over their heads. In so doing, the lenders could make money in origination fees and in sales of these mortgages to other banks who then could step in and bat cleanup, foreclosing on a considerable portion of the real estate market. People took out $200k loans to buy houses; they made as many payments as possible, and then lost the houses to the banks. Did the banks effectively steal the houses?

2) This is similar to the story told by John Perkins in his *Confessions of an Economic Hit Man.* Perkins tells how imperial powers would talk undeveloped nations into IMF, World Bank, and USAID debt, so those powers could control those nations when planned defaults occurred. The global lenders made loans they knew the undeveloped world debtors couldn't pay. The lenders wrote draconian loan contingencies in advance, ordering the countries to pay up using their valuable natural resources upon default. The borrowing nations had to submit to the harsh loan terms permitting multinational corporations to extract their resources for cheap, if not free.[8]

3) Following the Great Recession, Greece began to lose its sovereignty to the European Central Bank and the IMF, institutions the wealthier neighbors, Germany, France, and Belgium control. First, leading up to the Great Recession, Goldman Sachs Bank sweet-talked Greece into loans it knew the country could never pay back. Upon default, the ECB and IMF paid off the bank and took on the Greek debt themselves. The ECB and the IMF told Greece to sell and privatize its national sovereign assets in turn for two more successive loans that perpetrated austere living conditions for the Greek citizenry. Many concluded Germany had found a way to resume taking over Europe again. This time, instead of twentieth century neocon world-warring, it was done surreptitiously by neoliberal debt control.

Subterfuge is the theme that ties these three scenarios

together. It took a varied mix of incompetence and negligence to bring them about: incompetence from an inability to manage naturally occurring external forces and negligence from the willful desire to manipulate markets to profit unethically. Some are not so charitable and call it piracy.

The Reality Creators inadvertently and intentionally perpetrated the Great Recession. Compared to how unequal people were before the Great Recession, inequality is much worse after, making the Reality Creators far more wealthy. This disaster is a good example of how individual Reality Creators would not see themselves trying to rig the economy to collapse in their favor. Nonetheless, in aggregate, they had a material effect resulting in the collapse of the economy. The most benign interpretation of how the recession started requires viewing the Reality Creators as Idiot Savants.

The Great Recession altered the ratio of wealth in the developed world, where all people lost money, but the middle-class and poor lost more than they could afford compared to the Reality Creators. Food, fuel, and housing are necessary expenses we incur. The inability to pay for those items impacts our quality of life. In contrast, the wealthy don't know what food and fuel costs or what they pay on their multiple mortgages. The crippling of the economy concentrated wealth into the Reality Creators' bank accounts by reducing the overall amount of money in the world-pile, causing millions to lose careers, houses, and even their middle-class standing. In a contrast that is stark as the inequality, the plutocrats lost a bit more in their haircut but surged in wealth relative to our holdings. People don't begrudge others' wealth as much as they begrudge the injustice of persistent and institutionalized inequality.

There is also greater inequality in the justice served. Small-time bank robbers typically go to jail for years, while none of the bankers and corporate CEOs have seen any jail time for their malfeasance since 2008. Indeed, they got to keep their hidden spoils, similar to their privateer forebears who buried their treasure. Neos reduced the absolute amount of wealth in the world by trashing the financial markets. As a result, they came out relatively ahead of the rest of us. Most people have too small or no cushion to land on when an economic collapse occurs. People hit hard ground when neos push austerity during recessions because state-funded programs close. The wealthy can afford the collapse, land on their soft piles of cash, and still buy lavish luxuries with their excess. No amount of austerity ever hurts the plutocrats.

What can explain the neo drive? Pure, unabashed colonial imperialism incentivized by greed. It comes from the "Empire of the Self," or ego, where profound narcissism plays out in real life.[9] As referred to earlier, a certain percentage, as high as 10% in the financial sector, are psychopaths. All imperialism starts with imperial individuals. We've met these folks before; they can take over an entire room and even the world. These people know, "Some are born great, some achieve greatness, and some have greatness thrust upon them."[10] They also know that some are born inferior, some achieve inferiority, and the rest must have inferiority thrust upon them.[11] Indeed, neos thrust inferiority onto others as a matter of principle. Having lower peers allows dominance over them.

Neos rub the American Dream in our faces, saying we can all be successful if we work hard and smart enough. Why do so many people struggle to get by and cover their cost of living? Could there be that many lazy and stupid Americans? Or is the game of Monopoly being played out in our lives with the neos raking in our cash each time we pass *Go*?

People work for the neos in the same manner farm animals work for the farmer, and the compensation is not worth the debasement. Farm animals did not evolve to be subservient to farmers; farmers hunted down animals and forcibly domesticated them. When wealthy landowners did it to people, we called them slaves. What do we call ourselves today, civilized or domesticated wage slaves? In Freud's crowning work, *Civilization and its Discontents*, he points out how civilization limits our freedoms, but he never pointed his finger at those who accrue the power to control the political economy to enrich themselves further. He did not critique the Reality Creators for fabricating an excessively artificial civilization engineered to increase their wealth accumulation. Discontentment is due to the ruinous provisions of the so-called Social Contract we became a party to when we were born. We must create reality ourselves and rewrite the Social Contract.

"I wonder who they are/ The men who really run this land / And I wonder why they run it/ With such a thoughtless hand. Tell me what are their names/ And on what street do they live?/ I'd like to ride right over/ This afternoon and give/ Them a piece of my mind/ About peace for mankind/ Peace is not an awful lot to ask"

David Crosby's "What are Their Names"

"The Earth is not dying; it is being killed. And the people who are killing it have names and addresses."

Utah Phillips

CHAPTER SEVEN

Reports Of A Conspiracy Are Suspect

A colony of ants is not a conspiracy, nor is the single queen. They are part of a social order that precedes them in birth and phylogeny: one that existed before any of them were born in the recent past and one that existed when the ants' ancestors were something a bit different a million generations ago. The same holds for our colonization of the Earth: it existed before all of us were born, and it existed when we were a bit different. That's not a conspiracy. While there are striking differences between human colonies and ant colonies, we have meaningful similarities that give perspective on ourselves: ants work, store food, build housing, and war with different smelling ants.

A central point in this book is that the Reality Creators don't work in conspiratorial collusion with each other so much as they compete with each other, chasing after the same goal, which is the wealth we create extracting natural resources and adding value to those resources. We should interrupt this practice and favor ourselves instead. Reality Creators generally work out in the open, although there are some tasks done behind closed doors. The second half of this chapter touches on that. The first part of this discussion is less about what is hidden from us and more about what we have become accustomed to: we miss facts that are right in front of our faces.

It is easy to see an extreme minority of humans managing

the majority since that is the dominant paradigm throughout history. Countless people have pointed this out generation after generation in their own ways; it's not a new idea; it's not a secret. With fringe exceptions, we have always been the labor force of the few owners to provide them with luxury living. In return, they let us live on their land and use limited amounts of their goods and services. Each era and locality may discover this fact for themselves and study history through this lens.

As contemporary post-agrarians in the developed world, we go to work and then go shopping from the same stores and owners. On farms, the goats and chickens need to live, so the farmer feeds them what is required. The farmer eats chicken for dinner, eats eggs for breakfast, and drinks milk all day long. This much is not a conspiracy; it is how we have evolved to live.

We work where we shop. We are the chicken and the egg. We are both eating and eaten. We are at the table and on the menu. We consume ourselves. We comprise the body of Hobbes' Leviathan precisely because that sea monster feeds on us: we are what it eats. Given the nature of our social structure overseen by the terms and provisions of our Social Contract, Reality Creators need all of us to supply the labor to create the leisure world in which they live, and we need them for those jobs and all that we buy from them, in a relationship that is fragile as it is unfair.

The current empire is not a choreographed conspiracy staged by folks in a particular space and time. The Reality Creators view themselves as going to work like everyone else, except their job is to extract our capital by any means. That's what they do when they're at work. It's not dissimilar from how the wolf naturally hunts the sheep: there's some creeping around. They don't tell us this is what they're doing, and they don't think of it as being any more immoral than the wolf does hunting domesticated sheep.

The Reality Creators ask: 'Is it my fault if I'm successful? Would you give up your success? Would you expect me to live in the stalls and sleep with the goats? No, and you'll live in the nicest house you can too. You'll buy all that you can afford and satisfy your wants as much as possible. Heck, that's what you do already, no matter how unsuccessful you are!' Anatole France would say we don't have that much success to give up. Since we want to be successful, satisfying ever-expanding wants, many of us look at the Reality Creators' argument with reason because we forget that the irrefutable math shows there is less than one percent chance we'll ever fit into their profit-sluicing cohort.

Our current social structure evolved since we began agriculture over 12,000 years ago. Each succeeding generation passed down its practices, some of which disappeared, while other traditions held on or even reappeared. In all, history has not conspired to evolve the way it has: "history's actors"[1] have competed for power, and as a result, certain changes have held on and set up, in part, the way we live today, with questions about how we got to where we are, and where are we going from here.

There are times when we have no idea what's going on any more than fish know what's above the surface of the ocean. One problem we face is that it's hard to know what we don't know; too often, we're ignorant of our ignorance. How much goes on today about the inner workings of our political economy that we don't know? Untold amounts, not necessarily because it is always hidden, but because we're not always looking. The result is that we often don't know who or what to believe, or whom, besides our neighbors, to blame for our woes.[2]

Conspiracies did not exist before strategic planning and the dawn of sapience. Our earliest ancestors, who were "history's actors," handed down basic, non-conspiratorial stuff to live by. But, then the idea occurred to humans to plan ahead, which begat thoughts of conspiracy, which is to plan in secrecy. Secrecy is a function of awareness, and conspiracies are a function of awareness. People call out conspiracies because they believe something is going on but do not know about the plan or were left out of the planning. Plans are ubiquitous and left all over, everywhere; however, the vast majority of people don't know what's going on beyond their area of expertise or local awareness.

Many people don't know what state plans are in and even if they exist at all. The mess of an empire is who knows what's going on and who doesn't among many competing interests. The former are the planners, and the latter are the planned. Confusion exists at all levels: on one level, there are planners, but from higher up, they are the planned. Confusion exists through time, where plans are made by some and then changed by others.

Alan Moore says: "The main thing that I learned about conspiracy theory is that conspiracy theorists actually believe in a conspiracy because that is more comforting. The truth of the world is that it is chaotic. The truth is that it is not the Jewish banking conspiracy or the grey aliens or the 12-foot reptiloids from another dimension that are in control. The truth is more frightening; nobody is in control. The world is rudderless."[3]

Moore is correct about the presence of chaos; however, he conflates a lack of conspiracy with chaos, and by extension, suggests order necessitates conspiracy. This is not correct. Conspiracy and happenstance can mix and match with order and chaos. Inasmuch as there is chaos, there is order too. The vast majority of all that occurs is by happenstance. Some of it looks orderly but is unplanned, and some of it looks chaotic and is planned that way. Plans are not necessarily hidden. Only when the plans are secret are they conspiracies; otherwise, the plans are just business as usual. Reality Creators obfuscate by confirming some plans and denying others, while also neither confirming nor denying plans: this is the chaos Moore sought to describe.

Because the Reality Creators are not so much in cahoots with each other to the extent that they compete with each other to control the resource we possess, they constantly struggle with each other. This competition makes them appear as if they are coordinated because they are all in alignment, seeking the same goal: our wealth and political support. Of course, there is significant engineering to our political and economic system, but that evolved in plain sight over millennia in each locality across the globe.

This notion touches on the complexity of the world in which we live. Things may appear to be a mess on the readily observable level, but zoom in or out a few levels, and they look orderly. Long before James Gleick's *Chaos Theory*, which posits that from chaos comes order and from that order comes more chaos, Scott Nearing said this in 1922:

"The economic muddle in which the world now finds itself is one of many transition periods in the history of civilization, a phase of the great revolution. Like any period of chaos, it is the seed-ground of the new order the demolition which precedes construction."

Nearing was talking about how the Reality Creators were struggling to manage this new world order. For sure, the people had little to no agency in that process. He follows up his statement with this comment about the Reality Creators:

"Out of this chaos, men must bring order, and to do this they must discover the foundations upon which the new order can be successfully built. This is the work of the engineers, the constructors of the new society."[4]

While much of what humans do is not a conspiracy, we must admit that there is some planning done in secret by powerful

Reality Creators. For example, they were fit-to-be-tied when Edward Snowden exposed the extraordinary NSA spy ring that scours every bit and byte of our digital lives worldwide, and they still won't get past their resentment of Julian Assange for exposing the U.S. State Department's bracing lack of diplomacy. State secrets and the protection of intellectual property are expected and accepted activities; they are not in the same class as the fatuous conspiracy theories of so-called secret cabals and other obscene speculations.

When the Reality Creators are not planning in secret, which is most of the time, many of their ideas remain secret due to our lack of awareness. Our reality is similar to the goats who have no idea what the farmer is thinking, and no one ever accuses farmers of conspiracy. Just because we don't know what's going on doesn't mean it's necessarily being hidden from us.

The Great Colonatus

On the global "farm," the *Great Colonatus*, there is a system to how the farm looks and how it operates. We are subject to the Social Contract and controlled by the expansive social system under which we live. Yet, we feel like we are under our control because we can choose what cereal to buy from which grocery store and for whom we can vote. *Choice Architecture* is the term used to describe how we are fenced in and allowed to select from a limited number of options per the provisions of our Social Contract. This includes acquiescing to the terms of our employment and capitulating to buy whatever they choose to sell in their capacity as propagandizing supply-siders.

After working five days per week, we figure it's rational to go shopping and consume the goods and services we made from the same places we work. No worries, right? We take for granted that corporations hire us to bring good things to life, working five days per week for up to 50 years. We don't take notice when they profit by skimming off from the laborer on the left and the consumer on the right: we think that's normal.

As mentioned in chapter four, on the left is a person under-selling their labor, renting their personhood for eight or more hours per day to the owner, and on the right is that same person, a consumer, who feels entitled to buy back whatever they can afford. We are all labor-consumers, supplying and demanding. It is a harsh dual personality, liberal vs. conservative, we endure. Reality Creators exploit this political duality during elections, knowing they have us coming and going when we have to decide which side of ourselves we will vote for: the supplier or the demander. It's so normal; we have come to accept it.

Workers who sell their labor are concerned about what they can earn. On the other hand, consumers are all about me, me, me: "My money, my rights, my property, I bought it, and it's mine." The more concerned the laborer is, the more selfish the consumer is. Consumerism begs the prioritization of individuals taking care of their needs first before anyone else. On the other hand, laborers cannot survive alone and benefit from having dependable community support. Consumer morals are at odds with labor morals. Reality Creators favor their conservative consumers more than their liberal laborers because the consumers pay money back to them, whereas the laborers extract money from them.

Reality Creators used to view labor as an asset, a good thing that made them money. Nowadays, however, labor is a cost of doing business, a liability they seek to minimize. How did this change in perspective happen? Technology and globalization have influenced this change because artificial intelligence, robotics, and cheap labor from developing nations managed to alienate humanity from the idea of personhood. No longer are humans a part of the economy as much as it is the work they do that is important. Our humanness has been cleaved from our bodies, our corpus. Now it's overseas labor, robots, and hired hands. The terms *employee* and *contractor* have lost their humanity. Corporations treat the person driving the delivery truck or gig-economy worker as an automaton.

For over 200 years, our laws have argued that a corporation is a person. This idea helped remove humanity from personhood by expanding the concept of what a person is: in this case, a sociopathic entity that the law calls a *legal fiction*. Our acquiescence to the alienation of humanity from our persons is part of normal life today. This generations-long evolution is not a conspiracy. Certainly, however, the most prescient Reality Creators took notice of it over the years and nudged it along.

As for the consumer, the change occurred when shareholders became the number one cared-for constituency, knocking down the customer from the top position. Now the Reality Creators view the customer as the mark or patsy who's gullible enough to fall for the advertisements and marketing like children for candy. They now see customers as part of an equation: $L+C=W$ (Labor + Consumer = Wealth). The consumer, like the laborer, is a factor, a thing, and no longer a human.

The old-fashioned concept that *the customer is always right* came from the idea that we were humans who deserved compassion and had our needs met with care. This made business sense. We still see this at farmers' markets, nonprofits, and mom & pop shops. But, for the portion of consumerism that is *Too Big To Fail* (70% of our GDP), shoppers have become necessary operators compelled to buy too many ephemeral goods and services not explicitly for themselves inasmuch as for those very few who profit off selling them. Their mass media tell us we will all suffer if we don't keep up the mad consumer habits that comprise most of our GDP revenue. The term *rat race* comes from this propaganda.

Customers of multinational corporations are no longer *always right* and don't *come first* anymore – at least not for ethical purposes. Instead, they are viewed with favor solely as a source of profit. While there always was an implicit rationale by shop keepers to ingratiate themselves to their customers, now the reason to please shoppers is strictly for the shareholders' benefit. Workers have been forced to accept lower wages to motivate the consumers to shop while still leaving considerable room for shareholder profit margins. Somebody has always got to pay, and beating up the laborer has been easy since no one but the unions have ever said they come first.

You could imagine the laborer and consumer getting frustrated with each other when the laborer can't make enough money for the consumer to get by. Imagine what this does to all of us since we all labor and consume. It tears us apart. The Reality Creators maintain a delicate balance to keep us from getting too frustrated with ourselves. They spend much of their time figuring out how to keep us pushed to the limit without pushing us over our limits working too hard, and paying too much.

In striking this balance, they increase our work productivity through technological advancements and by imploring us to consume harder through supply-side economics. The latter is responsible for inspiring us to buy much more than we need through mass-marketing, while the former, productivity, gets more work out of the same people by dehumanizing them. Depressed wages, increased productivity, and supply-side economics contribute to the high rate of profit multinational corporations and their owners make. Reality Creators save money by underpaying the workers around the world and by over-selling to the consumers. (They also do it by lobbying for low taxes, but that is another topic.) For us, the result is dehumanized work, cluttered garages filled with ephemera made worthless through planned obsolescence, and loads of consumer debt.

We don't pay much attention to the management of the political economy because we're immersed in it, trying to get by day-to-day. Suppose we did have time to reflect on our lives more often than we do. In that case, we might be inclined to consider how our personal missions align with the work we do during the best waking hours of our adult lives. On average, we work 90,000 hours in our lifetimes, and few of us ever step back and ask ourselves what we have accomplished. The harsh truth is that we spend our lives building the plutocrat and oligarchs' wealth. This is not a conspiracy; it is a glaring fact for all to see if they choose to look at the extraordinary income inequality in our society.

Gaslighting the Goats

Reality Creators monitor our awareness of how they run the political economy. When it seems like we're not paying much attention to certain facts, they don't bother to hide them. In the past generation, however, we've started to complain about inequality, so they have sought to deny that the labor-consumer duality is a problem for us or that it even exists. They recognize what a loss of revenue it'd be should we acknowledge that they use us to build their wealth because more of us might try to work for ourselves instead. When we ask too many questions and want to know why our society has extreme economic inequality, they tell us that they are better at building wealth. This is true, but more to the point, what they're good at is getting us to work for them. Money is a force tool, and those who have it can force others to work for them.

The top 1% in the U.S. own 20% of all the wealth. The bottom 90% of all Americans only own 25% of the nation's wealth. This means the top 9% own the rest, 55% of the nation's wealth. Economic inequality in the U.S. is extraordinary. How did this come about? Well, Carter C. Price and Kathryn Edwards of the RAND Corporation explain that if the income trends from WWII to 1975 held true going forward to 2020, we the people would have accumulated $50 trillion more in our pockets, which would have doubled our annual incomes over the past four decades up to the present.[5] Sometimes, we don't believe the facts because they are so outrageous; most of us think the numbers just can't be true. The Reality Creators worry that if we comprehend facts about their wealth extraction, then the relative wealth gap between them and us would shrink because we would do something about the injustice.

God forbid we start creating our own reality, so Reality Creators use plausible deniability, a form of gaslighting, to stem this potential disaster. They sow doubt about exploitative business functions at times when it'd be too obvious, and we would not put up with being patsy serfs to them any longer. For example, they cultivated ambiguity about whether tobacco is a poison and if climate change is bad for the environmental health of the world we live in: both result from smoke, and they have used smoke screens to obscure our understanding.

Plausible deniability is the brilliant sleight of hand that casts doubt about facts, evidence, and proof. Their criticism is that we can't trust what comes to mind. The *availability heuristic* is our failure of cognition, they say. It is one of their greatest achievements in sowing plausible deniability and doubt: 'maybe what comes to your mind isn't quite right,' they suggest. They do this in every way possible 24/7/365 in their media.[6] Many people still question whether or not it's accurate that we are their wealth builders, proving the point.

The farmer can milk and slaughter goats right in front of each other, and they do not flinch when each goat gets its turn. When the farmer offers grain, the goats fight to get first in line. We are no different when we show up to the job each day and work for the owners, then walk out the back door at the end of the day, go around to the front entrance, and shop from the same owners for all the stuff we built earlier in the day. Some send their kids off to war cheering. This is a form of slaughter when the wars are unjust and perpetrated on lies such as Vietnam and Iraq were. People who work in the gig economy and claim to be working for themselves are in a state of denial about their dehumanized status. As one prescient worker states: "You're one step above an Amazon drone."[7]

While we complain about corporate abuse, unfair provisions of the Social Contract, and how the government does not ease our plight, the Reality Creators deny that they have any power over our government or corporations. Reality Creators promote the false notion that the government is an out-of-control, headless spending monster, run by second-rate, vindictive and power-hungry, anti-social-management careerists who were not born of mothers. If anything, they blame us for why the government doesn't serve our interests.

Historically, the longest-lasting and most effective idea to control our adverse reactions to their rule was how religious Reality Creators, such as the priests and bishops, in collusion with the kings, lords, and nobles, told the populace that God's place for you was set in this lifetime. If you're poor, don't complain or fuss because, in the end, we are all equal in heaven. They said, if you do complain about the lack of socioeconomic mobility and rise up in a revolution, not only will we kill you, but God will punish you for not accepting the place he gave you in this lifetime, and to Hell you will go. People thought the rulers would know about this since they got their ideas from God because they were rich.

Then came along capitalism, a secular economic system that permitted indefinite wealth accumulation by a tiny minority. To obscure this unjust feature of capitalism, Reality Creators had to promote the lie of class mobility, that anyone can be rich if they work hard and smart enough. Hence the story of *Manifest Destiny* and the *American Dream*. The outdated religious model had outlawed class mobility to enforce poverty. In contrast, the new secular model promotes class mobility with a quiet understanding that it is mathematically impossible for the majority to succeed and become wealthy. The Reality Creators sought political cover for this impossibility by shutting us up with democracy, a false sense of political equality. They said: "You control your government. You all have one vote per person, no matter how much currency we take from you." They figured it was cheaper to give us political equality than to give us economic equality, especially since we'd mostly end up still voting for them anyway.

A few Reality Creators involved in forming the U.S. political economy looked around and saw revolutions spitting up blood during the eighteenth and nineteenth centuries. They thought that the people would not swallow capitalism for very long because the power base would master the game of this new economic system too quickly and give away their hand, if not their heads. They were concerned that if the populace was overthrowing monarchies, any uneven form of governance, such as capitalism, would put the rulers at risk. The Social Contract has never been a fair or just agreement; conning us to believe otherwise has been an ongoing effort.

The future corporate captains of America were, in many cases, politicians: wealthy landowners and businessmen who went to university. They saw that the Enlightenment philosophies about liberty, equality, freedom, and justice could also apply to the nascent capitalist economy as it did their plans for democracy. Reality Creators figured that democracy would provide political cover for their economic plans by promoting a false sense of power among the populace: they knew that no amount of voting could ever build up enough democratic power to counter the economic power the richest have. There were romantic dreamers among the bunch who were not as cynical as the rest; however, they came to the same result by more inadvertent means.

The Reality Creators set plans to game the new economic system and establish under-regulated capitalism by applying the new Enlightenment ideas of personal freedom, liberty, justice, and equality to making money: these were their terms in the Social Contract. Liberty to make money with freedom from any restraints or constrictions was at the centerpiece of their idea. This is the rapacious economic system called economic liberalism mentioned in chapter six. The Reality Creators argued that personal freedoms should not be infringed, particularly their acquisition of wealth. Their version of justice is the dark side of the Enlightenment. These days, their descendants claim that spending money is free speech, and in 2010 they got the U.S. Supreme Court to make this nutty, fictional idea into case law.

How we got to where we are today is a wonder. It's as if the Reality Creators sat around and thought about ways to counter the effects of financial inequality that capitalism would generate without countering the real effects of inequality too much. Perhaps they were looking for a way that seemed to balance power, but that did not actually do so. Sitting around a nice fire, one of them said: "If people can't have money, at least they can pretend to control the government, which is an enormous apparatus and center of international power. That will shut them up." They each raised a glass as they quoted Proverbs 22:1: "A good name is more desirable than riches." Not to be outdone, a cynic in the bunch said: "If they can't have fortune...then let them have fame!" They all cheered.

Colonial Reality Creators said among themselves while drinking gin at the club, "let's get them to call our Republic 'a Democracy.' We'll tell the people we are their special agents of change they want to see in the world...Of course, it's not true because we'll do as we please...But it sounds so good, they'll believe it." When they wrote the U.S. Constitution, the already-educated and wealthy were concerned about the uneducated populace trashing the government. The Reality Creators did not want them influencing the government, so they gave the right to vote only to white landowners who were wealthier than other citizens. It was a throw-away bone on which to chew: one white landowner, one vote.

The one landowner, one vote scheme created an entire period of dreamy free-love with folks writing about personal rights, freedoms, thoughts, expression, privacy, and money. "The only purpose for which power can be rightfully exercised over any member of a civilized community, against his will, is to prevent harm to others."[8] Books on economics by Ricardo and Malthus despaired about the impossible conditions of the poor, but others hammered home the idea that individuals had inalienable rights to be happy as if in heaven.

Apart from the poor who lived in squalor, all this dreaming led the middle sliver of the populace to wrongly believing that democracy and capitalism worked together. They thought if they labored hard and voted their conscience, they would be financially successful and free to live a life of their choosing, of their creation. However, as time progressed, the glaring inequality between the few and the many remained obvious and grew. As desirable as capitalism is, it is likewise difficult to pull off without complaints such as those during the Gilded Age and the protests happening apace these days. Strife has long been the Reality Creators' concern because it eats into their profits.

To pull it off, they had to pretend to make us all equals, giving slaves, non-land owners, and, eventually, even women rights to vote. Saying we all had political equality was to prevent us from complaining that we lacked economic equality. The Reality Creators told people they were all equals, so those who were women or were not wealthy could no longer complain about being unequal. It is hardly cynical to argue that this is the reason for democracy in America and how it functions in the U.S. republic.

Capitalism promotes much more inequality than democracy ensures equality. Democracy is no match for capitalism. What is one vote compared to billions and trillions of dollars? Instead of going hand in hand, capitalism and democracy have conflicting goals, and what's surprising is how weak democracy is. Not even millions of voting U.S. citizens can counter the inequality of capitalism.

In just 240 years since 1776, the Reality Creators concentrated our wealth into their pockets like never before. They gained complete control of the government we elect and created a domestic colonial system in the process, all by the unjust terms of our Social Contract. Upton Sinclair said: "It is difficult to get a man to understand something, when his salary depends on his not understanding it." With the diminishing wages and pervasive income inequality these days, it appears we don't have the salaries to blind us, and we're beginning to take notice.

We have started seeing what's behind the curtain, which is unnerving to the owners and managers of the political economy. The gross misrepresentations in the media discussed in chapter one are becoming noticed by an increasing number of people. The political and social movements on the left and the right are one big class of people who share core, foundational issues at heart despite glaring, diverse cultural differences among those on either side. They are opposites on the surface, but they share substantial concerns down below in the undercurrent. This cohort is the future political bloc that will change the way we live in the twenty-first century.

The Reality Creators don't want us paying attention to these foundational core issues that they agree are mission-critical to their management of the political economy. As mentioned earlier, the way you can tell what the Reality Creators' red and blue teams agree upon are the issues they don't talk about. These are the issues that matter to us. Indeed, the concerns they openly debate and fight over are wedge issues, distractions designed to drive us apart like skittering water bugs, diverting our attention from the silent undercurrent issues that flow throughout society. These undercurrent issues are concerns that we have taken for granted and not thought to question, inspect, or critique too much until recently. They are capital flows. But now, folks are starting to see all this right in front of their eyes. They're starting to feel it in their hearts, and they're starting to hear it in their imaginative minds. Gaslighting us has become more difficult.

What we have in common is far more important than the wedge issues that they hammer day in and out, driving us apart. The constant and well-documented alienation effort by the Reality Creators has kept us divided and skeptical of each other. As a result, we have struggled to unite over important issues. They have noticed in the recent past that we have begun to realize what we have in common. They've seen our kids playing in the park together at our barbecues. They've seen us at our churches, schools, and ball fields, and they have noticed we go to the movies together, laughing and crying at the same parts.

We are beginning to have a simultaneous realization about what's going on in our lives. It feels like we are using our ability to see our lives, culture, heritage, and the greater society we live in as a reality created by others outside our sphere of control. Our present moment results from using our intuition to wonder about the world in which we live. Stanley Milgram would say we are on the road to becoming our own agents, our own sovereign bosses, and that is good for society.

"In God We Trust, Everyone Else We Monitor."

Traditional Motto of the Armed and Espionage
Services, Author unknown

"No matter how cynical you become, it's never enough to keep up."

Lily Tomlin

CHAPTER EIGHT

People Eat and Poop,

Corporations Feed and Lay Waste

There are many ways the Reality Creators control us to extract our wealth efficiently. Beyond manipulating our government as an HR department to manage us through their executive, legislative, judicial, police, and military control; beyond marketing purchases to us as if we had a meaningful choice; beyond controlling us through our labor-consumer-voter function; even beyond the debt-control they have over us, there is one necessity closely related to our immediate, everyday existence that's worth noting above all else at the core of our daily lives: eating. It's been said, "you are what you eat." In this chapter, we're going to explore what we've become.

Farmers feed their flocks and have control over the animals' sustenance and water. It may seem no big deal, but if they're late with hay in the evening, the goats complain noisily, and if the chickens haven't gotten their food scraps on time, they flock like crazy when they do. The farmer never considers missing a feeding, as that would be an utter catastrophe when the animals started revolting. The noise, the maltreatment of each other, the structural damage done to the stalls, and the eventual attack on the farmer when the feeding resumed would all but prevent being late for feeding, ever.[1] It would not be unlike urban riots.

Our food production and distribution technology have

changed due to modern advancements. Now, the food we eat is processed and put in front of our mouths like we are babies. In the past, we were more self-reliant about feeding ourselves. Today we are reliant on the Reality Creators' corporations for the food and liquids we drink, from the chlorinated municipal water supplies and well pumps we buy to the genetically modified and patented seeds to the scientifically engineered and processed fast food. An important distinction between the past and present is that we grew the food and fed the bosses. Today, it's the opposite, and they feed us.

There's a number line along which we find ourselves regarding how we acquire, prepare, and eat our food. That line, a continuum, has on the one side people incapable of feeding themselves, to those on the other side who can feed themselves from the dirt of the Earth. Before WWII, people could feed themselves in close-knit families. Often, families made home-cooked recipes from scratch, with bread, meat, and vegetables raised on the property or grown regionally. While the food was simple and repetitious, sometimes even downright trash, today, our food is surprisingly simple, repetitious, and junk as well.

After WWII, corporations developed agribusiness, producing mass quantities of corn, soy, wheat, rice, potatoes, dairy, and meat at economies of scale that reduced the costs below the prevailing wholesale prices at which small farms sold their crops. It was just enough to put out of business the dinner table economics of the family farm. In the last century, the U.S. went from having more than 50% of the population farming to only one percent.[2] People who kept the value of their labor on the farm by working their fields and preserving food to cook for themselves took their labor and gave it to an outside employer all day. They had no time to farm and preserve food for themselves anymore. Most people approve of this change and like living in a post-agrarian society.

China has moved 250 million people off their farms and into apartment buildings in brand new cities located right where the farms had been. Reality Creators in China are moving another 250 million people off their farms in the next 20 years. The reason they claim is that farmers have no need for shopping. China is trying to build up an American-style consumer economy, so they must condemn the farms through eminent domain. The Chinese government lavishes money on the farmers in exchange for their land to ensure that they can afford the new economic lifestyle. If they need anything, they now have to pay for it instead of digging it up from the Earth.

The rulers force the farmers to succumb to a helpless and dependent consumer-based lifestyle, whether they like it or not. This is a violent and totalitarian attack on their human rights. For sure, China is getting its "America on" using the stick instead of the carrot. The younger people acquiesce to this change much more quickly than do the elders, and in a generation, few will be left aware of what life used to be like.

In developed nations, Reality Creators could extract farming from our lives because technology advanced due to the Industrial Revolution and increased production after WWII. The western nations did this much more slowly than the Chinese, and we never noticed it. Farming resembles hard work and takes all day. Technology promised to take that away, allowing us to live like the nobility we wished we were. The promise that *work will set you free* became *technology will set you free*. Surely the Chinese farmers are told *shopping will set you free* as they move onto the 43rd floor of their new apartment building. Now they must pay rent for the rest of their lives. How is this racket different from being forcibly imprisoned? One difference is that they have to pay for their incarceration.

By the 1970s, U.S. corporations had consolidated smaller farms into giant conglomerates. Big-Ag farmers maxed out their production capacity, and the U.S. government gave them welfare subsidies as needed to reach an agreed-upon annual farm income (over-supply would drive down wholesale prices). This over-production was the exact opposite of the existing policy put in place after the Great Depression; indeed, it was the birth of neoliberal supply-side economics.[3]

The Reality Creators went to their brethren at the local, county, state, and federal levels and began lobbying them to pass additional laws favoring agribusiness to benefit the genetically modified plant-science, the petrochemical industry, the mega grain co-ops, the extensive production and distribution systems, the mono-cropping, the mass marketing, the industrial food processing, the lawsuits against saving seeds, the patenting of life, and the so-called "Nutrition Facts." This lobbying included asking for draconian regulations to be put on their industry because only large corporations would have the economy of scale to comply with such regulations. Small farmers went out of business, cursing the government the whole way. Instead, they should have been cursing the Reality Creators who control the government ahead of them.

Taking control of family farming is profitable, which led the Reality Creators to conclude it would also be profitable to control our kitchen. Now they feed us cooked ingredients three times a day. The number of people who do not eat at home has skyrocketed; only half of U.S. adults cook on any given day.[4]

The following explanation demonstrates how people get by these days, described along a continuum. There is a correlation with an increase in financial wealth as the continuum goes from 1-2-3-4. It goes down in financial wealth as the continuum nears its end at 5-6:

1) More than a quarter of U.S. citizens now get their sustenance at a fast food joint at least once each day.[5] Fewer people eat at home because they are served pre-processed foods at cafeterias located in schools, prisons, homeless shelters, and work. They are also fed at gas station food warmers and standard

restaurants. Too many of us were never taught to cook and saw little of it growing up; we never went into grocery stores more than a few times per year and now have no idea how to navigate the aisles and products for sale. No wonder gardening is far from home: on average, the food we buy travels 1,500 miles, which is how restaurants and grocery stores stock out-of-season foods all year long.

2) Here, folks eat fast food too but will shop at the grocery store and buy more of the frozen and canned instant meals such as all those products you microwave in its plastic container and eat. These processed food meals are no more or less healthy than the prepared fast food at a drive-thru, but you take it with you to work or home and feel like you're cooking and eating with a little more self-reliance and choice. People eat this way because it is far cheaper and easier than cooking from scratch. Given the lack of free time and finances working for the demanding bosses building their wealth, it is understandable why such food gets consumed by so many.

3) Folks here will eat fast food on the way to the soccer game or the road trip touring a theatre show, but mostly get their food from the grocery store, shopping in the middle aisles, where the semi and fully processed, multi-ingredient products are located.[6] Cooking is heating the tomato sauce and boiling the spaghetti, making a salad from a bag, baking foiled garlic bread, but not cooking from scratch. Shoppers will venture out to the store's perimeter to buy fruit, cheese, and meat when they come to the end of aisles. Those items are similar to what we would have raised fresh on the farm. They are expensive and bought sparingly. Still, getting together around the table is a near impossibility most nights with so much going on in the family: food is eaten around the clock and around the house, whenever individual family members are home, and dishes stack up in the kitchen sink until someone is fed up enough to do them.

4) These people have the cash to buy organic food and linger around the perimeter of the grocery store, acquiring expensive single-ingredient items such as fruits, vegetables, dairy products, and select cuts of meat and fish. They go in a few aisles and buy oils, flour, rice, sugar, coffee, spices, and pasta. They buy occasional exotic items if they feel flush or if they're wealthy and don't care about the cost. They will buy ice cream and brie. They don't go to fast food joints but maybe a few times per year and say they regret it each time. These people will cook their food and save leftovers for later. They learned all this behavior at home when they grew up with parents who shopped and cooked. They may have had parents who had a small garden plot with a few tomatoes and like the romance of attending the farmers' market each week. These people may try to start a window box of herbs or a small garden plot of tomatoes after one or two seasons attending the farmers' market and "shaking the hand that feeds you."[7]

5) These people are less than 1% of the population.[8] Most of them live on a small family farm and produce more than half of what they need at home. They buy the other half from corporate boxes and the rare mom & pop shop. Of 2.1 million farms today, about half make under $10,000 per year, 44% make up to $250,000 per year, and shop for what else they need. The remaining 6% are gigantic agri-businesses.

The poor half have a cow or two, perhaps goats to milk and eat, chickens that lay eggs, an acre or two of gardens. For those busy-bodies, extra food, plants, and seeds are sold at the farmers' market. These folks live like *The Waltons* on T.V., half on the land and half on the corporation. They are subsistence farmers scratching out a simple existence and thumbing their smartphones. They hunt and fish. They preserve their food by canning, freezing, and drying, and they save their heirloom seeds for the next year's planting. They spend much of their time living; sometimes, it takes them all day long to live. They share two or three homemade meals together every day.

6) These people don't exist in the developed or developing world and are thought to be nearly extinct. They don't have anything to do with the corporations; they don't do cars, stores, utilities, nothing that they can't get from the Earth, there at their feet. They build their shelters, hunt, gather, grow, raise their food, and live as many people did before the Industrial Revolution. Homeless folks and hermits such as Christopher Knight of Maine are not part of this group because they wear clothes, eat processed food, collect various manufactured goods, push shopping carts, and live in tents made by modern industrial processes.

For perspective, hominids began walking around the Earth about 2 million years ago. Humans became intelligent and wise less than 200,000 years ago. Greeks fought wars and staged tragedies only 2,000 years ago, and the Industrial Revolution began just over 200 years ago. The Industrial Revolution has been around a $1/10,000^{th}$ slice of time, compared to the 2 million years, and just $1/1,000^{th}$ of the time since we became sapient, and only ten times since Oedipus left his mark on his mother and plucked out his eyes.

We humans have radically changed how we live and eat during a 200-year blip in time. Our extreme division of labor has exploded into existence. Now life is more different for "i-people" than biological evolution could have ever envisioned or kept pace: even smartphones have radically changed life in just 15 years. The results are just coming in because the effects are precipitous and recent.[9]

Given this massive and rapid change, we can see why feeding humans has become the new way for Reality Creators to control people and keep them as dependent as babies. We are served what we need in life; all we have to do is pick it up off the shelf. All of us are "shelf pickers," and our fought-for freedom is whether we choose to pick off the Walmart shelf, the Costco shelf, or the Amazon URL, pushing around our finger and cart. Perhaps more optimistically, we're driving our tractor-cart down the aisles like it was our plow, mower, and combine. Shopping is not an expression of freedom. We have no alternative to fuel, feed, clothe, and care for ourselves. *Choice Architecture* should be called *Choice Stricture*. We have to get our necessities from a box to survive. There's no other way for 330 million U.S. citizens, 700+ million Europeans, and so many others in the developed and developing world to make do. You can tell you are not independent and free if you cannot be left on your own with a community to live outside the box.

Down On the Farm

The goats live in a box-like stall along a nice hillside under trees and among the over-browsed brush. Since it's fenced in along the river, the goats have eaten everything down to the nubbins. At first, we didn't need to feed them any hay, but now that's all they get, except grain for the three milkers. We pay to buy the hay from afar and truck it in a few bales at a time. We are their Reality Creators.

Goats are escape artists and try to get out of our fenced area because they like to browse. Our market gardens and fruit trees are covered with food for the goats, whereas their fenced area is now all brown and dusty compacted earth. Our goats prefer feeding themselves always, but if there is no food for them to eat because they've been fenced in an area that's been beaten down, then they'll take the food we give them. If we ration the food too tightly, the goats will be pushy at feeding time; otherwise, if well-fed, they'll take note of the hay tossed into the feed rack but won't get up from resting and chewing their cud. People are contented too when there's enough food to go around.

Goats will eat a surprising array of wild vegetation, but they won't eat stepped-on food unless they're hungry. People won't eat stepped-on food unless they're hungry. They eat a surprising array of food if one considers the global diet of indigenous peoples and not just the processed food made by the corporations. For instance, the goats will eat hundreds of species of plants when they browse through natural vegetation but eat only a few species when served processed food supplied by people: hay, corn, barley, and oats. People from different cultures worldwide have eaten most plants or animals and have the recipes to prove it. When the corporations got involved with farming, the diet of people in the U.S. and around much of the world became simpler, made of the same few ingredients that we feed to the livestock we milk and eat. The nanny corporations feed the stock animals and people in pretty much the same manner and with the same intention: to get value out of them.

Developers who planned the cities and suburbs after WWII did not leave enough open space for gardens and farming, nor did they plan for agricultural infrastructure. All they planned for was densely packed housing, commercial buildings, industrial facilities, and shared utilities. Density increased in the formerly rural areas and arable lands. Now people live in clumps across the country. (What they're doing in China is much faster, about 250 million people over 20 years are moved off farms into apartments.) People live in areas that are "over-browsed," or, better put, *over-developed*. In this sense, over-developed means living in such density that people cannot grow their food and must go into corporate-owned boxes to survive. There is no agricultural value left to the land that hasn't already been extracted by developers, who scraped, paved, and sold it off. There is too little value left to the land for farming, where most people live. The U.S. is not a developed nation; rather, it's an over-developed nation.

Urban in-fill is necessary to prevent further damaging sprawl in the backcountry and works only if the massive food production and distribution systems keep people filled up.

It would be a pity if 330 million U.S. citizens continued to sprawl all over the country, throughout the golden plains, up and down the California Central Valley, and out across the fields of the old south because all the natural habitat and beauty would be destroyed far more extensively than it already is today. America looked bucolic when there were only 100 million citizens, half of whom dotted their homesteads in and amongst the fruited plains. Today, there are too many people to spread out on five to 40-acre homesteads. Urban in-fill and tightly packed suburbs are necessary to accommodate our population explosion since the Industrial Revolution.

The Reality Creators have no other way to deal with such a large breeding stock of worker-consumers. Cities are necessary because they use density to mitigate large populations. The prevalence of cities above a certain point is evidence of over-population because the trade-off with density is total reliance on a fragile social structure. There is no consensus defining what is too great of a population, either regionally or globally. However, the vast majority of people rely on modern systems beyond their control for survival, and this precarious circumstance is unprecedented in history.

Some of the more prescient Reality Creators are worried about taking care of us because they see the problems of managing highly reliant residents living under extreme metropolitan density. In low-density rural areas, country-folk live like people in the suburbs and cities, buying all they need from stores except for the occasional garden item. With 85% of people in developed nations cooped up in suburbs and cities, and the rest living as if they do, it's fair to say they are in the same situation as the fenced-in goats, except that the goats always want to find a way out to browse, and the people don't. Why?

With a culture that does not teach farming; with land-use planning that does not provide sufficient agricultural space around homes; with a corporate box-like place providing everything we need to live without having to pick it off a tree or dig it up out of the ground; with a scheme of selling off our labor to the corporations to afford their products we build for them; with the invention of debt that allows us to sell off less of our labor than the value of products and services we consume, and with the constant fabricated media messages blaring that all of this is exceptional, how is anyone ever going to want to live or survive outside the box? Where's the incentive to do otherwise?

Choice Architecture is a form of poverty, where the real cost is the freedom we give up controlling our lives. A few people may want to live outside the box and rough it, even though they have become accustomed to living with technology and no self-reliance at all. Not everybody can be Scott and Helen Nearing, who believed others could live on the Earth the rural way they did. Those few who want to become more self-reliant and live outside the box need to find affordable land and farm it; they need to hunt and fish and do endless housework. But the majority cannot afford to quit their jobs, pay off their mortgages, move their whole family, and buy arable land to farm.

The Nearings were well-off, highly educated, competent, and lived four generations ago when folks had a fighting chance. Today, most people wouldn't know what to do if they ever got to a rural piece of land besides just living on it like a suburban resident. Grandma and Grandpa never taught them how to homestead. It's a different way of life with a set of skills to develop that takes years to master. It's not a book-learning field. No more people than those who already farm want to or can afford to live by their own means; otherwise, we'd see more of it.

The vast majority of rural folk have no interest in farming. Some prefer natural settings over urban ones and want to live in a bucolic environment in the same manner people live in cities with amenities. There is funding available to build more structures and roads as the population grows, and little to none for tearing up the streets and parking lots, returning them to bare earth. Expensive construction equipment usually rolls around while diesel fuel is cheap, and the bank loans are plentiful. Concrete and pavement are the last crops we'll ever reap from the Earth once installed. It's a pity we paved over so much of the fertile land. The over-developed areas are permanent and are like big stock pens. The proof of this is in the capacity for containment: the people cannot escape, and when a hurricane or fire wipes out a city, everyone flees to another city and comes right back as soon as they can.

The Reality Creators' corporations feed, bathe, and house the people. The people paying their mortgages, utilities, food bills, waste management, insurance, and other expenses are all paying to the corporations. They care for us like parents who give us a select few choices we can make. If one day the Reality Creators have to sell the farm and cannot feed, bathe and house the people, there will be problems for those who survive by getting what they need from corporate box stores, especially those who have to drive to get there.[10]

When times are good, the goats and chickens go to the feed rack or trough, eat the food farmers toss them, and pay rent with their milk, eggs, and lives. Because the Reality Creators don't milk people and eat their children, they make us pay rent with the value of the hard work our labor provides. They also periodically send our children off to slaughter in their wars every once in a while, and some particularly evil despots have even made soap out of innocents.

The goats run into their stalls, get locked in, and sleep for the night before they get let out the next morning, to the dry, dusty compacted earth they've over-browsed. Same with the people going to work, school, and prison. In all this, people struggle to acquire money to shop for food in the boxes. But there is a much bigger, lurking problem of once getting into the box, only to find it empty; no one shops in an empty box, regardless of wealth carted about in wheelbarrows. How did society get to the point where people must go into boxes to survive? The answer lies in the loss of knowledge, generation after generation, of how to live outside the box like people did before WWII, and to a much greater extent, before Industrial Revolution times. Will we go on forever with an increasing division of labor as technology marches on to save us from ourselves? Were we all born in a sweet spot of history and can't imagine a different reality?

A big box drought is unfathomable but not impossible. Exhibit A: for the simple reason of a political spat, Venezuela, the nation with the largest petroleum reserves in the world, collapsed and is experiencing extreme poverty and austerity. This resulted from political incompetence within the nation and external political forces punishing Venezuela for that incompetence. We know that it is easier to break nations than to build them (see Iraq); however, we live with a false sense of security that our developed and developing world nations are safer than they really are. It does not take much to bring them down, and politics is a much weaker force than Nature. The current political incompetence in the U.S. is renowned worldwide, and its citizens call it the *Greatest Nation On Earth*, foretelling a coming fall.

How long can the good times go on, forever? When the goats slide from the developed to undeveloped world living conditions, and they are left to fend for themselves and browse freely, to find shelter and safety, get fresh water and poop without concern, they'll be happy still, even as they have to run away from lions.[11] Us, maybe not so much.

PART THREE

How It Gets Worse

"This struggle may be a moral one, or it may be a physical one, and it may be both moral and physical, but it must be a struggle. Power concedes nothing without a demand. It never did and it never will. Find out just what any people will quietly submit to and you have found out the exact measure of injustice and wrong which will be imposed upon them, and these will continue till they are resisted with either words or blows, or with both. The limits of tyrants are prescribed by the endurance of those whom they oppress."

Frederick Douglass, 1857

CHAPTER NINE

Vertigo

Up to this point, we've explored the existential problem of our Social Contract and what it's like to be subject to a political economy we do not own or control, subject to a system that requires us to pay rent to the owners with our underpaid work and overpaid purchases that our daily labor produces. Our predicament is a form of debt bondage we cannot fully repay to the rent-seeking Reality Creators and therein poses a chronic existential threat to our lives. But we still have another pressing question that is not going away: what could happen when acute externalities strike this delicate and fragile system the Reality Creators run that we desperately rely upon for survival?

This chapter seeks to explore natural and human-made problems in the context of our dependence on technology, our extreme division of labor, and leadership provided by the Reality Creators. It is a fragile if not nasty circumstance to be reliant upon a political economy we don't control and could easily malfunction or even fall apart to one degree or another. Since it's come to the point when time is further along than it's ever been before, we need to get cracking on this discussion.

Expectations people have for daily life vary based on their wealth. A developed world resident will declare their day ruined because they ran out of gas and were made late to the shopping mall or work, while another person living in the undeveloped world had a bad day because their source of water ran out.

My close friend Al pointed out the difference between first and third world problems to me one day when I was struggling to close the annual fiscal budget on a year's worth of non-profit activity conducted on behalf of the community in which we worked dancing. He asked me how my roof was. Fine, I said. He asked how my health was. Fine. My running water, did I have any, and was it fresh? Yes, I said. And the trash, was it taken out this week, and did all the plumbing still work, least of which, did the toilets flush and had we enough toilet paper? Yes. While it was near the end of June, he did wonder if it wasn't a bit too stuffy for me in the loft-like office that had no air conditioning. Were I and the computers alright? Yes. Lastly, Al inquired about my feelings. How did I feel, a bit down, maybe a little burnt out from working so hard? Perhaps a short holiday would help once the budget was finalized. He was concerned for me: I had first world problems.

Developed world problems are known as luxury problems. They include such concerns as being late for work, over-drawing your checking account, waiting in long grocery lines, burning the rib-eye steaks on the grill, your house being too big to clean, and being stuck in traffic two hours a day (the equivalent of a full work-year every four years).

Undeveloped world problems include not feeling safe from juntas, war crimes, roving drug-thug gangs, HIV, malaria, cholera, dysentery, and not feeling protected from being raped, assaulted, and killed for being a woman. They include not having fresh water, education, children who survive to their fifth year, not having a place to defecate cleanly, a regular supply of food, a roof when it rains and snows, and earthquake-safe buildings.

If there's a false dream promoted by the likes of the UN, IMF, ECB, the World Bank, USAID, IAEA, NATO, OPEC, and the WTO about rising through the ranks from the third to the second to the first world, *joining the community of nations* as the Reality Creators say, then there's also a fact they ignore: falling backward off a cliff. The vast majority of people in the developed world don't know how to farm or live off the land. Even if they had enough space and equipment, less than one percent are set up to do this now. Should a lack of oil, electricity, or a combination of events such as a large-scale war, pandemic, or financial collapse of the dollar occur, there would be no second world stop on the way down to the undeveloped world. It is safer to already be at rock bottom in the undeveloped world than to hit bottom from up on high. Depressions are less of a concern to those who are already broke. When the power goes out in India, most of the population doesn't even notice.

But the modern, developed world lifestyle is an empire, and we notice the lights. What we do not realize, however, is how thin the line is between the relative affluence we have today and the poverty we could have in the future. We use electricity in our house the instant Reality Creators produce it, as do bankers who keep 92% of the world's currency on their hard drives. Militaries write malware should they want to disrupt economies by shutting down electrical grids in other nations.

Modern hospitals do poorly without electricity, as do financial markets, food production and distribution, manufacturing and transportation sectors, gas pumps, ATMs, cell phones, refrigerators, and lights. Our modern system is like a spider's web spun in three dimensions and tacked to the corner of the barn door by five elegant strands. Cut one elegant strand, and an entire side collapses into itself. Reach in, cut an arabesque strand from the center, and watch the same effect occur inside the globe-shaped web. It doesn't take many cuts to bring the entire web crashing down.

We are dependent on technology developed over the past 250 years to the point of a life-and-death addiction. Electricity and oil are interrelated energy supplies, and we need them for every aspect of our lives. Without both, the developed and developing worlds are not possible. In the nations that use up more than average resources, people expect to go into corporate boxes to get what they need any time of the day; this is our exceptional *First World Way*. We're willing to go to war fighting for our freedom to maintain our lifestyle, which, ironically, is a collective lack of independence. Like addicts, we'll fight to the death to perpetuate the political economy we rely upon no matter how potentially unreliable that system may be.

Our recent generations have grown to live like this. Citizens of the developed world cannot imagine any differently. We are not aware of the corporate veil that hangs in front of our face, filtering reality and shielding portions of the Earth from us such that we do not know from where our food comes or how to provide for our shelter, health, and happiness. Our culture is like a thin plastic film laid out and shrink-wrapped over nature to prevent us from contacting the earthy Earth. To catch up with us, the Chinese are paving over farmland as fast as possible.

Today we eat happy meals inside an Ikea-furnished condo while tooling around Facebook, watching T.V., and snacking on dietary supplements and meds. There's no muddy garden, hanging carcass, forest management, or computer server farms hogging energy in this scenario. Technology manages waste removal, so we don't have to deal with our own personal expression of nature, perhaps the closest we ever get to nature these days.

If it's hard to imagine that the Reality Creators can drop the ball, leaving all of us scrambling on our own with no resources to live, then the preconditions are set for what is called a Black Swan event.[1] The term is hundreds of years old and refers to an unbelievable occurrence or phenomenon, such as seeing a black swan. Today it has come to mean an event with three parts: 1) the event is unimaginable and unfathomable, hence unpredictable; 2) it is unprecedented in its short and long-term effects on our lives, and 3) it is seen in hindsight as having been capable of being predicted if someone had done so, and that others had sympathetically listened.[2]

Three hundred thirty million U.S. citizens who like to have it their way would be surprised in a Black Swan event to find out the doors were locked to the boxes or that the shelves weren't stocked well. We would all be shocked by long outages of electricity, fuel, food, fresh water, and no waste removal. Without the nanny corporations we rely upon, we would become helpless overnight because we live in such great population density and cannot go up the hill to fetch a pail of water. This lifestyle is not sustainable now and in the future.

Throughout the developed world, employees stock store shelves at night, putting back all the stuff we picked off them during the day. Gone are the many warehouses storing what we need before we buy it because much of the goods are stored in the delivery trucks and brought *just in time* to shelves that alert the logistics system when stocks get low. Warehousing on wheels is a fragile system where one link could break, and too much of it would come to a halt. Fuel availability could be a problem with the stability of this system by which we get our stuff. U.S. citizens and others in the developed world are dependent on this complex and delicate food and supplies distribution system.

The claim that this global system is decentralized and therefore robust is founded upon a false sense of security, not only because of the ongoing need to keep balanced diplomatic relations, but because the choke point is energy, and energy disruption is a significant existential threat. A failure of energy production and distribution could send some folks right into undeveloped conditions. Venezuela is one such example. This book has argued that true decentralization existed before the extreme division of labor and our utter reliance on technology took hold; now we have to worry about getting along diplomatically to get along.

Claims by the Reality Creators that their modern industrial production, distribution, and energy supply systems are decentralized and robust are gross misrepresentations of fact and contribute to the gaslighting they do to us. The irony of the existential threat hanging over us is that we cannot have real decentralization without suffering a fall back into undeveloped living conditions, and that would be a disaster since we require modern systems to care for us at an economy of scale made possible by technology and a division of labor. It is precisely this conundrum that drives the Reality Creators to push ahead, solving the problem of fragility with more of what has made us fragile.

Recall the few percent left behind in New Orleans who did not get out of the city before Hurricane Katrina? That group managed to loot many of the stores in a matter of hours after the storm had passed, and they even took broken durable goods they couldn't use. In the event larger scale events occurred, we would start hunting and gathering for food and supplies. First, it would be called looting; then, after a day or two, it would be called terrorizing when frustration broke out with neighbors attacking the Joneses.

The 1973 oil crisis resulted from the Saudi Arabian government turning down the oil spigot over a dispute with the U.S. We had a small disjunction in the supply and demand for petroleum. We can have most of the oil we need but cannot refine and transport it to the pump if we don't have all the oil we need. People had trouble getting gas; the decade from the mid-70s to the early 80s was a financial mess because of the disruption in the oil supply.

With a greater disjunction in oil supply in the future due to any number of reasons, demand would create huge first world fights. Getting to work, dance, and soccer practice late, or worse, maybe having no fuel at all, would spur bouts for weeks on end. Acclimating would not be easy or desirable because the U.S. has to be a growing economy for capitalism to exist. Less oil means contracting and not having it our way.

We elect to start Gulf Wars to show the rest of the world we are willing to fight tooth and nail to ensure the security of the oil regions so that when we do have to buy their oil, we can do it on our terms. The U.S. military is the world's single largest consumer of petroleum. Its sole mission is to protect and preserve the U.S. economy, which, incidentally, is reliant on petroleum. Without oil, that mission is dead in the water, and the U.S. Dollar would no longer be backed by petroleum. Military leaders know they would be lost at sea if they ever had to ration energy use with the Air Force and Marines fueling up on Mondays, Wednesdays, and Fridays, and the Army and Navy fueling the rest of the week. The idea that the military can come up with a non-petroleum-based energy supply is an all-consuming concern: the Air Force cannot run on batteries, solar panels, or nuclear energy, and like the other fighting branches, they need constant, secure supplies of portable energy.

Running parallel to these concerns is this fact: U.S. citizens own half the world's small arms. There are more than 390 million guns in the U.S., owned by people with billions of rounds of ammunition. When are all those rounds going to be shot off? Is there an expectation that they will eventually be shot off, or has the production of this ammunition been an empty threat? Forty-thousand annual U.S. gun deaths require an infinitesimal amount of our domestic ammo supply. To what degree are these citizens a match for the U.S. military? Are sectarian violence and uncontrollable mayhem possible, as we have seen in Syria, Iraq, and Afghanistan? Are we capable of another Civil War due to a breakdown of our fragile way of life coupled with our resentment toward each other and a subsequent struggle for resources?

The media soothes us, saying tomorrow will be the same as yesterday, but what they don't tell us is that the further we look into the future, the more life will repeat the past equally far away. And it won't necessarily look like the good ol' times because we can't live the way our great-grandparents did; technology took that lifestyle away from us. Rather, we can expect that the horrors of the past can always be made worse in the future.

We are at the top of the developed world tower; vertigo is setting in, with some folks starting to feel as if the construction is not safe and there's no way down from the top. Perhaps we have played King of the Hill for too long; being a top predator has its drawbacks. Anything that has happened in the past can happen again. New events can happen for the first time. Tragedies can be worse than they were before. Doubting that the worst excesses of the past cannot be replicated or topped by what we do in the future is the worst expression of denial. Such denial already creates a false sense of security in the present moment that's necessary for the precipitation of future events we refuse to imagine. If we think the worst atrocities from history cannot be repeated or that future nightmare scenarios will never become a reality, then the stage is set for the atrocious past and nightmarish future to happen in the present.

If we are ever to enjoy our rights and possess real stability and security, we must have more agency running the system we rely upon, or we will always be at unacceptable amounts of risk. Relying on the Reality Creators to make all the decisions is no longer tenable as it once was: they can't help but use us for their own benefit, and that abuse is no longer sustainable. We must gain more control of writing, revising, and enforcing the terms and provisions of our Social Contract to favor us in a manner that is sustainable into the long-term future. Therefore, we must gain control of Hobbes' Leviathan – the corporate-government complex. To start, we must be aware of our situation and speak openly about it. This book seeks to inspire compassionate social action along these lines.

The following discussion will look into this unsafe pinnacle-like structure made up by the Reality Creators, symbolized by the new ironically-named "Freedom Tower," erected despite the 9/11 attacks.[3] One World Trade Center indeed.

What Would Pollyanna Do?

Everyone wants to help. OK, not everyone, but most folks admire the idea of others helping people, especially when the assistance is non-partisan, like getting people out of burning buildings, car crashes, collapsed mines, flooded caves, and cats out of trees. We are stuck at the top of our Freedom Tower with nowhere to go; who wants to help get us down?

Whenever someone makes a list of problems, they're expected to have a list of helpful solutions; otherwise, critics lump them with the "nattering nabobs of negativism"[4] and call them rock throwers. If I were to offer a solution, it would be for everyone to come up with their own helpful solutions, to see the world from their viewpoints, and forge their realities, all set in the context of shared experiences and compassion for themselves and others.

We should pursue our visions, our missions, and our goals in life and share them together for our common welfare. We should stop resenting each other for how we see the world differently, for looking and sounding different, holding this or that opinion, or resenting each other for the jobs, education, and public support we get. We should replace corporate persons who influence our government with human persons through populism and populist control of our political economy.

Populism is an opponent to corporatism. We should work to reframe our partisan political parties along this dichotomy: one party of the human persons and another party of the corporate persons. Some might say we should rid ourselves of corporations altogether; however, we must recognize how dependent we are on them for everything we need in life and focus our critique on creating balance and learn to live with them as a necessary evil until a more just and sustainable idea comes along. Those who cheer on corporatism are, naturally, already members of the corporatist party; they are the neoliberals and neoconservatives.

But, there is a lingering question: are we too divided by the Reality Creators to cooperate among ourselves as populists? Is our alienation from each other permanent? The problem lies in finding a solution to empower ourselves together, so we do not give in to the gravitational force of competitive self-interest that tears us apart. The challenge is in broadly sharing success among all humans; this is the discussion we must have if we are to form a compassionate and moral countervailing force to the party of the corporations. Think about it: the Reality Creators vacuumed up $50 trillion from us over the past 45 years by virtue of their control over the government we elect. Broadly sharing success doesn't mean forced communism; rather, it means stopping the extraction of wealth from us in the same way wealth is extracted from Nature. Utah Phillips said:

> Have you seen what they do to valuable natural resources? Have you seen a strip mine? Have you seen a clear cut in the forest? Have you seen a polluted river? Don't ever let them call you a valuable natural resource! They're going to strip mine your soul. They're going to clear cut your best thoughts for the sake of profit unless you learn to resist...

You might say there are too many people on the Earth to

share equal success. If that were true, that would define a cynical new metric of the Earth's carrying capacity. However, the Reality Creators' domination has long existed and reaches back to times when the human population was smaller by an order of magnitude. The numbers of people deserving of equity today cannot be disregarded because there are too many of them. People have been tossed out of the life raft and forced to swim alongside forever. There have always been disenfranchised poor. Because the Reality Creators insist on taking so much for themselves, they make the existence of the poor a mathematical, logical necessity. (Recall, the 26 richest people on the Earth own the same amount of wealth as the bottom 50% of the world's population: that's 26 vs. 3.5 billion.) But let's explore, if not indulge, the claim that there's not enough to go around, hence the reason for all the poor people.

Worrying about the quality of life in the future picked up pace during the Industrial Revolution and its subsequent devastation of the ecology. Before industrialization, our ancestors did not worry about the carrying capacity of the Earth the same way we do today. The term *surplus population* came from the overpopulation of the British Isles in the sixteenth and seventeenth centuries, but people saw the density as a problem in their present moment to deal with; they didn't focus on the long-term future in the same way we do today.

One exception was Thomas Malthus, who pioneered the paranoia of the population boom in the early 1800s; however, his concerns fell silent for nearly 150 years until after WWII, and the real effects started showing as a function of atmospheric carbon. But there were always poor people with wealthier types complaining about them. In her work *White Trash: The 400 Year Untold History of Class in America*, Nancy Isenberg recounts a score of names that refer to the "trash people."[5] Saying there are too many poor people littering about for others to care is a cop-out; the poor have always been denigrated, yet, their numbers have not always been as great as they are today.

There is no factual basis that too many people on the Earth necessitates the existence of the poor. Rather, the fact is that plutocrats and their hirelings extract so much wealth, they necessitate the existence of the poor. Too many people in the top 10% say they can't help those below them because they don't want to fall back down into the top 20%, as explained by the phenomenon called *last place aversion*. The problem reaches all the way to the bottom: the second poorest person in the world does not want to become the poorest person in the world.

In lieu of trying to tackle the Reality Creators from the top of King of the Hill and leveling the peak into a plateau, there are those who help the poor seek various solutions within our existing social structure. This is good, hard work, and it must continue apace. They focus on immediate needs people have right now, while others work on the long-term horizon. We can generally view folks who address humanity's problems from these two perspectives.

First, many people work their entire careers to make the world a better place for others in the present who do not have any chance of escaping the problems that negatively impact their lives. They are working with individuals at the moment when they are hungry, tired, cold, wet, frightened, sick, alone, broke, mourning, spiritually eviscerated, or all of the above at once. Volunteers and missionaries of all kinds bless the world and reflect the best in human society. They drive people to voting centers, assist in nursing homes, food banks, homeless shelters, aid refugees, fight injustice, and support their local churches.

Second, there are those people who fight for the future. They are not as focused on the minutiae in the present moment helping people in the here and now; instead, they focused on preserving the future for succeeding generations. They work on changing the structure of society from the minor issues to the grandest ones of them all. They let others feed the homeless because they are focused on ending homelessness. Their goodwill is palpable. They have committed their entire careers to the cause of a stable and livable future for humanity and the Earth's flora and fauna. Perhaps it's a little reductionist to segregate those working in the present and those working for the future; certainly, some do both, but it helps explain the general tendencies of the work.

The former Archbishop of Canterbury has the temerity to call the Reality Creators down from the top of the hill:

> And yet, human beings still have the ability to put themselves right with the power that lies around them. Such ability depends on their readiness to loosen their grip on the world that is crushed and torn by the force of their holding. Only in doing so they can achieve a fusion of natural and human energy, and a beauty that is so intensely harmonious that it hurts. It is anything but a passive response to the world.
>
> It requires our own focused attention, listening for the flow of life to discover an energy that pulls together and not apart. This is what human power is when it is "put right": an alignment with nature that, rather than being destructive, leaves behind the violent battles for control and domination.[6]

Efforts to replace the current social structure dominated by the Reality Creators with one that is egalitarian and community-based is a fraught but worthy solution to the central problem of lacking agency discussed in this book. Ironically, the former Archbishop, a Reality Creator, has called on his crew to step aside to open passage for ordinary people to step in. He calls on his peers "to put themselves right with the power that lies around them...to loosen their grip on the world that is crushed and torn by the force of their holding." He says: "This is what human power is when it is "put right": an alignment with nature that, rather than being destructive, leaves behind the violent battles for control and domination." The Archbishop calls for real populism, not the neoliberal debasement decried by those in power who fear ordinary people getting involved in the political economy beyond working, shopping, and voting for them.

Societal change can work in tiny nooks in undeveloped nations. Since everywhere on the Earth is local somewhere, change to a broad-based populism would only become global if enough localities were to evolve simultaneously. To change the imperial structure of the world would require that the populace unites and that our economy is replaced with another system that does not put as much emphasis on investment of excess wealth and rampant competition. This change would require replacing governments worldwide with political systems that are more equitable and locally based: this is the challenge because Reality Creators will mobilize armies against anyone who contests them for power.

Is populism possible? Can the modernized populace, the multicultural stew of people, get along in a sharing kind of way by partnering to achieve mutual, beneficial goals in a developed world lifestyle fit for all? Can we peacefully coexist with corporate persons better than we are today? Adherents to conventional wisdom argue that a return to the kind of mythical communal life is only possible if all the modern-day accouterments are junked since it takes a worldwide corporate-colonial empire to bring good things to life like blenders, toasters, turbine engines, and nuclear weapons. It's impossible to have your GE and Apple products without nukes and capitalist wage-slavery because the latter two make the former two possible.

Technological advancements gird the empire. So long as the

advancements are in place, the empire will not fade away, with the result being a more fair system. To say you can have the best, beneficial technology of today, along with the communal structures that existed thousands of years ago, is illogical. Communal structures do not permit the colonial domination required to build and maintain the large-scale technological advancements we've come to expect and enjoy in the developed world. Why is it silly to sing Kum ba yah by reading the lyrics from a smartphone in your hand? Because the folks who suffered to make that phone in undeveloped nations aren't feeling it.

To imagine a utopia where we all get along on the Earth requires fracturing the globalism that the Enlightenment and the Industrial Revolution developed and return to the earthy, local-based living of the premodern era. This is called *Primitivism*. Before imperialism, days were spent locally. Somewhere, wherever you were, it was local. There was no globe, everything was flat, and you couldn't use technology to call from one continent to the other. We couldn't buy goods and services from around the world because that would have required an imperial-industrial complex with colonies to make the stuff in the first place. All you could do was lug water, stay dry, and defend against marauders: local living was often harsh.

Can the current world population live in the primitive fashion as the pseudo-mythical Ingalls family did on *Little House on the Prairie*, where they take care of themselves together with their neighbors in a small community out on the hinterland precisely because no one else will take care of them? I cannot see a Pollyannastic view of that future because there is not enough land for everyone to have forty acres and a mule, and very few know how to farm or live like peasants. That skilled lifestyle is the opposite of where we are now, and most do not want to go back.[7]

It's shocking to have to say it, but there are some people who believe reducing the human population will solve the modern human crisis. Seeking to resolve the problem of human overreach that results in a long-term catastrophe by rushing up that timeline to the short-term is a worse diabolical terror than the very worst evils the world has ever seen.

The idea that we should reduce the number of humans to a small, primitive population to avoid the problems we have now is to cause a problem more severe than the one it seeks to replace. The idea of solving the existential crisis humans face in the twenty-first century by destroying existence for all but a small percent is unfathomable. But, some people believe this is the only just solution to respect the Earth's flora and fauna because they see humans as a tyrannical species ruining life for all – including humans. Their solution to the problem is worse than the problem.

On the other hand, trying to sort out how human persons and corporate persons can get along on the Earth without the pain, suffering, and inequality so many currently experience is not an easy task. Reality Creators who want to keep their wealth and promote helpful solutions believe that technology will set us free and solve the overpopulation and natural resource problems we experience that cause widespread poverty and unrest. They don't agree we need to slow-up; they argue we need to double-down and push forward. They blatantly ignore the problem of minority management by plutocrats and the extreme division of labor present in modern society because they benefit from this status quo. This school of thought came from the engineers at IBM who believed smart and intelligent machines would take over all the dull, repetitive tasks we humans have had to do to make the modern world possible. They coined a phrase called the *Pollyanna Principle: Machines should work. People should think.* IBM theorists idealized a future in which we'd get to think creatively and do the few remaining jobs artificially intelligent robots could not. They did not conceive of Ian Bremmer's admonishment that artificial intelligence will do to humans what the internal combustion engine did to horses: "...when technology starts actually getting at the basic functionality of the human being, then human beings start becoming the equivalent of horses." Horses became pets for the rich. Pollyanna is not smiling.

It is precisely technology, our extreme division of labor, and management of our political economy by the Reality Creators that have gotten us into our current problems of ecological overreach, an explosion in population, and the potential to wipe ourselves off the map with nuclear weapons. They have wrought the problems that have gotten out of hand and put our society at significant risk; yet, we can no longer live without them because we lack ancestral skills and the will to live directly on the Earth without our thin plastic-cultural film protecting us. Technology is making human skills obsolete. For the first time in history, people will not necessarily find other work because technology is able to think and act like humans. But, we're being told by wealthy tech magnates that a little bit more technology and productivity will make our future more secure. Theirs is not a viable solution.

There comes the problem of a growing population of people with not enough to do all day long. For a historic example, in 1095, there were too many young men hanging around with little to do in Europe, and they were starting to find trouble among themselves. Pope Urban II took control of the political struggle and vacuum in the region at the time by calling for a Crusade. The Pope said, "Hey, let's all go on a long camping trip to Jerusalem and bring our swords." In the months while they waited to go on their first trek, they busied themselves slaughtering Jews. The cumulative effect of the Crusades was to make 13 long excursions down south, pillaging every speck of ground along the way, causing the worst humanitarian crisis until 800 years later with the onset of WWI. What will happen with eight billion humans sitting around with not enough to do but make art while the machines do much of our work for us? People like to be busy doing productive activities besides arts and crafts.

Many economists have considered the scenario where a lot of loitering humans can't earn a living anymore because technology has taken over most of the work. They have studied what happens when idle humans can't afford to buy what the robots make because the humans have little to no income. The economists project a reduction in what the robots will produce because the demand for goods and services will drop since the corporate owners will never give away their products for free to the unemployed nor go back to hiring humans.

Speculation on this scenario begins to break down with economists differing on the next outcome, but suffice it to say, the billions of humans on the Earth will still get hungry three times per day, need a place to live, defecate, require fresh water and healthcare, and they will still be having babies. Some work will still be done by humans, which is not in dispute. Economists dispute what all the idle hands will be up to. They may go on crusades raiding the robot factories. If the police haven't been replaced by drones at this time, then the public safety and incarceration sector will have full unionized employment.

An Island Dream

The United States of America arrogantly calls itself *The Greatest Nation On Earth*. It's more like *The Greatest Show On Earth*, and one day the curtain will fall; it always does. What will we do to make the future better than it is today? Will we only ever double down on our problems, making them worse? If so, poverty will not abate, nor will over-population, nor pollution, nor the fights over resources and struggles for security. We live like there is no end to our present moment in time. This bias for a short-term perspective over a long-term vision must be a phylogenetic failure of human nature we have not yet evolved beyond.

As with other developed and developing nations, the U.S. has nationalistic nearsightedness – visual jingoism. The myopic, self-oriented attitude comes from needing and desiring way too many worldwide resources. A central problem today is that most of the Earth's citizens need to live impoverished lives to absorb the cost of producing the goods and services they provide the developed nations' people. If the majority didn't absorb the costs of their own natural resources and labor, then the minority in the developed world would buy much less. Our economic-ethical system says we won't ever have enough for ourselves, much less enough to share with anyone else. No matter how much we have accumulated, we always want just a little bit more. Such a desire for wealth applies to all the developed and developing nations in the world. That's why we compete with each other and enforce our militaristic border fences.

The U.S. is 5% of the world's population, yet we take up 30% of the Earth's natural resources extracted each year.[8] This ratio will not last forever with China increasing per capita consumption. It's hard to see how Pollyanna can spin this one in a positive light. What happens when a dozen nations are all getting their third? How many pies are we going to have to bake to make enough slices? What if we can't bake any more pies, as some analysts are now suggesting?

What if there were 20 people on an island, and one of them used up a third of the available resources as the U.S. does? The other 19 folks would have to be followers to let this imbalance perpetuate and not kick Him off dry land. How they would allow such an imbalance to start is a curious notion: perhaps the lone chap already had a gun, booby-traps, and a castle, and none of the rest did. Or maybe He lulled them into a slumber about an *Island Dream* of each having their own third of the island's resources if they worked hard enough and followed Him, joining his effort: "Get started with me, boy, and one day you'll have your own island!" He might have even said that they were going to suffer after death if they challenged Him and his place on the island: "...He should know such truths," the 19 others thought, given the fact He is rich in the island's resources. "Compared to us and our meager lifestyle, He must know something we don't."

A leader who uses up six times their fair share is indeed followed by others to learn his secret. Such leaders arise after much growth and consumption. By the time they are using up one-third of the island's available resources, it's hard to stop them because they have considerable defenses built in to ensure the continuation of hogging. It's hard to think one guy could influence and overpower 19 others on an island, yet the U.S. does just that. (Incidentally, the U.S. military garrisons troops in 150 countries to keep the peace.[9])

One such way 19 others could let one accumulate a disproportionate share of the island's resources is if they stood around and watched the one work and were lazy. But that didn't happen since they all still had to make ends meet, morning, noon, and night. If they did look, it was brief because they wanted to know how The Man over there managed to acquire one-third of the annual resources dug up from the island: "...what was He doing differently from us?"

After planting season one year, a certain fellow of the 19ers looked around and began to understand the way to power: The Man had a helper. He whipped that helper hard, constantly. When the helper-horse died from its maltreatment, one of the 19 stepped into its place and said he'd work for wages instead of whips. The Man agreed since his arm was getting sore, and He had a gift for drawing on paper, which was a more civilized activity, anyhow.

This was early on in the colonization of the island when The Man only had twice his share of resources dug up annually. It was quite an advancement to have gotten this one other person from the other 19 to subject himself to The Man's imperial efforts. Like Scrooge, The Man made the 19er work exceptionally hard. This was much harder than the 19er ever labored for himself back when he wasn't working for wages and lived for himself like the other 18. When the 19er finally got his wages after the first week, they came in the form of handwritten script to buy simple food and toilet paper, both supplied by The Man.

The 19er began to think his life sucked since he had to work hard, not for himself, but somebody else, and because the wages were not worth the effort since the food was poor and the toilet paper was very thin. He thought about going back, and it was at this time when The Man asked the 19er if he'd like a better job: "Go out and recruit three people and bring them to work here for me, and you'll be their mid-level manager, with increased pay: more, better food and thicker toilet paper."

The 19er went out and convinced two people to shed their sovereign life on the family farm and go work for The Man to get paid wages. The third person was nowhere to be found, and the mid-level manager didn't know what to do: no one else of the remaining 16 islanders wanted to work for wages. The Man counseled that if he took someone against their will, they'd eventually come around and see how great working for wages is. The manager kidnapped a young girl and forced her to work for The Man.

Then one day, it occurred to the remaining 15 that this one man had people working for Him and that together they helped Him attain massive amounts of the island's natural resources. Indeed, at this point, He was getting about 25% of the island's resources with their help. The remaining 15 noticed the workers were taking home wages worth less than the value of their work because the workers' lives were not better compared to those who still worked for themselves. The Man, they figured, was getting about 21% of the island's natural resources for Himself, and his four workers were each getting about 1% in the form of wages He still paid to them as food and thin toilet paper.

After a time, it got to the point where The Man was raking in a full third of the island's natural resources and had about six people working for Him. They built weapons for The Man in addition to buildings and houses. When He was feeling generous, He would even share a small portion of his excess with his workers, above and beyond their wages, and they always appreciated that. They learned to love The Man like a father. They wanted to defend his rights to the island's natural resources because, oddly enough, they had a feeling deep inside they owed Him something, perhaps it was themselves they owed Him, and indeed it was. They became so accustomed to owing Him their labor, their person, that they became 'subject to The Man' in a way that showed a total lack of personal sovereignty: they gave up their personhood for The Man to defend his rights to power on the island. Such loss of individual sovereignty in trade for oversight is the birth process of Hobbes' "Social Contract," unmistakeable from patriarchy.

The workers provided security for The Man, as the other remaining 13 islanders often complained about the unfair consumption of The Man-In-Charge. He sent out his workers to quell the unrest, first with diplomacy, second with force. Patriarchy enabled the six worker-police force to align themselves with The Man to defend his rights because He was their sugar-daddy protector. No amount of irony can upset this fact: because He was their protector, they protected Him. As time went by, three workers got a bit wealthier. With the grand patriarch, the four of them controlled 80% of the island, with the remaining 20% left to the other 16 islanders, which is how the world ratio is today. And yes, the Earth is an island, and we cannot each have our third.

"Earth provides enough to satisfy every man's needs, but not every man's greed."

Mahatma Gandhi

CHAPTER TEN

On Our Own Together

In his introduction to a collection of essays, *Toward A Steady-State Economy*, Herman E. Daly critiques the *growthmania* economic model that states: "aggregate wants are infinite, and should be served by trying to make aggregate production infinite, and that technology is an omnipotent deus ex machina who will get us out of any growth-induced problems."[1] This was back in 1973. He explains that we would be better off not burning through all of our natural resources as fast as we can, polluting the ecosystem. He laments the insatiable greed of those who cannot control their desires.

For example, Daly notes Bertrand Russell's famous essay called *In Praise of Idleness*,[2] and tells the tale of the pin industry debacle (previously told by Russell's erstwhile friend G.B. Shaw and drawn from a discussion on pins in Adam Smith's *Wealth of Nations*). A chap comes by one day with a technological invention that doubles the daily capacity for factories to turn out straight pins. In the growthmania system, the bosses decide not to send home the workers at lunchtime with the same full day's pay as before but to double the output of straight pins, thereby increasing profit for the owner. Of course, the straight pin market gets flooded, and the price for pins drops in half. Then half of the pin factories go out of business, reducing the entire straight pin workforce in half.

To be clear, corporations are savvy about minimizing over-supply; it's one of the terrors that keep their CEO's up at night, their board members pounding the table, and their shareholders setting fires. Though not mentioned, the more likely option in this scenario was for the bosses to lay off half the workers and keep the rest employed full-time, thereby reducing overhead costs, keeping the supply of pins constant while still boosting profit for the bosses only. Either way, the workers lose half to the bosses who get the 50% boost in income. Now we know the primary reason owners seek more sophisticated technology no matter the consequences on the rest of us.

Russell believes it would be better to keep all the workers employed the same as before with the same wages but employ them as needed, such as half a day. That would have maintained the pay for the workers and the owners' existing profit level, but it would have cut into the increase in the profit potential for the bosses. This is the central distinction between what would be a political party made up of those who favor human persons and a political party made up of those who favor corporate persons. Those who lack agency in their lives but also support The Man as described in the previous chapter, are so enmeshed into the co-dependent system fabricated by the Reality Creators that they will defend their oppression out of a bracing fear that they can't care for themselves and live by their own means. This behavior is indiscernible from addiction.

The U.S. economy is 70% consumer-driven. Our commensurate addiction to the production of goods and services keeps about 60% of workers solvent in the developed world. Given the oversupply of goods and services in our over-developed world that do not suffice to enrich us so much as clutter our lives, we are now an economy of make-work to a significant degree. This activity is unsustainable for human persons in inverse proportion to corporate person profits.

We face a critical fact that John Kenneth Galbraith noted

back in 1958 in his acclaimed work, *The Affluent Society*: our society cannot live on production and consumption to such a great degree when so much of it is of marginal importance to our lives. We live in a social structure that is already fragile and put at increased risk by our failure to address resource depletion, waste pollution, and overwhelming population growth. Maybe when the world seemed indefinitely large, the over-production of ephemera to earn a living to keep dinner on the table wasn't seen as much of a problem. Sixty years later, after Galbraith's warning, the knowledge we have about the externalized expenses of resource depletion, waste pollution, and overwhelming population growth make it untenable and unethical.

Put another way, trashing the planet for sheer survival is more understandable and forgivable than trashing the planet only to make more short-lived goods and services that primarily benefit the corporate extraction of our wealth. In the former, we'd eventually die on a wasted planet, at least trying to survive, *die trying* as it were. In the latter, we'll all die on a wasted planet and be the waste itself. Supply-side production of ephemera will be the end of us all as more nations seek to emulate the consumption habits and carbon footprint of western nations that are not just developed but over-developed.

Our social process is irrational because too many of the results and effects are hurtful. To argue that harm can be rational, or above and outside the distinction of morality, is more of the Reality Creators justifying their injustice for short-term gain. Milton Friedman inspired the idea that *Greed is Good*; now they repeat that vulgar tripe on Wall St. and Main St.[3] If we accept that hurting ourselves or allowing ourselves to be hurt are potentially rational choices, then that consent is irrational in and of itself. These days, there is insufficient consent of the governed.

Our utter reliance on technology, on our extreme division of labor, our wasting of the ecology, our sizable population of the Earth, our political economy supported in large part by make-work producing ephemera for a living, our ability to overheat and nuke our planet, our birthing billions into inexorable poverty, all of this, is irrational. Ceding the power and control over these crises to < 1% of our human population is flat-out reckless; the Reality Creators have never addressed the problem because they lack the will and the skill. All of this comes down to insatiety, the domination of greed over love, and the Reality Creators herald their greed as a moral good.

It is unrealistic to reason that *Back to the Landers* and the homeless can extricate themselves from the system when they must use many of the goods and services provided by the global marketplace. Christopher Knight, a hermit who lived for 27 years in the Maine woods, relied completely on gathering goods from his neighbors when they were not present. No one can effectively opt-out of our never-ending growth model by which we live. This lack of freedom forces us to participate in our destruction. We can't opt out of the Social Contract; indeed, we can't even modify the terms and provisions because we don't control the corporate-government complex that the Reality Creators control. Our lack of agency prevents us from contesting the Reality Creators' behaviors and actions. We are forced to live irrational lives. This is an assault on our freedom and an affront to our liberty.

If the Reality Creators considered others more than they do, they wouldn't be hell-bent on burning through our natural and human resources, crashing the market for straight pins. They would be interested in bringing good things to life more for our benefit than solely for their bottom line profit. Magnanimity among the Reality Creators is a public relations cost of doing business, not an end in itself. Slavery has many shades and subtleties. Not much changed in the phylogenetic mind of the Reality Creators since U.S. slavery or even the time when Roman slaves abandoned the collapsing empire and rushed to the landed nobility for security. The Reality Creators are in it for the power, which is the wealth derived from their property (both real and virtual) and laborers living on and in it. They have never wanted anything else.

Insatiety is how freedom plays out these days, where we see the great potential of our consumer wants ahead of us: *shopping will also set you free*. The problem is that we can't all get along if all our wants exceed the resources on the Earth, a finite planet.

There has been an unfortunate focus on the quantity of growth over the quality of growth. It is better to have an insatiable pursuit of quality than quantity, but the Reality Creators have us creating bunches and bunches of goods and services we don't need, such as the plastic that breaks soon after you buy it or the junk they feed us that is as cheap as it is unhealthy, in direct proportion. Quantity makes money in the short-term for the few, and quality builds wealth over the long-term for the many. As a result, we have the paradox of poverty and waste in modern society. This paradox is a unique feature of over-developed nations.

Reality Creators won't relinquish one bit of control over the power they have; indeed, they will always pursue more until the day they die. Who do you know who gives up all their money? Warren Buffet? No. He's obsessed with making as much money as possible no matter how he patterns himself as a concerned liberal. Rather, he's a neoliberal racing to see how much money he can make in a lifetime. His billionaire peers all want to set a world record for wealth and top the Morgan, Carnegie, and Rockefeller names. When is it ever enough? How many billions will do? He'll die knowing his legacy will be paid for by donating all his wealth to the foundation of his multi-billionaire friend, Bill Gates. Such a donation is not giving up his wealth; he will spend it to shame-wash his legacy claiming he made it to give away in what is a cynical act of glib magnanimity.

Why is it better to accumulate all that cash only to later give it out rather than having let the people of the world make money for themselves in the first place? Are we too stupid to be trusted with the cash? Can only a neoliberal foundation spend it justly and efficiently? Yes, that is what they believe. If the Reality Creators didn't accumulate so much of our money off our backs and store it in tax havens, fatuous artwork, derivatives bets, and credit default swaps, then we wouldn't need foundations trying to fix the problems their owners caused. They stole $50 trillion from the middle and lower classes over the past 45 years, and they have the audacity to say they will now give a fraction of it back. Their philanthropy is self-aggrandizing propaganda purchased for a couple of pennies on the dollar.

The over-developed world keeps the poor folk in the undeveloped world impoverished through rampant colonialism renamed globalism. U.S. and European corporations have exploited every undeveloped and developing nation on the Earth for hundreds of years. Bill Gates' foundation is a patronizing public-relations device to lionize him and other Robber Barons as they go save the undeveloped nations from themselves. Denying their brilliant Madison Avenue marketing scheme is ground zero for their gaslighting. It is blinding hubris that they don't see how they caused the problems these nations face, and it's notably more pride that they think they can fix the problems they created.

Some plutocrats just don't care and want to promote a saint-like legacy and pay for the image-making instead of having ever acted as real saints. All Reality Creators want to buy their legacy to live long after death, lasting much longer than the short time they lived on this Earth. They want to live longer than poor people who are entirely forgotten.

Who has forgotten the Vanderbilt, Carnegie, Rothschild, and Rockefeller names? When they die, Reality Creators still want to control society from the grave with their bequests. They know it will take generations to spend all the wealth they each accrued in their lifetimes. They want to polish their images since, deep down in the Wall St. of their heart, they acknowledge what scoundrels they had to be to get all that "excess" capital from us in the first place. We knew this was going on when we coined the terms Robber Baron and wage-slave in the nineteenth century. None of this is new; many of the wealthiest have said they recognized their rapaciousness too late. Charles Dickens' *A Christmas Carol* is a cautionary tale about dying before repentance. Plutocrats worry about whether "it is easier for a camel to go through the eye of a needle than for a rich man to enter the kingdom of God." Their self-interest motivates the formation of their foundations: that's rich.

Real Wealth

Real wealth is the kind of benefit that cannot be quantified like fake wealth, which is all about volume but not about content. And of course, fake wealth is shown to be a charade as it changes in value, deflating and inflating on the Reality Creators' whims. For example, since the real estate bubble popped in 2008, your house is worth less money, but the physical structure is still there, just the same. But then it rose in value again. Real wealth can be qualified, and that is what matters. Real wealth is in the essential structure of the house that lasts any number of bubbles that inflate and deflate its fake value.

Should the Reality Creators' paper money, nowadays electronic 1s and 0s, become devalued, most of the houses would still be left standing. And in the financial downturn of 2008, all the Reality Creators could do to fight back against their investments' devaluation was to claim the real structures back from the families who thought they had bought the houses. The Reality Creators know real from fake. They saw the houses lose fake value and decided they had better at least foreclose on them to get them back since the structures were still inherently the same. They set a new standard for rapacious behavior.

Real wealth is innate to a person or object; fake wealth is attached like a price sticker. Love and community support represent real wealth. Nature and our Earth represent real wealth. The commodification and monetization of real wealth attach fake value to resources that already have inherent real value. Commodification and monetization overtake and smother real wealth. Reality Creators use math to create complex financial instruments as a form of alchemy to monetize life: commuting labor to wages takes a natural human resource and turns it into a fake-fiat value for others to own.

Fake wealth is all the rage; it is the current paradigm for how we imbue value in our lives, and it is wrong. If you don't have fake wealth in our society these days, it's impossible to live. This extortion is a crime against Nature. It should not be easier to live with money but ask those who don't have it, and they will tell you under the system they were born into, life sucks without it.

It is sad to see people use their limited free time shopping, buying stuff that represents wealth, items that signify wealth, but that are not real wealth itself. People buy totems to wealth in place of having an enriched life. We seek an enriched life by making money and shopping; this is no way to live a life of liberty. Wealthy people speak about being unhappy: fake wealth cannot buy happiness, *Can't Buy Me Love*, as The Beatles would sing. It's hard to imagine why money isn't all it's cracked up to be until we understand that it is a way of measuring the power one person has over others: it's the force tool, yet money cannot force peace, love, and happiness.

To paraphrase Frederick Douglass, the extent that we put up with a fake wealth system rigged against us (a system that is unjust equal to its artifice) is the "exact measure of injustice and wrong which will be imposed upon" us. Our tolerance for pain is the tribute we pay to the Zeitgeist: a carved-out portion of our spirit collateralizes our contemporary ephemera-based lifestyle, an offering made to the Leviathan.

The innate fear we have in the developed world is living outside the Reality Creators' contrived modern political economy. None of us have the skills or fortitude to live on the Earth as our ancestors did in the recent past. We calculate that giving up a part of ourselves per the terms of our Social Contract is worth minimizing this fear. But this fear does not go away; rather, our contract binds us to it by threatening us daily that if we do not keep putting out, we will be put out onto the street and under the bridge.

On the topic of pain: the suffering that people experienced in the old world was less than today's suffering when you consider the huge amount of pain, loss, and anguish that's required to keep the expensive twenty-first century U.S.-led empire red-lined, running at full-tilt. Across the world, people live impoverished, war-torn lives as a direct result of northern-hemisphere imperialism. The U.S. led empire puts petty dictators in charge of whole nations, displaces indigenous peoples, destroys their land and way of life in pursuit of their natural resources, disrupts regions by arbitrarily drawing borders, thereby creating decades-long wars and suffering between traditional enemies, and indebts nations to make them subservient to central banks, the IMF, ECB, and World Bank lenders, creating austerity and poverty among previously autonomous and sovereign societies.

Human suffering is comparable across generations and

geography. No matter how advanced a place or time has become, there is always hardship. Suffering has worsened because the human population has increased worldwide. As a result, technology has advanced its crushing blow against more people born into the lower classes through no fault of their own. The undeveloped world suffers today to make gross consumption in the over-developed world possible. This pain is the most acute example of the effect fake wealth has on humanity and why we seek protection under provisions of a Social Contract that can only be described by the analogy of addiction: the more one relies, the more one has to rely.

Contraction is the opposite mission of capitalism. Capitalism must expand and grow the economy to survive by chewing up the ecology, digesting it for its energy and utility value, and excreting the waste onto the Earth. Currency tabulates that value into dollars, pesos, pounds, rubles, yen, and euros. Millions suffer for it around the world. Indeed, we are burning out our economic engine, which in turn burns out our greater, worldwide ecological system. While the planet is circular, unlike pure mathematics and economics, the Earth is not infinite. If we were honest with ourselves, we'd have to admit that our overall human mission on Earth is to take the ecology and turn it into the economy to use it up as hard and as fast as possible for our insatiable desires.

Now we never have enough time in our real lives. Not enough seconds in a minute, not enough minutes in an hour, not enough hours in a day, not enough days in a week, not enough weeks in a month, not enough months in a year, not enough years in a lifetime. When is it ever going to stop? "You Americans...You never have enough time in your lives. We here in the old world, we know that's all we have, the gift of time..." said an elderly Tuscan gentleman.[4]

Time is all we have. Sure, space is always around so long as time is; perhaps space can get limited too, but having time get limited is worse. Before sapience, time was spent without notice, perhaps because as apes, we weren't aware of our own death, but drumming and dancing put a stop to that, and time was invented with rhythm. People started and stopped notes and beats along their way to speaking. Shortly after the dawn of consciousness, they began to communicate, to catch each other's rhythm. Often we danced, often we fought each other, all in rhythm, just to get along. We sustained life for tens of thousands of years on a local level because that's all there ever was. Our problem is going from having been local to becoming global. We have not taken the time to reflect on what that implies, although many have thought about the nagging issue that we could nuke ourselves to oblivion and overheat the Earth, making life untenable for billions.

In our modern age, we treat all problems by suppressing the symptom from the top down. If we are ever to have agency in our lives, we need to build strength from the bottom up and fix what's wrong for real, first in our minds and bodies, then radiating out to our families, communities, countries, and continents. Maybe that's the kind of global reach we should be considering.

We each need to create our reality. We need to be self-reliant enough even to begin considering reality creation. Yet like the chicken and the egg, we need to create reality to become self-reliant. Analogous to the benefits of having a diverse investment portfolio and gene pool, it's better to have many people each creating their own reality than a few nannies doing it for them. The call of populism is to decentralize leadership. Arguments against this call are by those who risk losing wealth-power over people and fear getting trampled – the same fear a farmer has of their livestock living freely off their property and on their own.

Maybe we will begin creating our reality by first becoming agents of our destiny, not subjects to somebody else's. We can be agents together. That is the task: we are individuals, and yet together, we are one community. Individuals build community. This is not irony; it is a gestalt, where the sum is greater than the individual parts. When done well, in aggregate, such communities are a positive force for the welfare of humanity. It is precisely because the Reality Creators are an effective dominating hegemonic force that their collective presence and actions form a negative phenomenon. We have been driven apart into every corner possible by the Reality Creators' constant arguing over political and social wedge issues that are never resolved. Folks can't help others when they see their neighbors as enemies on issues we care about but have no power to change substantially.

We need to create ideas and put them in place of those for whom we work and from whom we consume. We need to vote for ourselves. This is not to say we can't come together in a *united we stand, divided we fall* manner; rather, it means we each need to support each other and not try to use each other solely for our own indulgence.

If there's going to be a fight, it will be the Reality Creators going after anyone who gets into their game and starts making up a life of their own. There is a way forward; there always is, for better and worse. Whether any paths are decent remains to be seen. We ought to determine to move forward with great intention regardless of the wide-open ambiguity the future holds. We will only know what to do among the choices the future holds if we act now with great purpose and a leap of faith. We cannot know what the future holds. We might as well embrace the time we have as the future unfolds. Instead of being Participators, we need to become our own Reality Creators.

"If a town is suffering from a break in the water-main, there are two things that may be done! The old pipe may be patched or a new pipe may be put in its place. It is sometimes possible for the engineers to patch the old main temporarily, while they are getting in a new one. The same situation confronts the people of the world. Their economic life is disorganized and chaotic. Shall it be reorganized along old lines, slightly modified in the light of experience, or shall it be built on fundamentally different lines?"

Scott Nearing, 1922
"The Next Step: A Plan for Economic World Federation."

AFTERWORD

The Reality Creators' media tell us we are moving forward: we will continue to refine inventions, new ones will arrive, progress will be made, and humanity will be better due to technology.

No.[1]

We will continue to waste the air, land, and sea. The population will eventually exceed the Earth's carrying capacity, and catastrophic failures will occur given enough technology, time, and the right climatic and political conditions.

Is it an ethical responsibility to find a way for our species to live forever on this planet? This is not a rhetorical question because our lack of consideration for flora and fauna on the Earth is the same disregard we have for ourselves. We will only stop or reverse the destruction and extinction of humanity inasmuch as we're concerned for other species: we are all canaries now.

When humans lived before the modern era 500 years ago, we had to go up the hill to fetch a pail of water, and that sucked. Without industrial technology, our population grew slowly and held relatively steady at one billion. Our pollution was mostly human and livestock effluent; our species' future was not at risk of extinction. To say we live *the good life* today just because we can live longer lives that are more luxurious than those of our ancestors is selfish and short-sighted. Not only do we trade in our liberty for luxury in the present, but our profligacy is the cause of our impending doom as a species. We trade in a longer, more luxurious life now for all the potential future lives and generations to come.

We are not adapting to the environment around us. Instead, the opposite is occurring: the Reality Creators have fabricated a dynamic, virtual environment that is smothering us. Darwin never imagined we would build an artificial environment around ourselves faster than we could adapt to it.

By uncritically participating in the political economy, we are complicit with the coming fallout; indeed, we are the particles comprising the fallout. No one knows how many more generations humans will last, how likely we will or will not nuke the planet, or how likely a bad pandemic, world war, or financial collapse will bring us to our knees. Nor do we know how badly climate change will exacerbate all of the above. We're on a one-way elevator down. The longer we wait to get off, the more steps we will have to climb to get out of the hole into which we are descending. When we hit rock bottom, some will ask, "Why we didn't quit earlier?"

Winston Churchill said of Americans: "You can always count on Americans to do the right thing after they've tried everything else." This applies to any of the people around the world, not just U.S. citizens. So long as we fail to admit facts about our lives we have been denying, we will never take sufficient corrective action. Negative impacts will continue to worsen in the long-term until there is no slack left in the system in which we live.

The modern world developed under the Reality Creators' leadership over the past three centuries by taking out loans on future generations' potential for existence. They did this in a literal fashion by extracting the stored energy of the sun that was buried in the Earth's crust in the form of carbon-based fuels. Prior to the Industrial Revolution of just 200 years ago, people mostly used the sun's energy as it shone down upon them in real-time; at most, they harvested food that grew over months or manually cut wood for various uses. Deforestation on a global scale is a recent activity made possible by carbon extracted fuels and industrial machinery. Ignoring the negative impacts of such extraction, the Reality Creators still seek to increase productivity in the present by turning even more of the ecology into the economy despite the bleak prospects for the future. They are gaslighting our grandchildren by claiming a brighter future tomorrow. They know carbon extraction expanded the world population from one billion to eight billion in just 200 years, and now they do not have an alternative fuel source that is fluid, portable, cheap, and plentiful as carbon.

Because of our intertwined social structure, there is no option for only some of us to begin the long journey trudging up the steps back to sustainability while those still on the elevator continue down until they have reached the *Seventh Circle of Hell*. Not the back-to-the-landers, the hermits, the homeless, nor isolated islanders can escape the coming pain and suffering unless we all do it together. No one on Earth is isolated from the effects of the dominant hegemonic forces of the western political economy that exist today.

We cannot escape it alone any more than we can get off this rock in the solar system. It is grossly ironic that the wealthiest magnates dream of spending their money generated by great economic inequality on escaping to outer space, building bunkers in New Zealand, and funding foundations in their name to fix the problems they created. Their vast wealth is the root cause of the problems driving their zeal to escape; it is also their means to do so.

We must gain control of our lives from the Reality Creators by creating our own lives. In so doing, maybe we can step back from the precipice and find a way to live in a measured manner that balances the opportunity for all future generations to live with our present desire for longer luxurious lives in the short term. Barring this choice, then we are left with the question of why bother even having a human species in the first place.

We must ask ourselves, why do we exist, and for what purpose do we need to inhabit the Earth? Compared with the houseflies buzzing about, annoying as they are, why do they have to live? What vision or mission do houseflies have in life? To answer these questions, note that humans are a top predator, and all the lower species would be fine without us. The housefly feeds animals that support human life: the fly is more important than humans to the food web.

Some say the expansion of human consciousness into the universe is the real purpose of humanity; however, there are possibly 40 billion Earth-like planets in the universe. Frankly, there's already enough consciousness out there not for us to be driven by pride when we can't even care for the consciousness of our grand-babies and their children here on Earth. Those who claim that human consciousness is so important to the universe are simply projecting their narcissism onto the cosmos. They can't even experience humility in the presence of the great expanse of the universe: they look into the deep, infinite starry sky like Narcissus did the shallow pool of water. And yet, they are our leaders. Let that one sink in for a minute.

Why would the universe want our consciousness, anyway? Writ large, if the Reality Creators had their way, they'd eventually trash the galaxies too. This reminds me of the bumper sticker: *Earth First! We'll Destroy the Other Planets Later.*

If we like our first world fatty footprint lifestyle and do not want to give it up for the present and the future welfare of the human species, then the honorable, honest position is to come to terms with whether we are all that important in the first place. It's time to admit our humble status: we're now a species that only cares for itself at the moment. Other species do not care for us, and we have proven to ourselves that we really can't be bothered to care for future generations of our kind given our myopic behavior in the recent past and the present.

Are we so prideful and lacking in humility that we soothe ourselves about *life ever after* to cover up our lack of care for ourselves on this Earth? Is it because of the idea we are elsewhere important that we shrug when we destroy the future potential for human life here on Earth? Are we perpetrating species extinction on ourselves as we have on other species but resolve the angst by imagining life forever elsewhere? Are the tech magnates dreaming of a secular heaven when they promote human life on Mars?

We need to use our sapience not for concocting a palliative narrative about our selfish lives ever after, but for figuring out how to live our lives together so we may benefit all those lives who follow ours.

"First off, this is all about our fragility. We are as nothing. The fragility of man, in respect to God. We are nothing but creatures."

Monsignor Patrick Chauvet, Rector of Notre-Dame
following the great fire of 2019

"The most successful people in life recognize, that in life they create their own love, they manufacture their own meaning, they generate their own motivation."

Neil deGrasse Tyson

ENDNOTES
& FURTHER
DESCRIPTIONS

---

[1] **Introduction**

David Graeber and David Wengrow, *The Dawn of Everything: A New History of Humanity*, (New York: Farrar, Straus and Giroux, 2021).

By proof of archeological evidence, the authors destroy the conventional wisdom that a mythical dawn of agriculture – a so-called *Neolithic Revolution* – necessarily led to the development of states controlled by ruling classes. So much has to be rewritten in our cannon. *Sigh...* Or, perhaps in lieu of laying waste to entire libraries, a great many books need to be asterisked.

The debunked conventional wisdom strongly suggested that ruling classes were natural and unavoidable – even fated. The consequence of such deterministic mythology is that a ruling class is inevitable and must therefore come to be accepted as the natural order of things: when faced with a problem they cannot control, people come to accept it. One could cynically suggest that this fabricated narrative was too good for the ruling class to pass up. But now they cannot persist in this drama. For over 200,000 years, our socio-political evolution has been episodic, complicated, unruly, uneven, and interesting. The outcome was never fated; there is no clean, neat, and tidy trajectory that necessarily led us to the metastasized social organization of the world we find ourselves in 2022.

The archeological record now shows that urban civilizations over tens of thousands of years were not necessarily ordered in states ruled by a minority class of wealthy individuals. Since, however, the formation of states did metastasize over time in different geographic areas, the Reality Creators have been lording over the vast majority of humans as livestock. This metastasis is the real *Agricultural Revolution*. Fuck Cancer.

Also,

Edward S. Bernays, *Propaganda*, (New York: H. Liveright, 1928).

Bernays influenced the entire twentieth century on how to organize society and run it. To many people today, Bernays' influence feels timeless, and his ideas, *a priori*. Hence, many think his ideas always existed. His thoughts, however, are recently descended from *The Enlightenment* philosophers and others closer to his time, including Gustav Le Bon, who wrote *The Crowd: A Study of the Popular Mind* in 1895, Wilfred Trotter, who wrote *Instincts of the Herd in Peace and War* in 1916, and Walter Lippmann, his mentor who wrote extensively on the need for the enlightened few to lead the many herd-humans. (The ruling class perpetrated a Tragedy of the Commons in their reckless behavior running the herd of humans that we now all find ourselves in such a mess today with climate change, regional wars, unstable trade supply lines, a population run amok, and the potential in 30 minutes to nuke the world's major cities.)

Bernays opens *Propaganda*, explaining the circumstance we live in [**Emphasis added**]:

> THE conscious and intelligent manipulation of the organized habits and opinions of the masses is an important element in democratic society. Those who manipulate this unseen mechanism of society constitute an invisible government which is the true ruling power of our country.
>
> **We are governed, our minds are molded, our tastes formed, our ideas suggested, largely by men we have never heard of.** This is a logical result of the way in which our democratic society is organized. Vast numbers of human beings must cooperate in this manner if they are to live together as a smoothly functioning society.
>
> Our invisible governors are, in many cases, unaware of the identity of their fellow members in the inner cabinet.
>
> They govern us by their qualities of natural leadership, their ability to supply needed ideas and by their key position in the social structure. Whatever attitude one chooses to take toward this condition, it remains a fact that in almost every act of our daily lives, whether in the sphere of politics or business, in our social conduct or our ethical thinking, **we are dominated by the relatively small number of persons—a trifling fraction**

of our hundred and twenty million—who understand the mental processes and social patterns of the masses. It is they who pull the wires which control the public mind, who harness old social forces and contrive new ways to bind and guide the world.

And Bernays closes his book by saying:

"Intelligent men must realize that propaganda is the modern instrument by which they can fight for productive ends and help to bring order out of chaos."

[2]Sigmund Freud, *Civilization and It's Discontents*, (New York: W.W. Norton, 1961).

In this work, the author discusses how the act of civilizing people relies on our inner sense and predisposition to experience guilt (feel shame), and how people ultimately become discontent because their freedom, liberty, sense of equality, and experience of justice are necessarily limited by being civilized. Their sense of guilt shames them into staying within the box and adhering to *social norms*. Not all dogs will sit on command.

It should be noted that Freud is Edward S. Bernays' uncle and had an influence on him.

[3]Edward S. Herman & Noam Chomsky, *Manufacturing Consent*, (New York: Pantheon Books, 1988).

The authors describe five filters that obscure, color, and manipulate the way we see the built environment/ developed world/ contemporary society: the fabricated reality in which we live.

The media lights the way for us to see the artificial, fabricated world how the Reality Creators want us to see it. The Greeks thought our eyes projected the world out in front of us; in the modern era, we understand the world enters our eyes. The Reality Creators project images into our eyes using a hybrid form of archaic Greek and modern concepts, and we grasp the world however it is presented to us. This is how propaganda functions, and as Herman and Chomsky describe it, the Reality Creators are *manufacturing our consent* to control us, ultimately for our capacity as wealth builders.

When Reality Creators manufacture our consent, it's not just to play along with their casting, props, and scenery, all dressed up in their costumes to work, shop, and vote for them as their herd of livestock; it's also to consent to the racket in its entirety, to consent to the unfair provisions of the Social Contract they have constantly rewritten without our consent. Their ultimate effort has been to gain our consent to give up consent, to vote away the power of our vote. This is the liberty Kafka and Orwell envisioned would go away, and it was Herman and Chomsky who demonstrated how it would actually happen.

In addition to training the populace to think by manufacturing their consent, the elites have driven the populace apart for generations, most notably as political partisans. When it comes time to blame the people for believing utterly ridiculous conspiracy theories, they have no further to look than at themselves – the next endnote below touches on this issue.

[4]Joseph E. Uscinski, Casey Klofstad, and Matthew D. Atkinson, "What Drives Conspiratorial Beliefs The Role of Informational Cues and Predispositions," *Political Research Quarterly*, University of Utah, 2016.
https://www.researchgate.net/
publication/290474440_What_Drives_Conspiratorial_Belie
fs_The_Role_of_Informational_Cues_and_Predispositions

Manufacturing Consent is the most effective system in history to direct the attitudes and behaviors of the populace to conform them to the modern political economy and therein extract the value of their human resources as they go about working for and shopping from the owners of capital. Here, the authors of this paper, "What Drives Conspiratorial Beliefs The Role of Informational Cues and Predispositions," say [**Emphasis Added**]:

"It is beyond the scope of this paper to determine the factors that drive the predisposition toward conspiratorial thinking. But, we suggest that political socialization and psychological traits are likely the most important influences. It is worth noting that elite political thought in the United States is generally skeptical of conspiratorial logic (Bratich 2004), and there appears to exist a mainstream norm of anticonspiracy thinking. **Most people are socialized into the political system and begin to trust political institutions at an early age** (e.g., Sears 1990). This being the case, mainstream American citizens should be generally resistant to conspiratorial logic. **Nevertheless, many citizens—to one degree or another—are not socialized to mainstream political values** (e.g., Avery 2006)

and others have psychological traits that overwhelm mainstream socializing influences (Dagnall et al. 2015, Miller, Saunders, and Farhart, 2015)."

It is worth noting that the elite who manufacture consent bristle at the notion that others outside of that wealthy cohort would generate fiction that is equally damaging to the populace. In the authors' critique, there's a detectable sentiment that disagreement with the neoliberal dominant hegemony must be derived from conspiratorial thinking.

It's not ironic that the authors can't "determine the factors that drive the predisposition toward conspiratorial thinking" because they would otherwise have to step outside the neoliberal orthodoxy to recognize that people are prone to conspiracy theories because they have been primed for years to believe those damaging fabrications and propaganda churned out daily by the corporate-government complex. Edward S. Bernays is laughing from the grave and his mentor, Walter Lippmann, is inconsolable because the manufacturers of consent have become victims of their own machinations. 70 years of manufacturing the consent of the developed-world citizens has brow-beaten them down to accept pretty much anything that is contrived, construed, and conspiratorial.

[5]Anna Grzymala-Busse, Francis Fukuyama, Didi Kuo, Michael McFaul, "Global Populisms and Their Challenges," Freeman Spogli Institute for International Studies -- Stanford University, March 2020, https://stanford.app.box.com/s/0afiu4963qjy4gicahz2ji5x27tednaf

The authors, and by extension the institute for which

they work, and by inference the audience for whom they write, stridently conflate despots, autocrats, dictators, totalitarians, and fascist wannabe's with populists to discredit both populists and evil malefactors, forging one opponent out of two very distinct, opposite political ideologies. The authors do this to benefit the established mainstream political parties in the U.S. and Europe, which are not, by contrast, dissimilar and are in need of a plan to survive a changing political climate.

Populists seek to represent the citizenry and their interests first and foremost above the neoliberal interests of corporations and their entrenched allies in government. Unfortunately, there is an increasing number of despots, autocrats, dictators, totalitarians, and fascist wannabe's who are threatening the social structure in the U.S. and Europe. The authors of this white paper seek to rally their established neoliberal political parties into action by taking down both of their competitors in one shot: 1) the compassionate, caring populists, and 2) the evil, destructive malefactors. They attack in one swipe by conflating the two as one. This is shameful, dirty politics for which neoliberals have become renowned.

Who are populists? We, the populace, are the populists. Our leadership is decentralized. Our leaders represent us instead of manage us, and they come from a groundswell of genuine support quite apart from the nepotism, cronyism, favoritism, and elitism that beget neoliberal leaders who disproportionately benefit plutocrats and oligarchs. The despots, autocrats, dictators, totalitarians, and fascists are dangerous malefactors who seek power by extracting support from the populace; they are despicable. In no way does their leadership of whole nations imply they are populists any more than saying the neoliberals are populists because they too extract support from the populace and lead whole nations.

In "Global Populisms and Their Challenges," the authors scold their establishment team, saying that "These weaknesses of mainstream political parties have created the permissive conditions for populist politicians to emerge and thrive." Frankly, this white paper appears to be driven in part to salvage Francis Fukuyama's thesis that liberalism is the end point of all human progress that we reached back in 1989; an event he called the end of history. His thesis is absurd as the naive physicists of the nineteenth century who thought Newtonian physics was all that was to be known about the subject. If the neoliberals were not acting from a place of fear and loathing, they would rather speak more truthfully, saying: *'The failures of our mainstream political parties have created a vacuum for well-intentioned populism to grow, which is a good result, but, unfortunately, our lapse in leadership has also created space for malevolent despots, autocrats, totalitarians, dictators, and fascist wannabe's to rise up as well.'*

But the neoliberal establishment allies are not fair dealers. The list of political malefactors they deceitfully call populists includes only bad actors, none of whom are populists: Viktor Orbán of Hungary, Jaroslaw Kaczyński of Poland, Matteo Salvini & Silvio Berlusconi of Italy, Rodrigo Duterte of the Philippines, Recep Tayyip Erdoğan of Turkey, Vladimir Putin of Russia, and Donald Trump of the U.S.

Trump recently inspired a violent insurrection against the U.S. Capitol. These leaders are not interested in the welfare of the citizenry compared to their self-interest and desire to aggrandize themselves by accumulating political and economic power. Populists, on the other hand, are genuinely and sincerely concerned with the citizenry, first and foremost, not themselves. It is cynical and disingenuous to call these self-serving malevolent leaders *populists* because they are the exact opposite of populists; they are sociopaths.

The authors of "Global Populisms and Their Challenges" ought not to be singled out for such criticism; rather, they are just one very good example of the widespread neoliberal effort to malign populists by conflating the aforementioned malefactors with populism. A great many others have criticized populists for being boorish and paranoid. For example, the authors name Cas Mudde in their article as an ally, referencing his work and quoting his statement that populism: "...considers society to be ultimately separated into two homogeneous and antagonistic groups, 'the pure people' versus 'the corrupt elite,' and which argues that politics should be an expression of the volonté générale (general will) of the people."

This, too, is a gross misrepresentation and facile simplification of what populism is. Such an error can only be intentional. Populists focus on the welfare of the populace and not that of the <1% neoliberal minority who currently own and manage the political economy and control the mainstream, established political parties and media. Populists point out the vast economic inequality that exists today; the simple math is enough for the division between the people and elite to be revealed, all on its own. Just because populists focus on their own welfare is not cause for the plutocrats' allies in academia and journalism to denigrate populists by saying it is us who label one side pure and the other corrupt. It is cheap name-calling and defames populists as sarcastic cynics.

All political parties – partisans – structure their public relations messaging as "us vs. them" and to single out populists for doing so is brazen hypocrisy.

Others malign populists simply by disparaging them, making ad hominem attacks, instead of aligning them with evil despots, dictators, et al.:

Richard Hofstadter, "The Paranoid Style of Politics," *Harpers Magazine*, 1964, https://harpers.org/archive/1964/11/the-paranoid-style-in-american-politics/

Richard Hofstadter often came running to defend his contemporary neoliberal brethren who rule the political and economic spheres. He pushed back against the non-elite outsiders who questioned how the elite managed the corporate-government complex by attacking easy, soft targets. In particular, Hofstadter criticized ignorant people who posited the existence of secret organizations and made ludicrous assertions about those groups. "The Paranoid Style of Politics" catalogs a short history of misinformed people reading between the lines of reality and getting their suppositions wrong. By selecting crackpots to critique, he painted all of those who legitimately question authority as conspiracy theorists who speculate about tiny cabals secretly consolidating power away from the citizenry. Such intellectual dishonesty is dirty politics; it's disingenuous that Hofstadter only includes paranoid people to excoriate. His examples are a few outrageous boors any reasonable person would deride. He does so to suggest the rest of us are likewise unreasonable. His deceptiveness is a sleight of hand, and it's ironic to have to call him out his subterfuge: paranoid indeed!

Astonishingly, Hofstadter could get away with boorish ad hominem attacks calling people "paranoid" when in proper society and debate, erudite academics would never tolerate such lowbrow below-the-belt hits. Denigrating ordinary people and their credibility when they begin to close in on why their lives are hard has been considered a sport among Hofstadter's neoliberal class in more recent times. Thorstein Veblen would be shocked by the lack of decorum and dignity.

Walter Lippmann, *The Phantom Public*, (Rutgers, New Jersey: Transaction Publishers, 1925).

Walter Lippmann, who I discuss in the book and these endnotes, spent a lot of time complaining about having to "live free of the trampling and the roar of a bewildered herd," arguing the point that a "specialized class" needs to corral us. Lippmann's class of elite bosses has always run the government and corporate sectors, while the rest of us are the livestock they kick about while we build their wealth. The farmers will never tolerate any closing of the gap in intellectual awareness between them and their animals any more than neoliberals will tolerate reducing economic inequality.

To his credit, Lippmann's opinions and suppositions

evolved throughout his life; suffice to say, he believed populism was an impossible ideal that could never work. The populace was not sufficiently educated in school nor informed well enough by the press to make good decisions for themselves. Such a blunder could never have been happenstance. This naturally led to an idea that Cass Sunstein promoted.

Cass Sunstein has argued that we need to be nudged in the right direction because we can't be trusted to think for ourselves. He calls our 'thinking errors' the *availability heuristic.* These so-called errors are actions and assumptions we make outside the box on what we think is the next right thing to do. The Reality Creators set up the *Choice Architecture* box containing the selections they want us to make, and they nudge us to stay within the box. Ironically, too many people fail to recognize that this is just one more sleight of hand to manage us by hook and crook. Populists reject such patronizing leadership.

To epitomize the point and conclude, Donald Trump has been called a populist by the neoliberal establishment; yet, he could not get the popular vote in 2016 and 2020, nor electoral college majority to win the 2020 U.S. Presidential election. Trump committed sedition by calling for an insurrection on the U.S. Capitol on January 6, 2021. The neoliberal established political parties impeached him a couple of days later because he posed a legitimate threat to the nation. To be clear, Trump lost because he did not have popular support, and his insurrection consisted of only several thousand citizens.

David Sanger describes Trump's authoritarian behavior in his

November 19, 2020 analysis for the New York Times:

> President Trump's attempts to overturn the 2020 election are unprecedented in American history and an even more audacious use of brute political force to gain the White House than when Congress gave Rutherford B. Hayes the presidency during Reconstruction.

Sanger goes on to say:

> The first test will be Michigan, where Mr. Trump is trying to get the State Legislature to overturn Mr. Biden's 157,000-vote margin of victory. He has taken the extraordinary step of inviting a delegation of state Republican leaders to the White House, hoping to persuade them to ignore the popular vote outcome.

Trump is an authoritarian and wannabe totalitarian dictator. His plutocratic wealth and self-interested behavior alone bar him from the ranks of populism. No amount of hand-wringing and misrepresentation by the authors of "Global Populisms and Their Challenges" will ever make Trump and his ilk populists. We must call out the neoliberals' mendacity as no better than the lies of the malefactors whom they falsely call populists.

[6]A brief discussion on the tension between Liberalism and Populism:

Liberalism is the idea that individuals will rise up by virtue of their merit to run the political economy on behalf of the populace who do not possess the skills to do it for themselves. The scarcity of elites in the free market justifies compensating them at exponential levels compared to the rest of the populace. This arrangement is unmistakable from a farm.

Liberal elites wrestle control of the free market from Nature by how they choose to shape laws, including those that permit low tax rates for themselves and allow campaign financing and lobbying to further ensconce their control of the political economy so that they can further aggrandize themselves financially and politically. This is a corruption of the system. A feedback loop of power and wealth that begets more power and wealth spins out of control; as such, liberalism's elites abuse their heightened position at the expense of the populace. Any individual among the elite may be a lovely and thoughtful person; however, when they are together, or rather, as a gestalt, they are a menace to the public.

Populism is the idea that the populace should run the political economy via true representatives who are not aggrandizing elites. As such, populism is at direct odds with Liberalism. By definition, populist leaders are caregivers who do not exploit their elected position for financial gain or wish to abuse political power for their personal benefit. Liberalism eschews populism (true democracy) because elites fear losing control over the political economy and the aggrandizing financial and political benefits they enjoy. Populism cares for the populace as an end purpose; liberalism, on the other hand, is a racket that only benefits the populace as a side effect – only as much as needed to maximize the elite's wealth and power. This is the downside to a social system that concentrates political and economic power in a tiny minority.

Liberalism came into existence as a struggle for power between those who could succeed by virtue of their merit and those already in power by default of their birthright. As such, the fight between the nascent, upstart liberals and the existing monarchs in the eighteenth century was a fight, among the Reality Creators, for who would control the political economy. Both parties could not succeed because success was only possible if there was sufficient scarcity of winners; otherwise, too large of an elite group would dilute the winners' political power and wealth, and by definition, it would not be very elite.

The complaint by liberalism (and their extremists, neoliberals) that the populace is prone to being hapless fools and patsies to propaganda – such as falling for despots, authoritarians, and crazy conspiracy theories – is hypocritical: not only have the neoliberal elites led the charge driving us apart from each other, but they have created the most fabulous, fantastic, fabricated reality the world has ever known by sucking us into their media, fantasia-like built environments, corporate identities/ brands, and advertising, all to manufacture our consent to be governed by them for their financial and political aggrandizement.

[7]Steven Erlanger, "European Populists Who Looked to Trump Now Look Away," New York Times, January 13, 2021. https://www.nytimes.com/2021/01/13/world/europe/ trump-europe.html?searchResultPosition=15

The author writes an article ostensibly about how Trump has given a bad name to populism in the wake of his call to his supporters to attack the U.S. Capitol; however, the overriding message is quite different and deceitful. The article makes the claim that populists are dangerous leaders of mobs who want to tear down governments. The strident misrepresentative claims in this article include repeating the hackneyed stereotype that populists make *Us vs. Them* narratives necessarily leading to violence. All mainstream political parties – partisans on the left and right – structure their public relations messaging as *Us vs. Them*. The neoliberals and neoconservatives structured the entire Cold War, and then later, the War On Terror as *Us vs. Them* which has been the gravitational center of violence in the world over the past 75 years. To single out populists for *Us vs. Them* is cynical hypocrisy and demonstrates their propensity for dirty politics and lack of intellectual honesty.

The NYT author writes that:

> Heather Grabbe, director of the Open Society European Policy Institute in Brussels, said the unrest showed how the populist playbook was founded on "us versus them and leads to violence."

> "But it's very important to show where populism leads and how it plays with fire," she added. "When you've aroused your supporters with political arguments about us versus them, they are not opponents but enemies who must be fought with all means, and it both leads to violence and makes conceding power impossible.

Donald Trump and the numerous malefactors written

about in this article are no more populists than are the neoliberal establishment politicians and their cheerleaders who rule over the western hemisphere and Europe with their grip on political and economic power affecting more than a billion voting citizens. Calling authoritarians, despots, autocrats, totalitarians, dictators, and fascists the term *populist* just because these evil malefactors attract public support is disgraceful and dishonest.

Both the evil malefactors misnamed by the neoliberals and the neoliberals themselves have in common the desire to use lies and deceit to manufacture consent among the citizenry in order to rule over them for the benefit of the minority rulers. Populists, in contrast, seek to represent the interests of the populace and elevate the citizenry as the beneficiaries of the political system. Populists are neither the malefactors nor the neoliberals; they are the populace caught in the middle of this dogfight.

[8]Charles Mackay, LL.D, *Extraordinary Popular Delusions and the Madness of Crowds*, (New York: Three Rivers Press, Crown Publishing Group, Random House, Inc., 1980) Originally published (London: Richard Bentley, New Burlington Street, 1841).

While many failures of competencies have wracked societies throughout the ages, it is not wrong to have an implicit bias in favor of humanity: an *a priori* sense of humans as being smart, decent, kind, and caring is morally responsible. Given this ethic, I also am very much aware of and troubled by the errors of the populace and the undifferentiated result Margaret Atwood refers to when she says, "stupid is the same as evil if you judge by the results."

For example, the 19th-century book, *Extraordinary Popular Delusions and the Madness of Crowds* details many significant errors by large groups of humans. These errors were set in the context of rules, laws, and regulations under the ruling elite's control. *The Reality Creators* emphasizes the culpability of the ruling minority for their bad behavior resulting in countless atrocities the populace has perpetuated throughout history. I argue that the ruling leaders have often been riding herd on the atrocities many others committed.

If the members of the ruling class want all the power and wealth they can get by running the corporate-government complex, then they ought to take responsibility for how members of society act. The ruling elites write laws and shape the economy to benefit themselves. In the past, they promoted slavery and the genocide of indigenous Native Americans; they poisoned everyone to varying degrees through grotesque processed foods sprayed with pesticides; they offered their tacit approval and permission for the lynchings by their failure to stop them; they legalized segregation and imprisoned African Americans at incomprehensible rates, and they have divided the populace by pitting cultural, racial, religious and other identities against each other. All major wars of the past couple thousand years have been inspired and run by the minority ruling class who used the populace as cannon fodder. The U.S. garrisons troops in 150 nations and has installed petty dictators in dozens of nations as just one facet of control by a very small ruling class; Pope Urban II's call for the

Crusades is another example; the twentieth century fascists and authoritarians who killed hundreds of millions is the most extreme example.

The Reality Creators cannot blame the populace for poor leadership because we've never had agency in the political economy; we can, however, blame them. Exceptions to this are obvious as they are rare: evil soldiers who blindly accepted orders to perpetrate genocide on Jews during WWII were, by all measures of humanity, responsible for knowing they had a moral duty to reject the authority they were under. We the people have a moral responsibility to reject the Reality Creators' orders when it is clear their leadership is dooming humanity's posterity; at the least, we should use our power to elect representatives of our best interests, not overlords looking after their own.

Chapter 1

[1]The Enlightenment secured a new paradigm for how elites would manage political and economic power. The previous manner was by kings, lords, landowners, and church leaders, all who wrote laws, decrees, and made threats of force and damnation to control how people lived and who got the most money.

The Enlightenment opened up new ideas on how politics and economies work, focusing on the liberty to do anything a person could want to do, limited only by how much money they possess and by the rule of law the wealthiest people enforced. In this new paradigm, the political economy functions on a feedback system between political power and economic power: the more money one has, the more political power they have; the more political power they have, the more they can shape the laws making favorable conditions for economic wealth accumulation. This system derives ideological and voting support from the populace because they are told they too can be rich and that they too can have political control of their government by virtue of having one vote each. The facts show that over 250 years, only a tiny minority can become wealthy and that no amount of voting has ever upset this feedback system where those with wealth accrue more wealth while those with less or none do not meaningfully improve their lives crawling up the ladder of financial success.

The difficulty in creating and enacting a new paradigm results from a serious and worrisome concern that the current system would have to collapse to leave room for another to take its place, and in collapsing, the billions of humans who rely upon it would suffer immensely, with untold numbers dying. This is unacceptable. The difficulty in changing to a new paradigm is also problematic because those very few in power would fight tooth and nail to stop any change to the current system, using the police states and militaries as well as institutionalized propaganda to beat down any potential leaders of a new way that promoted greater access to wealth by reducing its concentration in so few people.

[2]We all chip in a part of ourselves, a bit of our soul, spirit, heart, and flesh, to create the government, a being, an entity, a gestalt made from all of our parts. We have also done the same for the corporations who are also entities called legal persons. Together, both the governments of this world and thousands of large corporations are living creations made

from our flesh, bone, and blood, from our spirits, minds, and emotions. These two species of creatures live as fraternal twins, as an order among the gods.

One goes about energized by our votes to rule over us and manage the world we live in. This would be fine if it benefitted us, but the Reality Creators sit atop this animal, holding the reins and control it for their benefit ahead of us. They use this creature's power to write laws not so much to represent us and our interests but rather to manage and corral us in ways that benefit them. They also sit atop the other beast for which we must work all of our best hours of the week; 50 years of our lives we work and shop for and from this voracious creature who never is satiated by our offerings: it always wants just a little bit more.

At times, both entities become monsters, dragons flying through the air lording over the populace who huddle and hide when they swoop down upon the people, one with its laws, the other with its exploitative wage slavery and extortionary consumerism. We have given our lives over to these twins under false pretenses and lies about what we would get in return; we've been had; we've been set upon as marks; we've been used up for the wealth our physical and mental energies create. This has been going on for millennia. The only way it will ever change is if we control the twin entities that we empower with our votes and create with our very selves.

The Reality Creators misrepresent the Social Contract, the deal we are supposed to have struck with the government and corporate entities in a way that is no less than a scam. They deceive us by saying we elect a government that represents our interests when it acts mostly to manage us. They lie by saying their sociopathic corporate entities care for us, giving us goods and services in trade for the work we do for them when corporations act more to extract our wealth and concentrate it into the tiny minority owners' financial accounts. The Reality Creators commit subterfuge; they achieve their goal of accumulating our wealth by deceit, by lying to us about the benefits empowering the government has had for us, and by lying about the nature of our relationship with their corporations for whom we work and from whom we consume. This mendacity is the basis for the racket they run.

[3]Ben Hunt, "Why am I Reading This Now?", *Epsilon Theory*, October 7, 2018. https://www.epsilontheory.com/why-am-i-reading-this-now/

The author asks the rhetorical question about why we are reading certain articles or papers in current events and other media, particularly, why we are reading them in a specific context in which we find ourselves. He makes the argument that the owners and managers of the political economy constantly influence us in the course of their daily work. I liken it to how a farmer manages their livestock for income purposes. Here is Mr. Hunt's conclusion to his short essay:

> Who are the Writers of the World-As-It-Is? They are Republicans. They are Democrats. They are central bankers. They are pundits. They are politicians. They are oligarchs. They are in every nation on Earth. They have ONE thing in common. They're Writing for their own

political and economic advantage. *And they're really, really good at shaping our behaviors with their words.*

It's never been more important to read critically and think critically. Not because you're a nihilist or you believe in nothing. *But because you believe in yourself.* Because you're smart enough and wise enough to make up your own damn mind.

Here, the author is telling people to create their own realities. This is the same message of *The Reality Creators*.

[4]Kevin Draper, Julie Creswell and Sapna Maheshwari, "Nike Returns to Familiar Strategy With Kaepernick Ad Campaign", *New York Times*, September 4, 2018. https://www.nytimes.com/2018/09/04/sports/nike-colin-kaepernick.html

The Nike corporation celebrated its thirtieth Anniversary of the *Just Do It* slogan by rolling out a new marketing slogan: *Believe in Something Even If It Means Sacrificing Everything.*

Nike has turned a career-ending job loss for Colin Kaepernick into a potentially lucrative marketing and sales campaign by using this famous and wealthy football player as a retail sales symbol. Mr. Kaepernick could not get hired because of his political actions protesting systemic racism, abuse by law enforcement, and widespread social injustice. He knelt during the national anthem at professional football games.

This is hypocritical of Nike, a corporate name and brand synonymous with child sweatshop labor and for jacking up consumer prices on what are otherwise cheaply produced textile goods. This hypocrisy is the mendacity that defines our contemporary period, what I call *The Mendacene*. The media marketers fabricate dramatic stories to drive consumerism instead of realistic explanations that reflect our lives accurately.

If Nike were telling the truth, they would say:

We're a rapacious capital sluicing corporation appropriating the image of a divisive yet visionary civil rights activist to sell more shoes and shirts at inflated prices to people who care about the issues he raised, creating a false and misleading reality that your shopping, your consumerism, will somehow solve those problems, when in fact, all it will do is enrich us by accumulating your wealth at a faster rate, furthering those social injustice problems through poverty and blind affection for us, your corporate overlords, who dress you each morning.

We also understand that because you think something good will come out of all this economic activity (that benefits Nike more than it shoes your feet or covers your torsos), you will have done your part in a world where shopping from us is now seen as a moral duty, despite the irony that our brand name is synonymous with sweatshop labor and other such injustices. At the very least, the real effect of all this chicanery is that you will be able to enter retail establishments having been shoed and shirted, an irony we deeply appreciate.

For example, shoe and shirt consumers (a substantial segment of society and equally large potential consumer base) are led to believe this very wealthy football player has given up everything. That is patently false; he gave up playing a professional sport. He did not give up what poor people throughout the nation and the rest of the impoverished world give up daily. Indeed he has yet to give up what so many others have, whom his protest supports. The hyperbole that the football star gave something up that is everything is a gross misrepresentation of reality for the express purpose of selling more shoes and shirts to people. (Reports are that Mr. Kaepernick was paid close to $40 million for this play.) This is a perfect example of fabricating a dramatic reality to extract wealth from the populace: it also exemplifies how the Reality Creators fabricate a virtual reality in the course of managing the political economy. To put a fine point on this message, it is the figurative aspect of this circumstance more than the literal that matters: we all need clothes even if it means sacrificing everything. Nike is going to the mat to provide you those cheap clothes to ensure your freedom.

Of course, a gross misrepresentation such as Nike's misleads consumers that freedom and justice are achieved by shopping at Nike. Nike is one of the preeminent profit sluices in the world, directing the flow of capital from hundreds of millions of people into their ever-accumulating stores and then into the accounts of those very few who own and control the corporation.

The article's authors state:

> But the people buying their products, whether they are a millennial or a Gen Z consumer, those consumers want their brands to take visible, social positions, and this is an opportunity for Nike to do just that," said Matt Powell,

quoted in the New York Times. Mr. Powell is a sports industry analyst at the NPD Group, a marketing research company.

So Nike is the conduit, the vehicle, the corporation that serves as the standard-bearer for people to be represented in society in the area of civil rights; this is a stunning breach of honesty and reality, given the synonymity of Nike with sweatshop labor and consumer price gouging. Nike is now being hailed as daring as the football player who lost his job for protesting persistent injustice in law enforcement by aligning itself with him. The only truth in this sordid affair of mendacious marketing is that "Nike Believes in Corporate Profit Even If It Means Sacrificing Everything."

[5]Ibid.

To illustrate the virtual reality (the dramatic space), the addition to the real estate the Reality Creators have invented to increase the size of their property holdings, is this quote from the article referenced in the above endnote [**emphasis added**]:

> Indeed, on social media — **where the nation's youth live and breathe** — Mr. Kaepernick attracted more than one million responses on Instagram, Facebook and Twitter in the hours after he announced the Nike partnership, according to ListenFirst, a social media analytics company.

The youths' living and breathing are in service of the Reality Creators' wealth accumulation. They are capitalizing on a social justice cause, and that is why they have appropriated

Mr. Kaepernick, a taking, that is a form of servitude.

Coming around to the truth, the NYT reporter wraps up by saying: "In the end, there might be two simple explanations for Nike's move: money and attention. Mr. Kaepernick's jersey was among top 50 in sales during the second quarter of 2017, even though he was not on an N.F.L. Roster."

[6]To drive the point home, our effort to see ourselves and therefore address our problems is corrupted by the media company Nike hired. It goes about telling us what a famous football player says or does and then convinces us to live in a virtual world of costume garb made by the Nike corporation that is itself responsible for the sweatshops and other related injustices that we were trying to see about ourselves in the first place.

It's not only that they are making money from our plight, nor is it just that they are enticing us to increase our plight the more we listen and shop from them; rather, it's that we are mostly unaware of our plight as patsy serfs. We mistakenly think we are solving our problems by doing more of what is causing our problems. We cannot shop our way out of our serfdom; indeed, we cannot even ease the injustice we live with daily by doubling down on what's got us down. That all the other media reports on what Nike did as daring or compelling not only proves the point, but makes matters worse by orders of magnitude.

[7]See *The Social Dilemma*, 2020, Exposure Labs, Netflix, Director: Jeff Orlowski, Producer: Larissa Rhodes.

The documentary interviews tech executives who have

direct experience breaching the terms of our Social Contract we have with the tech corporations for whom we work and from whom we shop. These are among the largest corporations ever created on earth.

The tech executives explain that we are the product that's for sale to other corporations who advertise on the tech company platforms. The name of the documentary, *The Social Dilemma*, is more than just a play on words nodding to *Social Contract Theory*. Their argument is that we face a problematic choice when we agree to the tech companies' service contracts that no one ever reads: we trade in our time, our privacy, and our potential to build our own wealth for their electronic services they offer: entertainment, virtual human connections, and communications convenience.

This documentary points out how we agree to be marks, and that far from having a balanced contractual agreement to use the tech companies services in trade for giving up our personhood, we have an abusive relationship that any reasonable viewer would say is similar to the peasant-noble relationship in Medieval times.

Also, with great eloquence:

Edward R. Murrow, "Wires and Lights in a Box", *Radio Television Digital News Association*, October 15, 1958.

Mr. Murrow states [**emphasis added**]:

Our history will be what we make it. And if there are any historians about fifty or a hundred years from now, and there should be preserved the kinescopes for one week of all three networks, they will there find recorded in black and white, or perhaps in color, evidence of decadence, escapism and insulation from the realities of the world in which we live. I invite your attention to the television schedules of all networks between the hours of 8 and 11 p.m., Eastern Time. Here you will find only fleeting and spasmodic reference to the fact that this nation is in mortal danger. There are, it is true, occasional informative programs presented in that intellectual ghetto on Sunday afternoons. But during the daily peak viewing periods, **television in the main insulates us from the realities of the world in which we live.** If this state of affairs continues, we may alter an advertising slogan to read: LOOK NOW, AND PAY LATER.

 For surely we shall pay for using this most powerful instrument of communication to insulate the citizenry from the hard and demanding realities which must indeed be faced if we are to survive. And I mean the word survive, quite literally. If there were to be a competition in indifference, or perhaps in insulation from reality, then Nero and his fiddle, Chamberlain and his umbrella, could not find a place on an early afternoon sustaining show. If Hollywood were to run out of Indians, the program schedules would be mangled beyond all recognition. Then perhaps, some young and courageous soul with a small budget might do a documentary telling what, in fact, we have done--and are still doing--to the Indians in this country. But that would be unpleasant. And we must at all costs shield the sensitive citizen from anything that is unpleasant.

. . .

I am frightened by the imbalance, the constant striving to reach the largest possible audience for everything; by the absence of a sustained study of the state of the nation. Heywood Broun once said, "No body politic is healthy until it begins to itch." I would like television to produce some itching pills rather than this endless outpouring of tranquilizers. It can be done. Maybe it won't be, but it could. But let us not shoot the wrong piano player. Do not be deluded into believing that the titular heads of the networks control what appears on their networks. They all have better taste. All are responsible to stockholders, and in my experience all are honorable men. But they must schedule what they can sell in the public market.

And this brings us to the nub of the question. **In one sense it rather revolves around the phrase heard frequently along Madison Avenue: "The Corporate Image."** I am not precisely sure what this phrase means, but I would imagine that it reflects a desire on the part of the corporations who pay the advertising bills to have a public image, or believe that they are not merely bodies with no souls, panting in pursuit of elusive dollars. They would like us to believe that they can distinguish between the public good and the private or corporate gain. So the question is this: Are the big corporations who pay the freight for radio and television programs to use that time exclusively for the sale of goods and services? Is it in their own interest and that of the stockholders so to do? **The sponsor of an hour's television program is not buying merely the six minutes devoted to his commercial message. He is determining, within broad limits, the sum total of the impact of the entire hour.**

If he always, invariably, reaches for the largest possible audience, then this process of insulation, of escape from reality, will continue to be massively financed, and its apologists will continue to make winsome speeches about giving the public what it wants, or letting the public decide.

. . .

But this nation is now in competition with malignant forces of evil who are using every instrument at their command to empty the minds of their subjects and fill those minds with slogans, determination and faith in the future. If we go on as we are, we are protecting the mind of the American public from any real contact with the menacing world that squeezes in upon us. We are engaged in a great experiment to discover whether a free public opinion can devise and direct methods of managing the affairs of the nation. We may fail. But in terms of information, we are handicapping ourselves needlessly.

. . .

It may be that this present system, with no modifications and no experiments, can survive. Perhaps the money-making machine has some kind of built-in perpetual motion, but I do not think so. To a very considerable extent, the media of mass communications in a given country reflects the political, economic and social climate in which it grows and flourishes...We are currently wealthy, fat, comfortable and complacent. We have currently a built-in allergy to unpleasant or disturbing information. And our mass media reflect this. **But unless we get up off our fat surpluses and recognize that television in the main**

is being used to distract, delude, amuse and insulate us, then television and those who finance it, those who look at it and those who work at it, may see a totally different picture too late.

Chapter 2

[1]Yanis Varoufakis, *Talking to My Daughter About the Economy, or How Capitalism Works and How it Fails* (New York: Farrar, Strauss & Giroux, 2018).

I came across this book a month after it was published in the U.S. while researching comparable titles within the genre of *The Reality Creators*. Initially published in 2013 in Greek, it reaches out to those who have no background to comprehend dense, complex books on the political economy. This is an excellent work.

Also:

John Kenneth Galbraith, *The Affluent Society*, (Boston: Houghton Mifflin & Co., 1958).

Galbraith coined the term *Conventional Wisdom* to explain the outdated idea that production of goods and services was paramount above all else in the political economy because over-production set in and was depleting the earth's natural resources, littering the earth with waste, and interrupting the allocation of sufficient funds to the public sector. He argued there was far too much emphasis on using excess capital in the private sector and not enough in the public sector. He explained that corporations over-produced in the private sector by hard-selling goods and services consumers had no idea they needed. All of this was for wealthy private interests to vacuum up the wealth of the citizenry as hard and fast as possible. It was precisely because public sector investments and spending did not directly accrue to the accounts of the plutocrats who owned and managed the corporations that funding for public infrastructure, education, health, and other items withered on the vine. This critique helped demonstrate how and why the wealthy class had such extraordinary influence on our democratically elected government.

Also:

John Kenneth Galbraith & Nicole Salinger, *Almost Everyone's Guide to Economics* (Boston: Houghton Mifflin Company, 1978).

The authors brought economics to the commons. It is a nod and homage to the work by G.B. Shaw referenced in this endnote. Galbraith and Salinger discuss how neoclassical ideas of a pure market economy do not reflect the real world where corporate and political power have come together as a united force with enough power to shape, plan and direct the market, constricting the extent to which it is free by a considerable degree. Without explicitly saying it back in 1978, he suggests that it's socialism for the few in power and capitalism for the rest of us.

Also:

George Bernard Shaw, *The Intelligent Woman's Guide to Capitalism and Socialism*, (New York: Garden City Publishing Company, 1928).

A curt if not at times sarcastic approach to the economy of the early twentieth century that has in its bite a strongly developed sense of justice. All ways of looking at alternatives to the existing system come under critique, including the current paradigm of the early twentieth century, and it is clear that the sense of justice G. B. Shaw has is one that suggests the market is manipulated for the benefit of those who retain the power to do so.

He argues that "Just as Parliament and the Courts are captured by the rich, so is the Church." Shaw criticizes the use of public institutions to maintain the system by which 90% of the population supports the other 10%. Shaw is the first to point out that the wealthy are both the private sector bosses and the public sector bosses working seamlessly together to manage the work of the 90% to profit from them. Today it seems the percentage is more extreme; the <1% and >99% are more accurate measurements of who runs things and who's doing all the running around.

Also:

E. F. Schumacher, *Small is Beautiful: Economics as If People Mattered* (London: Blond & Briggs, LTD, 1973).

The author criticizes the political economy as it exists in western nations, arguing the lack of spirit, celestial wonder, and beauty in our interactions among ourselves and the natural world is responsible for rapacity filling in the void, leading to disregard for nature and humanity. The author skewers the notion that thinking big is always better, and he is passionate about why small is beautiful. Schumacher's concerns, written over 45 years ago, are the same as ours today, but the idea there's hope, as the author suggests, now feels quaint and naive: the future as it stands today compared to back then is not only much worse for not having ever changed in ways the author hoped, but it is worse than what he thought would happen if nobody cared about the concerns he so eloquently wrote about.

Also:

Charles Wheelan, *Naked Economics, Undressing the Dismal Science*, (New York: W. W. Norton & Company, Inc. 2002, 2010).

This book is a shameless cheerleader for the status quo that makes the political economy such a tool of the neoliberal establishment. It's written from the perspective of a neoclassical economist who believes that the free market exists in a pure form and defends whatever comes out of it as right and good no matter how appalling the facts are to a reasonable person. The author makes wide-ranging generalizations about people, taking the discredited idea that we all act rationally to heights not seen before. He then lists horrible human actions such as rainforest depletion as economically and politically justified. He also says, "different individuals have different preferences...For example, rich people have different preferences than poor people do." Indeed!

Wheelan makes trite statements about why he pays taxes, which is to "keep me from dying of typhoid or going to jail," which means much of what the public sector provides is not incentive enough to chip in; rather, incarceration is his motivating factor. In his discussion of Adam Smith, philosopher Samuel Fleischacker refers to a belief Smith held, that "people who care about social sanctions display better character than people who can be motivated to good action only by the law." Adam Smith, via Samuel Fleischacker, just pulled the pants down on Charles Wheelan. (See the citation for Fleischacker at Endnote #3 in Chapter 6 below.)

I hope Mr. Wheelan enjoys the roads he drives on and that his college students come to him well-prepared from public school. This book is an unmitigated disaster for those who think they are getting an honest accounting of what's going on in society. Wheelan wrote this book to mold minds into thinking the political economy and markets are as wild and free as nature, when indeed, they are highly manufactured tools under the ownership, management, and control of Charles Wheelan's favorite crew for whom he cheerleads.

Also:

Tim Harford, *The Undercover Economist* (Oxford: Oxford University Press, 2006).

Harford explains how an economist comprehends the world and also celebrates the team effort of the division of labor without even the slightest critique. Like "Naked" Wheelan, "Undercover" Harford tries to suggest there's a truth that's hiding he's going to share that the rest of humanity doesn't comprehend. That would be laudable, but his conceit is silly at best and instructs readers to take a shallow approach when assessing the deeply problematic political economy we must live through.

Like Wheelan, Harford reveals "how great" the economic system is without questioning how it overwhelmingly benefits those who possess large amounts of wealth. He refers to the everyday miracles of the system but fails to question the system. He blindly thinks all is well, like Pollyanna. He hopes to teach the reader to see the world as an economist – this is very different from *The Reality Creators*, where I hope you see the world for yourself. The author does seek to make the reader a more savvy consumer (become an expert shopper!), a more discriminating voter (be more precise choosing which person you want as your overlord!), and to understand what the politicians tell you (blame the government, not the private sector that controls the government!).

Both Wheelan and Harford are Reality Creators' obsequious hirelings mitigating the plutocrats' and oligarchs' concerns that we are looking critically at how the political economy truly functions. They're trying to nip in the bud the idea that the rich have any control over it. Their entry-level books are patronizing and insulting to the intelligence, deliberately written to quiet discontent by suggesting we are all at the mercy of the forces of nature and therefore cannot have any agency to take action to shape our world. This is the exact opposite thesis of *The Reality Creators*.

[2]Ciepley, David. "Is the U.S. Government a Corporation? The Corporate Origins of Modern Constitutionalism," *American Political Science Review* 111, no. 2 (2017): 418–35. doi:10.1017/S0003055417000041.

The author seeks to draw a technical distinction between a popularly issued corporate charter and the "social contract" concept that has been the traditional agreement between citizens and their governments. To be clear, the U.S.

Constitution functions as an agreed-upon set of terms and provisions the people must abide by. The scare quotes on "social contract" emphasize that the distinction lacks a difference when comparing it to the notion of a chartered corporation described below.

From the Abstract of the article:

> The U.S. Constitution is best understood not as a "social contract," but as a popularly issued corporate charter. The earliest American colonies were literal corporations of the Crown and, like all corporations, were ruled by limited governments established by their charters. From this, Americans derived their understanding of what a constitution is—the written charter of a sovereign that ordains and limits a government. The key Federalist innovation was to substitute the People for the King as the chartering sovereign. This effectively transferred the "governance technology" of the corporation to the civil government—including the practice of delegating authority via a written charter, charter amendment, and judicial review. Federalists used these corporate practices to frame a government that united seeming irreconcilables—a government energetic yet limited, republican yet mixed, popular yet antipopulist—yielding a corporate solution to the problem of arbitrary rule. Leading founders considered this new government a literal chartered corporation of the People.

[3]President Barack Obama, eulogizing one of the family members, John McCain 9/1/2018:

The Reality Creators genuinely love each other as family.

They respect each other as competitors. They are fiercely loyal to each other. They honor themselves for their moral code and ethical system to do the right thing all in the service of running the farm expertly: they take seriously managing the herd and keeping it safe, well-fed, and above all, ensuring the welfare of the livestock that is their income. No matter how they may fight amongst themselves about how to run the political economy for the benefit of all, they are ultimately united in running the political economy that benefits them above all. The following is a touching eulogy from a partisan on the left to a partisan on the right.

[Excerpts. **Emphasis added.**]

"President Bush and I are among the fortunate few who competed against John at the highest levels of politics. He made us better presidents, just as he made the Senate better, just as he made this country better.

After all, what better way to get a last laugh than to make George and I say nice things about him to a national audience. **And most of all, it showed a largeness of spirit, an ability to see past differences in search of common ground.**

We were standard-bearers of different American political traditions, and throughout my presidency, John never hesitated to tell me when he thought I was screwing up— which by his calculation was about once a day. But for all our differences, for all of the times we sparred, I never tried to hide, and I think John came to understand, the long-standing admiration that I had for him.

But he did understand that some principles transcend

politics, that some values transcend party. He considered it part of his duty to uphold those principles and uphold those values. John cared about the institutions of self-government, our Constitution, our Bill of Rights, rule of law, separation of powers, even the arcane rules and procedures of the Senate. He knew that in a nation as big and boisterous and diverse as ours, those institutions, those rules, those norms are what bind us together. They give shape and order to our common life, even when we disagree. Especially when we disagree.

And finally, while John and I disagreed on all kinds of foreign-policy issues, we stood together on America's role as the one indispensable nation, believing that with great power and great blessings comes great responsibility.

We didn't advertise it, but every so often over the course of my presidency, John would come over to the White House and we'd just sit and talk in the Oval Office, just the two of us. And we'd talk about policy and we'd talk about family and we'd talk about the state of our politics. And our disagreements didn't go away during these private conversations. Those were real and they were often deep. **But we enjoyed the time we shared away from the bright lights. And we laughed with each other. And we learned from each other. And we never doubted the other man's sincerity or the other man's patriotism, or that when all was said and done, we were on the same team. We never doubted we were on the same team.** For all of our differences, we shared a fidelity to the ideals for which generations of Americans have marched and fought and sacrificed and given their lives. We considered our political battles a privilege, an opportunity to serve as stewards of those ideals here at home and to do our best to advance them around the world."

[4]Walter Lippmann, *The Phantom Public*, (Rutgers, New Jersey: Transaction Publishers, 1925).

Walter Lippmann believed we were not capable of taking care of ourselves and that he and his educated elite cohort had to provide constant leadership to us lest we smother everything in our overwhelming lack of coordination and inadvertent ways. He was very skeptical of democratization efforts. He said: "The public must be put in its place...so that each of us may live free of the trampling and the roar of a bewildered herd." He feared the goats getting out of their pen. He believed there was no way for us to ever be educated sufficiently to take part in governing ourselves in a democracy. He didn't think we could ever know enough to cast informed votes. He felt we needed guidance from the bosses. His beliefs were always widely held among the elite; he just made a point of speaking their minds.

Lippmann's contemporary, Scott Nearing, put it this way in 1922: "The men and women who are responsible for the work that is involved in the economic reorganization of the world must see the whole plan as well as the multiplicity of detail, and must work with the whole plan vividly before their eyes if they are not to be blinded and led astray by the multitude of will-o'-the-wisps that flit across the path." (From *The Next Step: A Plan for Economic World Federation*)

The frustrating thing is that to a certain degree, Lippmann

and Nearing may have a point no matter how distasteful it is: after so many generations, centuries, of being managed by the elites, we the people lost a great deal of the skills and agency needed to live our own lives. For example, domesticated goats will have a much harder time surviving in the wild than deer. We have been voting against our interests for so long; we may be past the point of no return. The large number of voters who side with the political and economic bosses who rule against their interests do so out of ignorance that is not their fault. Their ignorance is due to a lack of self-reliance into which they were born, raised, and educated, causing them to depend upon the ruling minority elite.

Why do goats come running for their hay and stand for their slaughter? If they knew better, they would not just stand there. Because they are not free, they are penned up and have no other choice but to depend upon the farmer. Lippmann thought the populace could not take care of themselves because he saw how incapable they were navigating the modern, industrialized world. The real problem is that the bosses and farmers have corralled, boxed in, and cooped up the people and the goats, stripping them of their ability to live on their terms. In doing so, the bosses use their control over the populace like farmers manage their livestock, not to help them live their lives, but to control their lives to accumulate wealth for the bosses.

The story-line we've all been told throughout the years is that the bosses are ultimately benevolent, acting out of a sense of "Noblesse Oblige." This is not accurate. The bosses have always been acting out of pure self-interest, turning any benefit the people experience into a further gain for themselves. They care for us because we are their source of wealth, period. Adam Smith's trust in the magnanimous landowner to care for his tenants is quaint and naive when applied to corporate persons who are widely regarded as sociopaths. The farmer waters and feeds the goats and chickens just barely enough so the milk and eggs are plentiful and the animals are nice and fat for dinner time.

In Lippmann's first book, *Public Opinion*, published in 1922, he says that "a specialized class whose interests reach beyond the locality" must corral a "bewildered herd."

So, the bosses are the very few folks who comprise the "class of experts, specialists and bureaucrats" who have to figure out how to run this very complex modern world and feed us our currency like the farmer tosses hay into a hay rack. This is a critical point: the bosses are not there to help us; they are there to help themselves. No farmer ever wants to switch positions with their farm animals, and they use their power to keep it that way. Those in power never want to lose it by giving it up to those who lack it. Even the top 10% want desperately to avoid joining the bottom 90%, pretty much at all costs.

[5]Marc Santora and Vivian Yee, "Even with the ship free, it will take time to clear the backlog of ships," *New York Times*, March 29, 2021.
https://www.nytimes.com/live/2021/03/29/world/suez-canal-stuck-ship/clearing-backlog

From the article:

All global retail trade moves in containers, or 90 percent of it," said Alan Murphy, the founder of Sea-Intelligence, a maritime data and analysis firm. "Name any brand name, and they will be stuck on one of those vessels."

With the backlog of ships now stuck outside the canal growing to over 300 on Sunday, the threat to the oil supplies in Lebanon and Syria was an early indication of how quickly the disruption to the smooth functioning of global trade could ripple outward.

Virtually every container ship making the journey from factories in Asia to consumer markets in Europe passes through the channel. So do tankers laden with oil and natural gas.

The shutdown of the canal is affecting as much as 15 percent of the world's container shipping capacity, according to Moody's Investor Service, leading to delays at ports around the globe. Tankers carrying 9.8 million barrels of crude, about a tenth of a day's global consumption, are now waiting to enter the canal, estimates Kpler, a firm that tracks petroleum shipping.

[6] David Graeber, *Debt, the First 5,000 Years* (Brooklyn: Melville House Publishing, 2014)

This work has pulled together my thoughts to such a degree that I owe a great debt to this author. It occurred to me that my notion of lacking self-reliance is debt and that unlike the web of a village with members supporting each other, this is a web that imprisons us all because our constraints are more like leashes, or worse, like balls and chains, with the weight being our involuntary reliance on technology, an extreme division of labor, and dependence upon the owners of it all, the <1% Reality Creators.

While we are inherently a sharing and trusting species, we can become corrupted by the very few powerful rulers who change our "human economies" into rapacious "commercial economies." This is what the Reality Creators do, day and night. Debt is a form of community bonding built upon equality and trust, and the Reality Creators have monetized that into a violent form of bondage.

It is like the Reality Creators always to see a system that we like, then take advantage of and power over it for their own gain. Because the Reality Creators are so resilient and willing to change tactics to maintain their power status as owners of stuff and people, debt is a flexible through-line that connects each age, generation, and location on earth so the owners can maintain their control. Owning the land and the people on it is similar to owning the means of production and renting the workers every day for eight hours or more. Today, real control exists in the ownership of our political economy made possible through the advent of technology and the development of an extreme division of labor. None of us can live without the system yet, and so we don't dare upset it.

It is through supplication to the owners for our existence we find ourselves. As Graeber suggests, when the debts get too burdensome, revolution, unrest, or some sort of rebellion will occur, as has been historically demonstrated throughout the ages. It is my view that we're too scared to upset our way of life because we lack the skills of the past

10,000 years to fall back on. How we can gain new self-reliance by voluntary action today is an enigma. We may be capable only of an involuntary reaction in response to external events tomorrow.

[7] Alan Moore, "V for Vendetta," *DC Comics Vertigo*, 1982-2012

"Since mankind's dawn, a handful of oppressors have accepted the responsibility over our lives that we should have accepted for ourselves. By doing so, they took our power. By doing nothing, we gave it away. We've seen where their way leads, through camps and wars, towards the slaughterhouse."
and

David Graeber and David Wengrow, *The Dawn of Everything: A New History of Humanity*, (New York: Farrar, Straus and Giroux, 2021).

See Endnote #1 for the Introduction. The authors destroy the conventional wisdom that oppressive rule has been going on since the dawn of humankind by proof of archeological evidence.

[8]   Ron   Suskind,   "Without   a   Doubt: Faith, Certainty   and   the   Presidency   of   George   W. Bush,"   *New   York   Times   Magazine*,   October   17, 2004.   https://www.nytimes.com/2004/10/17/magazine/faith-certainty-and-the-presidency-of-george-w-bush.html

The aide said that guys like me were "in what we call the reality-based community," which he defined as people who "believe that solutions emerge from your judicious study of discernible reality." ... "That's not the way the world really works anymore," he continued. "We're an empire now, and when we act, we create our own reality. And while you're studying that reality—judiciously, as you will—we'll act again, creating other new realities, which you can study too, and that's how things will sort out. We're history's actors...and you, all of you, will be left to just study what we do.

Mark Danner, "Words in a Time of War: On Rhetoric, Truth and Power," in András Szántó *What Orwell Didn't Know: Propaganda and the New Face of American Politics*," (New York: PublicAffairs, 2007), p. 17.

"... the unnamed official speaking to Suskind is widely known to be none other than the self-same architect of the aircraft-carrier moment, Karl Rove ..."

Also:

Similar to this quote is one by Condoleezza Rice following her eight-years at the Whitehouse as noted by Michele Keleman, "Longshot Rice Would Lift Romney's Foreign Expertise," *National Public Radio*, August 6, 2012:

"One of the big differences is that I get up every day and I get my cup of coffee. I go online to read the newspapers. And I read them and I say, isn't that interesting. And I'm able to go on to other things because I no longer have responsibility for what's in the newspaper."

[9] Scott Nearing, *The Next Step: A Plan for Economic World Federation* (Chicago: Hammond Press W.B. Conkey Company, 1922).

[10]   Malcolm Gladwell, *Blink: The Power of Thinking Without Thinking* (New York: Back Bay Books, Little Brown, 2005).

Gladwell condemns prejudice and bigotry resulting from intuition; otherwise, he points out the extensive research on the subject of how intuitive conclusions are accurate as long-thought out rationalizations. Cass Sunstein's *Availability Heuristic* is the idea that people come to conclusions by the most readily available idea that comes to them and that Reality Creators can nudge people away from these conclusions to their way of thinking to profit off them. Of course, Sunstein couches the reason in a way that purports to benefit the populace, and that is just more manufacturing consent.

[11]   Stanley Milgram, *Obedience to Authority* (New York: Harper & Row, 1974) pp. xii, xiii.

"...the essence of obedience consists in the fact that a person comes to view himself as the instrument for carrying out another person's wishes, and he therefore no longer sees himself as responsible for his actions. Once this critical shift of viewpoint has occurred in the person, all of the essential features of obedience follow...the major problem for the subject is to recapture control of his own regnant processes once he has committed them to the purposes of the experimenter."

This is the central problem we face today and the subject of *The Reality Creators.* How can we go from being Participators to our own Reality Creators? Have we lost too much agency to ever get it back?

Chapter 3

[1]Ian Bremmer interviewed in *Capital in the 21st Century*, 2019, GFC (Capital) Limited and Upside SAS, a Justin Pemberton Film/ Netflix documentary. Based on the book of the same title by Thomas Picketty and published by Editions du Seuil, 2013.

[2]Edward N. Wolff, New York University and G. William Domhoff, Department of Sociology, University of California, 2010.

"In the United States, wealth is highly concentrated in a relatively few hands.

As of 2007, the top 1% of households (the upper class) owned 34.6% of all privately held wealth, and the next 19% (the managerial, professional, and small business stratum) had 50.5%,

which means that just 20% of the people owned a remarkable 85%,

leaving only 15% of the wealth for the bottom 80% (wage and salary workers).

In terms of financial wealth (total net worth minus the value of one's home),

the top 1% of households had an even greater share: 42.7%.

Table 1: Distribution of net worth and financial wealth in the United States, 1983-2007

Total Net Worth

	Top 1 percent	Next 19 percent	Bottom 80 percent
1983	33.8%	47.5%	18.7%
2007	34.6%	50.5%	15.0%

Financial Wealth

Top 1 percent Next 19 percent Bottom 80 percent
1983 42.9%   48.4%   8.7%
2007 42.7%   50.3%   7.0%
Also:

Robert Reich, "The Widening Wealth Divide, and Why We Need a Surtax on the Super Wealthy," Monday, March 12, 2012, robertreich. org.

"Over 90 percent of the nation's financial assets – including stocks and pension-fund holdings – are owned by the richest 10 percent of Americans. The top 1 percent owns 38 percent...The 400 richest Americans have more wealth than the bottom 150 million Americans put together."

[3]Christopher Hall, "The Corporate Colonization of Our Democracy," *Common Dreams*, March 7, 2011, http://www.commondreams. org/view/2011/03/07-3

The author makes the case that out-of-state wealthy corporate bosses funded the Wisconsin governor's race to help elect Scott Walker to enact union-busting legislation and other laws to control the citizenry. Scott Walker is the "puppet dictator" put in charge to rule his people on behalf of the outsiders who want to colonize the populace. This is similar to how the British and other imperial powers colonized American, Asian and African people, where the colonizers put in place puppet dictators to do their bidding, which is to rule over the people, controlling the manner of their labor, and extracting their natural resources.

[4]Tommy Douglas, The Douglas-Coldwell Foundation, Tommy Douglas Building, 300-279 Laurier Avenue West, Ottawa, Ontario, K1P 5J9, http://www.dcf.ca/en/mouseland.htm.

Clarence Gillis, a Canadian miner, labor advocate for miners and politician first told the story of "Mouseland" that Tommy Douglas used and made famous.

[5]Ezra Klein, "Our Corrupt Politics: It's Not All Money," *The New York Times Review of Books*, March 22, 2012.

Excerpts from reviewing two books, one by Jack Abramoff and the other by Lawrence Lessig (**bold emphasis added**):

"In addition to providing campaign contributions and employment prospects to outgoing elected officials and their staffs, he or she provides legislative expertise. Political scientists call this "the legislative subsidy" model of lobbying, and it poses a serious challenge to the view that lobbyists are little more than parasites.

The theory was first proposed by Richard Hall and Alan Deardorff in a 2006 paper entitled "Lobbying as Legislative Subsidy." Hall and Deardorff proposed an alternative: lobbying, they argue, is a matching grant of costly policy information, political intelligence, and labor to the enterprises of strategically selected legislators. **The proximate objective of this strategy is not to change legislators' minds but to assist natural allies in achieving their own, coincident objectives. Their budget constraint thus relaxed by lobbyists' assistance, already likeminded legislators act as if they were working on behalf of the group when in fact they are working on behalf of themselves. In other words, lobbyists act like a volunteer, and highly skilled, army for politicians who already agree with them.**

In this model, the point of lobbyists is not so much to change votes as to change the legislative agenda.

Lobbyists build up relationships with politicians they like and, in many cases, agree with. They give those politicians money and they invite them out for dinner, or to their corporate box to watch ball games. They argue for the client's interests, but they don't argue too hard, or cross any ethical boundaries. **And, over time, the politician comes to see the lobbyist as a friend. After all, the lobbyist is doing all sorts of things that, in a person's normal life, would lead to friendship, or at least a warm business relationship: he's supporting the politician's work and spending lots of time having interesting conversations with him and showing up at his events.** The lobbyists are smart and personable and interesting and connected. They have expertise he needs, and connections that can help him, and information about what other political actors are doing that gives him a leg up. It is a perfect mixture of ideological comradeship, financial perks, and personal affinity. **But it is the sense of comradeship and affinity that makes the whole thing work.**

In many cases, the lobbyist actually is the politician's friend. She is his former staffer, or a colleague he used to see three times a week at the Congressional gym.

But if one of your smartest, most persuasive friends, a friend you agree with on almost everything, is explaining to you that those environmentalist nuts are going too far again—they're always doing that, aren't they?—and they have sneakily tucked a provision into a bill that would make it more expensive for your constituents to buy electricity, that's very persuasive. And if it's also in your self-interest to listen to him—and lobbyists are good at nothing if not making sure it is in a politician's long-term self-interest to listen to them—then all your incentives are pointing in the same direction. You'll listen.

The outcome of this is that a disproportionate number of people who have access to politicians, and who are owed favors by politicians, are lobbyists. And so those politicians are listening to a lot of lobbyists—lobbyists who are being paid by a client to invest in their relationships with politicians in order to advance the client's interest.

The answer, of course, is that players with money are getting a lot more representation than players without money, not in sacks of cash delivered in the middle of the night, but through people a politician listens to and trusts and even likes having lunch with in the bright light of the day. That's why savvy and well-funded players will contract with a number of different lobbyists at a number of different firms. Every lobbyist will have legislators he's close to and legislators he isn't.

Lessig marshals ample poll evidence to show that Americans are angry about money in government and that anger is a contributor to their distrust of, and disgust in, the political system. None of that is in doubt. But Lessig is saying that it's the driver, the root of all our other problems."

[6]Martin Gilens, Princeton University, Benjamin I. Page Northwestern University, "Testing Theories of American Politics: Elites, Interest Groups, and Average Citizens,"

American Political Science Association, Perspectives on Politics, September 2014 | Vol. 12/No. 3, Pp. 564—581. https://scholar.princeton.edu/sites/default/files/mgilens/files/gilens_and_page_2014_-testing_theories_of_american_politics.doc.pdf

The central point that emerges from our research is that economic elites and organized groups representing business interests have substantial independent impacts on U.S. government policy, while mass-based interest groups and average citizens have little or no independent influence. Our results provide substantial support for theories of Economic-Elite Domination and for theories of Biased Pluralism, but not for theories of Majoritarian Electoral Democracy or Majoritarian Pluralism.

Chapter 4

[1]Tyler Durden, "The Dark Side Of The QE Circus," *Zero Hedge,* 06/26/2013

A rephrasing of an illogically-worded comment by *logicalman*:

"Countries are just the fences between fields that make controlling the livestock possible."

[2]Sherree Decovny, "The Financial Psychopath Next Door, Rogue traders are disturbingly common,"
CFA Magazine, CFA Institute, March/ April 2012.

[3]David Graeber, *Debt, the First 5,000 Years* (New York: Melville House Publishing, 2014)

Graeber takes issue, saying it is fatuous to think we are motivated by a contractual obligation to our forebears for bearing us. Farmers and rudimentary healthcare drove parents to have large families; we have not ever been expected to pay them back for being born to work for them. Rather, the message has been "no freeloaders," and everyone with a mouth has to pitch in and help. The Reality Creators rewrote this idea like a bad piece of fiction, saying, "Well, you can't really pay back your ancestors, so we'll take their pay for them since we own everything that was theirs; we are their heirs to the world and rightful owners of all the land and capital that you see." And so we go to work building their plutocratic wealth 40 hours per week, 50 weeks per year, for 45 years of our lives. We're supposed to work for our ancestors' heirs as if we were born to them in a big family, helping pull our weight – that is the contemporary primordial debt we cannot ever pay off.

[4]Wikipedia entry on Racketeering, http://en.wikipedia.org/ wiki/ Racket_(crime).

[5]Nicholas Shaxson, *Treasure Islands: Tax Havens and the Men Who Stole the World* (New York: St. Martin's Griffin, 2011).

Chapter 5

[1]Malcolm Gladwell, *David and Goliath: Underdogs, Misfits, and the Art of Battling Giants* (New York: Little Brown and Company, 2013).

Gladwell's *David and Goliath* trades on the feelings of sympathy people have for the underdog, and so it tells some tales where the underdog won. One such example is a rise out of the ashes of dyslexia by a well-known individual. The book received numerous scathing reviews for being pat, reductionist, and vapid. This book does not derive its argument in the same way his excellent book *Blink: The Power of Thinking Without Thinking* does, and criticism of *David and Goliath* is not evidence that Gladwell's other books are without merit.

David and Goliath does not prove that the Goliath corporations which rule the world are ever at risk by the people who labor for them and consume from them. David Korten's book, *When Corporations Ruled the World*, is a rigorous argument to the contrary.

Gladwell inadvertently reinforces the fact that *David and Goliath* is the only myth in existence that we must still use today when we want to refer to the concept. Ironically, the author had to select this very myth for the title of his book.

[2]David Korten, *The Great Turning* (Oakland: Kumarian Press & Berret-Koehler Publishers, Inc., 2006).

The author states: "Thus began the transition from rule by imperial monarchy to rule by imperial corporations." p. 127

He goes onto say, "Over time, the ruling monarchs turned from swashbuckling adventurers and chartered pirates to chartered corporations as their favored instruments of colonial expansion, administration and pillage." pp. 129-130

[3]Ibid.

David Korten explains: "It is no exaggeration to characterize those forebears of contemporary publicly traded, limited liability corporations as, in effect, legally sanctioned and protected crime syndicates with private armies and navies backed by a mandate from their home governments to extort tribute, expropriate land and other wealth, monopolize markets, trade slaves, deal drugs and profit from financial scams." p.132

Indeed, the Seven Years War was fought by warring colonial powers over each others' spoils, in an anarchic fashion that mirrored the wild, where there was no moral authority at all.

[4]Trustees of *Dartmouth College v. Woodward*, 17 US 518 (1819)

In this decision, the notion of a private corporate charter was upheld over the will of the state.
Chief Justice John Marshall said:

> A corporation is an artificial being, invisible, intangible, and existing only in contemplation of the law. Being a mere creature of law, it possesses only those properties which the charter of its creation confers upon it either expressly or as incidental to its very existence. These are such as are supposed best calculated to effect the object for which it was created. Among the more important are immortality, and, if the expression may be allowed, individuality; properties by which a perpetual succession of many persons are considered as the same, and may act as a single individual. They enable a corporation to manage its own affairs, and to hold property without the perplexing intricacies, the hazardous and endless necessity, of perpetual conveyances for the purpose of transmitting it from hand to hand.

Because a judge said this, it was deemed to be true as

a matter of law, whether or not it is naturally a Truth. Furthermore, countless legal orders over more than two centuries pressing corporate law has made corporations near human-like in all but voting and being able to face execution and imprisonment.

[5] Official Court Syllabus in the United States Reports, *Santa Clara County v. Southern Pacific Railroad Company* 118 U.S. 394, 396 (1886).

[6] Ibid.

[7] Charlie Savage, "Democratic Senators Issue Strong Warning About Use of the Patriot Act," March 16, 2012, *New York Times*, https://www.nytimes.com/2012/03/16/us/politics/democratic-senators-warn-about-use-of-patriot-act.html

The Obama administration is interpreting the Patriot Act in ways a plain reading of the law would not allow, and he's using the FISA Court to get around what a reasonable interpretation would be.

[Bold emphasis added]

The dispute centers on what the government thinks it is allowed to do under Section 215 of the Patriot Act, under which agents may obtain a secret order from the Foreign Intelligence Surveillance Court allowing them to get access to any "tangible things"...

There appears to be both an ordinary use for Section 215 orders — akin to using a grand jury subpoena to get specific information in a traditional criminal investigation — and a separate, classified intelligence collection activity that also relies upon them.

The interpretation of Section 215 that authorizes this secret surveillance operation is apparently not obvious from a plain text reading of the provision, and was developed through a series of classified rulings by the Foreign Intelligence Surveillance Court.

Note that the FISA Court had to "evolve" an interpretation of Section 215 over a number of classified rulings (secret decisions) and not by any one reading of the section. This means making one questionable ruling based on a previous questionable ruling, then followed by another questionable ruling, until down the line, the most recent ruling has no reasonable basis in law, only a sketchy trail of secret, questionable rulings. They modify the law by playing the *Telephone Game*. This is what passes for case law today: one questionable ruling after the other until the endpoint is wholly made up fiction with a spurious legal basis. This is very much like the way the Supreme Court acted when it made up the idea a corporation is a person via "case law."

[8]Adam Winkler, *We the Corporations: How American Businesses Won Their Civil Rights* (New York: Liveright Publishing, 2018).

Winkler explains all of this history on corporate personhood in great detail, stating in his introduction:

In the years that followed, the Supreme Court would invoke those corporate rights to invalidate numerous laws governing how businesses were to be run, supervised, and truced. Between 1868, when the amendment was ratified, and 1912, when a scholar set out to identify every Fourteenth Amendment case heard by the Supreme Court, the justices decided 28 cases dealing with the rights of African Americans-and an astonishing 312 cases dealing with the rights of corporations. At the same time the court was upholding Jim Crow laws in infamous cases like Plessy v. Ferguson (1896), the justices were invalidating minimum-wage laws, curtailing collective bargaining efforts, voiding manufacturing restrictions, and even overturning a law regulating the weight of commercial loaves of bread. The Fourteenth Amendment, adopted to shield the former slaves from discrimination, had been transformed into a sword used by corporations to strike at unwanted regulation.

[9] CONNECTICUT GEN. LIFE INS. CO. V. JOHNSON, 303 U. S. 77 (1938)

This is the dissent from the bench of the US Supreme Court by Justice Black in 1938. It is a prime example of what Adam Winkler is talking about in endnote #8 directly above. Sure, there are honest and decent judges appointed to the supreme court, but it always appears they are in the minority.

Below are excerpts from his dissent [**Emphasis Added**]:

I believe this Court should now overrule previous decisions which interpreted the Fourteenth Amendment to include corporations. Neither the history nor the language of the Fourteenth Amendment justifies the belief that corporations are included within

its protection. The historical purpose of the Fourteenth Amendment was clearly set forth when first considered by this Court in the Slaughter House Cases, decided April, 1873 -- less than five years after the proclamation of its adoption.

Certainly, when the Fourteenth Amendment was submitted for approval, the people were not told that the states of the South were to be denied their normal relationship with the Federal Government unless they ratified an amendment granting new and revolutionary rights to corporations. This Court, when the Slaughter House Cases were decided in 1873, had apparently discovered no such purpose. **The records of the time can be searched in vain for evidence that this amendment was adopted for the benefit of corporations.** It is true that, in 1882, twelve years after its adoption and ten years after the Slaughter House Cases, supra, an argument was made in this Court that a journal of the joint Congressional Committee which framed the amendment, secret and undisclosed up to that date, indicated the committee's desire to protect corporations by the use of the word "person." [Footnote 11] Four years later, in 1886, this Court, in the case of Santa Clara County v. Southern Pacific Railroad, 118 U. S. 394, decided for the first time that the word "person" in the amendment did, in some instances, include corporations. A secret purpose on the part of the members of the committee, even if such be the fact, however, would not be sufficient to justify any such construction. **The history of the amendment proves that the people were told that its purpose was to protect weak and helpless human beings, and were not told that**

it was intended to remove corporations in any fashion from the control of state governments. The Fourteenth Amendment followed the freedom of a race from slavery. Justice Swayne said in the Slaughter Houses Cases, supra, that: "By any person' was meant all persons within the jurisdiction of the State. No distinction is intimated on account of race or color." Corporations have neither race nor color. He knew the amendment was intended to protect the life, liberty, and property of human beings.

The language of the amendment itself does not support the theory that it was passed for the benefit of corporations...Both Congress and the people were familiar with the meaning of the word "corporation" at the time the Fourteenth Amendment was submitted and adopted. **The judicial inclusion of the word "corporation" in the Fourteenth Amendment has had a revolutionary effect on our form of government.** The states did not adopt the amendment with knowledge of its sweeping meaning under its present construction. No section of the amendment gave notice to the people that, if adopted, it would subject every state law and municipal ordinance, affecting corporations (and all administrative actions under them) to censorship of the United States courts. **No word in all this amendment gave any hint that its adoption would deprive the states of their long recognized power to regulate corporations.**

Yet, of the cases in this Court in which the Fourteenth Amendment was applied during the first fifty years after its adoption, less than one-half of 1 percent invoked it in protection of the negro race, and more

than 50 percent asked that its benefits be extended to corporations.

This was as of 1938 when Justice Black was dissenting, and since that time there have been so many more.

[10]   Parul Koul and Chewy Shaw, "We Built Google. This Is Not the Company We Want to Work For." *New York Times*, January 4, 2021. https://www.nytimes.com/2021/01/04/opinion/google-union.html

Excerpted from the Op-Ed:

Our company's motto used to be "Don't be evil." An organized work force will help us live up to it.

For far too long, thousands of us at Google — and other subsidiaries of Alphabet, Google's parent company — have had our workplace concerns dismissed by executives. Our bosses have collaborated with repressive governments around the world. They have developed artificial intelligence technology for use by the Department of Defense and profited from ads by a hate group. They have failed to make the changes necessary to meaningfully address our retention issues with people of color.

We are the workers who built Alphabet. We write code, clean offices, serve food, drive buses, test self-driving cars and do everything needed to keep this behemoth running. We joined Alphabet because we wanted to build technology that improves the world. Yet time and again, company leaders have put profits ahead of our concerns. We are joining together — temps, vendors, contractors, and full-time employees — to create a unified worker voice. We want Alphabet to be a company where workers have a meaningful say in decisions that affect us and the societies we live in.

Everyone at Alphabet — from bus drivers to programmers, from salespeople to janitors — plays a critical part in developing our technology. But right now, a few wealthy executives define what the company produces and how its workers are treated. This isn't the company we want to work for. We care deeply about what we build and what it's used for. We are responsible for the technology we bring into the world. And we recognize that its implications reach far beyond the walls of Alphabet.

Our union will work to ensure that workers know what they're working on, and can do their work at a fair wage, without fear of abuse, retaliation or discrimination. When Google went public in 2004, it said it would be a company that "does good things for the world even if we forgo some short-term gains." Its motto used to be "Don't be evil."

We will live by that motto. Alphabet is a powerful company, responsible for vast swaths of the internet. It is used by billions of people across the world. It has a responsibility to prioritize the public good. It has a responsibility to its thousands of workers and billions of users to make the world a better place. As Alphabet workers, we can help build that world.

Also:

Nicholas Kristof, "The Children of Pornhub", New York Times, Dec. 4, 2020, https://www.nytimes.com/2020/12/04/opinion/sunday/pornhub-rape-trafficking.html

> Mindgeek's moderators are charged with filtering out videos of children, but its business model profits from sex videos starring young people.

. . .

> The goal for a content moderator is to let as much content as possible go through," a former Mindgeek employee told me. He said he believed that the top executives weren't evil but were focused above all on maximizing revenue.

Margaret Atwood stated: "Stupidity is the same as evil if you judge by the results." Google's founding slogan "Don't Be Evil" could also be read as "don't be stupid" which, in the business world that cheers the slogan "Greed Is Good" as a moral imperative, suggests that not maximizing revenue is stupid, or as Milton Friedman alluded to in his NYT editorial from 1970 that impacted 50 years of business: "The social responsibility of business is to increase its profits." This is relevant since Google returns millions of results for searches related to Mindgeek, a corporation that has published untold numbers of pedophilia videos all in the name of profit.

In 2018, the Business Round Table, a collection of multinational corporations who periodically meet to discuss themselves, realized how bad all this looks and published a petition signed by 200 of their members saying corporations need to focus on more than just profit. Most people believe this was because the corporate leaders realized the bad press they were getting for focusing solely on profit for 50 years was hurting their profit.

[11] We have always lived in a competitive world. The wild is all about competition, and most people believe in the "survival of the fittest" concept. Political activity mitigates anarchy that's inherent to the wild world, either to regulate competition to make the weak last long enough to be consumed or to focus the efforts of the strong, so they are more efficient and strategic in their consumption.

As ideas and technology have progressed through time to become more advanced, our culture has become more advanced at *managed competition*. Managed competition is supposed to be an improvement over natural competition, and perhaps it is, while it lasts. As matter tends to dissipate and spread out in the universe unless a constant input of energy counteracts that trend, so too, managed competition requires constant effort, law enforcement, to prevent us from falling back into anarchy, the natural state of the wild.

We write political laws to push back against the natural laws we face daily, and this regulation is thought to be an improvement upon what happens to us in the natural world. This political activity is an artificial construct designed to counteract the natural world we live in, a shield behind which to live. We can call it civilization. Ideally, rules and regulations would benefit the majority; however, they have always benefitted the minority plutocrats.

Civilization is no more moral than nature; however, because we made civilization to mitigate nature, we think it is. Civilization is designed for managing competition on behalf of those who already can compete so that they can get more of what they want than nature can provide alone. Some people want castles, wealth, and luxury built by those who can't or won't compete. Others might think it is immoral to construct a system outside of nature to increase the competitive edge of a very few percent who seek to own and control others for their own benefit. There is no morality when a lion eats a deer; there is only morality when a human decides not to use another human for their benefit or decides that using other humans for their benefit is moral, that "Greed is Good." Morality is the result of civilization. What is considered good or bad is seen in the relative context of those who do the civilizing: the very few who compete to consume others who don't or can't compete.

Morality is also regulating consumption so that there is still something left to eat tomorrow while gorging yourself today beyond what nature would naturally provide. People use morality to justify a competitive advantage beyond what would be found in nature. Morality is like history: those who win determine what is moral, codifying the 'might is right' maxim. Those who lose can try to say what is right or what happened, but then they'd need to compete to push back, and by definition, losers don't have the ability to do so. Frederick Douglass quoted the poetics of this fact when he said: "Who would be free, themselves must strike the blow."

And so his great claim, that "The whole history of the

progress of human liberty shows that all concessions yet made to her august claims have been born of earnest struggle," demonstrates that we attain liberty by fighting to win. He is stating an obvious fact of civilization, that liberty is found through struggle and defended by continued struggle: "This struggle may be a moral one, or it may be a physical one, and it may be both moral and physical, but it must be a struggle. Power concedes nothing without a demand. It never did and it never will. Find out just what any people will quietly submit to and you have found out the exact measure of injustice and wrong which will be imposed upon them, and these will continue till they are resisted with either words or blows, or with both. The limits of tyrants are prescribed by the endurance of those whom they oppress." Reality Creators play king of the hill, fighting to keep others from pushing them back down, forcing the populace to fall back and start all over again like poor, old Sisyphus pushing the rock to the top of the mountain over and over again for eternity. As Douglass implied, liberty is not only had by those who can compete, but more importantly, by those who rig the competition so they can stay on top.

Rigging the competition is what we mean when we say building civilization, an artificial construct to mitigate the natural manner by which life exists in nature. Political acts are those efforts people take to enhance their natural ability to compete. It sucks to be consumed, and so much of human activity is spent trying to avoid being consumed while trying to live another day consuming. The USA and other developed nations have perfected civilization. They are "superpowers" seeking to consume the rest who are still developing (seeking to compete and fight back), and who are undeveloped, trying to survive the civilizing done to them in the name of colonialism.

Such activity exists at all levels, from between two people in a family, to neighbors, to townspeople, and within all manner of groups, organized or not. This is the civilized culture we live in. The respite in the fight for one's own liberty, for one's own life, is not in the political fight for survival where very few can ever win, but in not having to fight for life at all, which, of course, is the natural progression of time as each living beings approaches death. Ironically, being free of the struggle is the only way to liberty, for as long as you struggle, you are not free and have not liberty. Hell for Sisyphus was the eternal struggle. This is what Patrick Henry meant when he proclaimed: "Is life so dear, or peace so sweet, as to be purchased at the price of chains and slavery? Forbid it, Almighty God! I know not what course others may take; but as for me, give me liberty, or give me death!" In the civilized world, liberty and death are the same, and Mr. Henry was presciently conflating the two.

[12]   It should be clear that taking criticism of "artificial law" and the Social Contract too far is wrong since we obviously need some of laws and consensus to get along in our artificial-industrialized, civilized made-up world. I am highly critical of the concept of a "Nightwatchman State" called *Minarchy*, a government stripped to its bare minimum: a police state. Furthermore, it should also be made clear that extremism in the other direction is scary when some folks claim that the only legitimate laws are

those that come from God, and that humans may not (cannot) make up laws. The irony of those who claim that only God can make laws is that they who make such claims are indeed the ones making up the laws. Religious Reality Creators make up the laws they claim God makes. The bottom line is that laws should be made by the populace and their true representatives who care for their interests above the minority plutocrats.

Chapter 6

[1]"Power is nothing without control" is the well-known slogan of Pirelli Tyre Company. Keiichi Tsuchiya, a race car driver said: "What is power without control?"

The two words are distinct; they are not synonyms. Power is the engine; control is getting that engine to do work. Control can be either good or bad along a continuum, different for various interests and constituencies. Morality guides control and control guides power. The difference between control and power is that the former is subject to ethical critique, and the latter is not.

[2]From Lord Acton's 1887 letter to Mandell Creighton, *Historical Essays and Studies*, edited by J. N. Figgis and R. V. Laurence (London: Macmillan, 1907).

> I cannot accept your canon that we are to judge Pope and King unlike other men, with a favourable presumption that they did no wrong. If there is any presumption it is the other way, against the holders of power, increasing as the power increases. Historic responsibility has to make up for the want of legal responsibility. Power tends to corrupt, and absolute power corrupts absolutely.

> Great men are almost always bad men, even when they exercise influence and not authority, still more when you superadd the tendency or the certainty of corruption by authority. There is no worse heresy than that the office sanctifies the holder of it.

It is possible Lord Acton had this Latin phrase in mind: *Argumentum ad Crumenam:* the fallacy of supposing that a conclusion must be valid because the person making the argument is wealthy. The problem is that the office or responsibility of Pope's, kings, bankers, CEO's and other Reality Creators is too great to manage -- they are not afforded special powers to run the office because of the office; rather, they rise to their positions and bring to their jobs less than what is required.

The world's problems, no less economic inequality, are the sole result of humans being incapable of managing the power of such large governments and corporations. Just because they are in the position to control such massive entities and that they show up to work each day does not mean they are competent at what the job entails. Absolute power can and does corrupt. Most of the time, however, the officeholder is in over their head and cannot control the power afforded them.

[3]Susan Lund, James Manyika, Jonathan Woetzel, Jacques Bughin, Mekala Krishnan, Jeongmin Seong, and Mac Muir, "Globalization In Transition: The Future of Trade and Value Chains," McKinsey Global Institute, McKinsey & Company, January 2019.

https://www.mckinsey.com/~/media/McKinsey/Featured

%20Insights/Innovation/Globalization%20in
%20transition%20The%20future%20of%20trade%20and
%20value%20chains/MGI-Globalization%20in
%20transition-The-future-of-trade-and-value-chains-Full-
report.ashx

This 144-page report details how the expanding trend of globalization is shrinking. Over the past century, goods and services were shipped around the globe and laborers were split off from consumers: laborers would build something on one side of the world that consumers would buy elsewhere. This was called *Labor Cost Arbitrage*. Under this model, many of the laborers were never paid enough to afford the goods and services they produced and the stuff wasn't for them anyway.

With 1) the increase in productivity due to technological advancements, 2) an unrelenting drive to extract the ecology and shove it through factories and turn it into the economy, and 3) an embrace of capitalism by nations such as China, the sale of cheap goods and services has proliferated in poor nations allowing for "inexpensive progress" among a few top 20% who are fortunate to be socially mobile.

The resulting trend is the physical distance between the laborer and the consumer has shrunk from being global to regional. Now, more goods are being produced and consumed regionally. Since Globalization is the act of spreading out across the globe, a reduction in distance, even by a little bit, is a reduction in globalization. It would be a mistake to assume that the economies are becoming more equitable for the populace across the world because the relative number of poor and struggling working class persons is at an absolute all-time high and climbing. What's happening is that the top 20% wealthiest in certain, specific nations is getting to buy more stuff while the bottom 80% are still experiencing poverty and disaffection.

The reduction in globalism isn't a sign that the world's poor are getting richer; rather, it's a sign that the physical distance between the haves and have nots is shrinking. To be clear, it would be a grave error to confuse and conflate the shrinking physical distance with shrinking numbers of poor and financially struggling persons. Indeed, no longer is colonialism an activity exclusively perpetrated abroad; nowadays, colonialism occurs domestically within the borders and regions of the nations where the ruling elite reside.

[4]Price, Carter C. and Kathryn A. Edwards, "Trends in Income From 1975 to 2018". Santa Monica, CA: RAND Corporation, 2020. https://www.rand.org/pubs/working_papers/WRA516-1.html.

[5]Howard Zinn, "The Power and the Glory: Myths About American Exceptionalism," *Boston Review*, June 1, 2005. https://bostonreview.net/zinn-power-glory

Zinn explains how Reality Creators define and defend their use of power by misrepresenting that it is for the good of others when the exact opposite is the truth; their use of power is solely for their self-aggrandizement and wealth accumulation.

This is the heart of the Reality Creators' gaslighting activity. Zinn's description comes from the idea behind the immortal and somewhat mythical quote about having to "destroy the town in order to save it," as a U.S. Army Major is said to have characterized the USAF bombing of Ben Tre during the Vietnam War.

"… to bring civilization, or democracy, or liberty to the rest of the world, by violence if necessary…" as Zinn refers to U.S. propaganda, is a cynical and irrational calculation not unlike the t-shirt that proclaims: "The Beatings Will Continue Until Morale Improves."

[6]Fleischacker, Samuel, "Adam Smith's Moral and Political Philosophy", *The Stanford Encyclopedia of Philosophy* (Spring 2017 Edition), Edward N. Zalta (ed.). https://plato.stanford.edu/archives/spr2017/entries/smith-moral-political/

The author explains that Adam Smith believes in deriving morals from the local source where people live and not from ideas outside their daily lived experience, and that leads Smith to also believe that the people can be trusted to know what they want. This is a humanistic ideal – self-determination; it is distinct from having a deity-in-charge as in the premodern era. It is worse with politicians in charge who don't represent but manage us, and it's much worse when corporate leaders are in-charge [**Emphasis added**]:

> Smith's writings are permeated by a lack of respect for the sorts of people who go into politics: for the vanity that leads them to seek fame and power, for the presumption by which they regard themselves as morally superior to others, and for the arrogance by which they think they

know the people's interests and needs better than the people do themselves. He also believes that politicians tend to be manipulated by the preaching of merchants who do not have the good of the nation as a whole at heart (WN 266–7), and that they can rarely know enough to guide large numbers of people. Correlatively, **Smith has a great respect for the competence and virtue of common people. He shows no trace of the thought, common at the time and strongly held by Hutcheson, that a class of wise and virtuous people ought to rule over the common herd.**

[7]Boas, T.C., Gans-Morse, J. "Neoliberalism: From New Liberal Philosophy to Anti-Liberal Slogan." *St Comp Int Dev* 44, 137–161 (2009). https://doi.org/10.1007/s12116-009-9040-5

This article is a must-read. The authors begin with:

The meaning and proper usage of neoliberalism curiously have elicited little scholarly debate. Based on a content analysis of 148 journal articles published from 1990 to 2004, we document three potentially problematic aspects of neoliberalism's use: the term is often undefined; it is employed unevenly across ideological divides; and it is used to characterize an excessively broad variety of phenomena. To explain these characteristics, we trace the genesis and evolution of the term neoliberalism throughout several decades of political economy debates. We show that neoliberalism has undergone a striking transformation, from a positive label coined by the German Freiberg School to denote a moderate renovation of classical liberalism, to a normatively negative term associated with radical economic reforms in Pinochet's Chile.

...

One compelling indicator of the term's negative connotation is that virtually no one self-identifies as a neoliberal, even though scholars frequently associate others—politicians, economic advisors, and even fellow academics—with this term.

...

Related to neoliberalism's negative normative valence is the fact that it often denotes a radical, far-reaching application of free-market economics unprecedented in speed, scope, or ambition.

[8]John Perkins, *Confessions of an Economic Hit Man*, (New York: A Plume Book, published by Penguin Group, 2004).

The central claim of the book can be found in italics on page one of the preface. This book reads like a fictional John Grisham novel and is easy to read from start to finish in one sitting. He explains that his job was to sell (like a common salesman) loans to undeveloped third-world nations so they could join the developing and developed nations in globalism.

These nations would get cash from the IMF, World Bank, US AID, and elsewhere to fund infrastructure projects such as airports, roads, electrical grid systems, water and sewer systems, communications systems, and hotels and "green zones" in cities where multinational corporations' staff would stay when conducting business.

The infrastructure was necessary for multinational

corporations to 1) set up shop and function as colonial powers extracting the natural resources of the nation using cheap local labor and 2) to manufacture goods cheaply for export back to the home countries. The evil in the plan was that the Economic Hitmen would sweet-talk the poor nations into debt that they knew the nations could never pay back – John Perkins was a very competent snake oil salesman by his own admission.

The loan contracts had provisions stating that in the event a nation defaulted on the loans, then they could repay the loans by free transfer of their nations' natural resources, which benefitted the corporations and happened in nearly all the cases to varying degrees. This was a stitch-up, an evil scheme designed to take advantage of the undeveloped nations.

Perkins goes on to explain that if he and his crew were unsuccessful in talking a nation into the loans, then they would step aside and the U.S. and its European partners would send in the jackals who are strongmen enforcers working for the espionage and security/ defense services. Jackals would conduct special operations to take down leaders and install puppet dictators such as Augusto Pinochet of Chile, Mohammad Reza Pahlavi (the Shah of Iran), and others. Lastly, Perkins explains that when the Jackals fail, they just go to war as they did trying to oust Saddam Hussein.

The problem Perkins ran into is that the claims run counter to the public relations messages that the U.S. and European partners put out about being morally upstanding and working solely for an ethical system of democracy and capitalism for peace, freedom, liberty, and justice for all. The conniving special operations done by the first-world nations have been easily hidden by the false claims that the world's superpower and its allies are uniformly "good" and have the highest ethical standards. Of course, this is what every king and privateer thought when they went about the globe punking native peoples and terrorizing them under the regime of colonialism.

[9]David Korten, *The Great Turning* (Oakland: Kumarian Press & Berret-Koehler Publishers, Inc., 2006).

The author explains that people develop through different stages of life, with youths defined as "Imperial individuals," with the hopeful expectation that maturity would lead to outgrowing such a state. He decries the fact that too many people never grow out of this state, causing problems with the control people have over power.

[10]   William Shakespeare, "Twelfth Night," 1602, a quote by Malvolio that made the play famous.

[11]   My reversal of Shakespeare's quote by Malvolio: "Some are born inferior, some achieve inferiority and the rest must have inferiority thrust upon them" can be seen in a evolutionary biology context in which thrusting inferiority upon others is done by men in the course of their efforts to match wits with women. This explanation is at the heart of any neocon or neolib effort.

A General Theory Of Testosterone:

Why men concentrated so much testosterone and grew to

be so big and tall: men had to adopt an imperial evolutionary path to try and match wits with women, to compensate for the inherent power of women. Women give birth to humans; they have the greatest power of the universe in them, the power of life. To see a woman give birth is to see that raw power like a lion personified, roaring. To see your son or daughter come out of your wife, is among all things, the greatest humbling experience.

To match wits with women on this level is impossible in every way, thought man, but one day it occurred to him in the back of his evolutionary brain that killing was the equal power of birth, and with that, he could match wits with the power women have. Man killed any and everything to show he was powerful too. He killed deer, bear, bison, fish, and sheep. He fought lions and tigers while riding elephants. He has waged war with other men to show his power to kill en masse, therefore trying to upstage women's power. He has taken steroids to augment his vast reserves of testosterone that occur in him, and he's worked out to rip his muscles.

He came to the opinion that owning her was not only equivalent to having her power, but that in fact, it was better, because he did not have to go through the work carrying, birthing, and raising the children, and that fishing and hunting were much more fun. Man saw his wife as a baby appliance that spat out future workers and wealth builders. Testosterone poisoning such as this was the birth of patriarchy, sexism, and misogyny. Today, neocons and neolibs see all of us as appliances of one kind or another, and they'll either dump or recycle us (respectively) as soon as they can get their robot appliances working. Inferior, indeed!

Chapter 7

[1]Ron Suskind, "Without a Doubt: Faith, Certainty and the Presidency of George W. Bush," *New York Times Magazine*, October 17, 2004, https://www.nytimes.com/2004/10/17/magazine/faith-certainty-and-the-presidency-of-george-w-bush.html

[2]Walter Lippmann was famous for going on and on about how the populace was ill-informed and therefore incapable of governing itself. It's as if we were like children who couldn't possibly have the knowledge and wisdom to raise ourselves. He believed that the media was incapable of educating the populace in such a manner that they could cast informed votes, and so he felt like democracy was not only a failed ideal to seek, but that the populace needed strong, considerate, and reasoned leadership.

It's important to note that Reality Creators are of the absolute opinion that we are so uninformed that we don't even know we couldn't survive without the bosses: we're ignorant of our ignorance and can't even contemplate the limits of our abilities. Again, since we have lost the vast skillset to technology that our ancestors developed over the past 12,000+ years, we are dependent on that technology and the owners of it. We have become supplicants and the Reality Creators are prescient enough to recognize this and take advantage of our pronated and diminished circumstance.

Perhaps today the populace is too contented to know any better, to know that they are not free, and the Reality

Creators would rather keep it that way. Most of all, the bosses would very much like to keep their stature as Reality Creators hidden from us.

[3]Alan Moore, "The Mindscape of Alan Moore," Shadowsnake Films, 2003.

Mr. Moore writes comic books and graphic novels. He is among the best authorities on fiction.

[4]Scott Nearing, *The Next Step: A Plan for Economic World Federation* (Chicago: Hammond Press W.B. Conkey Company, 1922).

[5]Price, Carter C. and Kathryn A. Edwards, "Trends in Income From 1975 to 2018". Santa Monica, CA: *RAND Corporation*, 2020. https://www.rand.org/pubs/working_papers/ WRA516-1.html.

OK, so here's a shout out to the Reality Creators who pulled a $50 trillion heist:

The Reality Creators who decided that enough was enough after four decades of socialist policies from the 1930s up to 1970 were prescient and greedy; wise and selfish. They saw the enormous amount of wealth U.S. worker-consumers were creating through their vast production and commensurate increases in productivity and consumption. They thought that the capacity for inflation was a long-term concern that would reduce the value of their investments and financial holdings.

They figured that if they could divert the money away from the populace, not only would they get the money for themselves, but they would also stem the inflation they thought was coming because the rich don't spend their money like the rest of us; they hold onto it. For example, if the $50 trillion they took from the bottom 90% since 1970 had remained in circulation among the populace, the bottom 90% would have had twice as much money to spend on goods and services. The cash among the populace would have driven up the price of everything, which would have made the bank accounts and investments of the very wealthiest people worth much less. So, to counteract leveling the class structure, the wealthiest power brokers wrote laws to make legal their skimming off the bottom 90% of people and taking that money out of their hands. They took that money and drove up the stock market, buried lots of it on Nicholas Shaxson's "Treasure Islands," and they invested in land, yachts, jewels, art, and other ephemera that effectively kept the money from ever entering the so-called real economy.

To fully appreciate this, imagine that there are two different currencies, one that consists of denominations in the ones, tens, hundreds, and thousands, and another that consists of denominations in the millions, billions, and trillions. Sure, all this money is from the Federal Reserve, but the money in the higher denomination is so vast – so much larger by orders of magnitude – it is its own currency that we the people never trade in. This has the effect of creating two very distinct economies, one where 90% of the people has 20% of the wealth, and 10% has the other 80% of the wealth. In reality, this plays out in gated communities, elite private schools, very expensive haute couture, and a rarified existence far away from the crowds. The rest of us live in degrading towns, cities, and rural areas bereft of decent infrastructure, good schools, safe neighborhoods, and halfway decent goods and services. It really is as if the wealthiest live in the farmhouse, and we live out in the barnyard. We get food-like substances* sprayed with pesticides, and they get delicious organic food.

(*Michael Pollen's term)

[6]Zeynep Tufekci, "Twitter and Tear Gas: The Power and Fragility of Networked Protest," (New Haven: Yale University Press, 2017)

Tufekci explains how sowing doubt – plausible deniability – can be immobilizing and confusing to citizens who wish to understand their world, the society they live in. She explains the long renowned history by corporations and governments to counter populism:

> This tactic of sowing doubt as a means of forestalling opposition certainly predates the internet. Sowing doubt occurs through natural polarization in the populace (when each side challenges the other), grassroots efforts (organized campaigns), astroturfing (when corporations or governments pay people to create the appearance of grassroots efforts), direct nation-state intervention, or direct corporate campaigns.

The author goes on to explain that: "A 1969 memo by a tobacco industry executive was titled "Doubt Is Our Product," and it was a successful product."

This demonstrates how brazen and visible corporations have been about their efforts to control the fabricated media narrative in their capacity as Reality Creators. The cliché, *We Can Neither Confirm Nor Deny*, made famous by the CIA in 1975, has been around and in use since the early twentieth century. This cynical term has been employed to sow doubt for the express purpose of cultivating confusion.

The author goes on to explain that [**Emphasis added**]:

> **Confusion and doubt do not have the same effects on those in power as on the movements that challenge power; there is a fundamental asymmetry.** Social movements, by their nature, attempt change and call for action, but doubt leads to inaction that perpetuates the status quo. The paralysis and disempowerment of doubt leads to the loss of credibility, spread of confusion, inaction and withdrawal from the issue by ordinary people, depriving movements of energy. **If everything is in doubt, while the world is run by secret cabals that successfully manipulate everything behind the scenes, why bother?**" pp. 250-251

The author notes that: "Governments and powerful people also expend great efforts to control the public sphere in their own favor because doing so is a key method through which they rule and exercise power." pg. 8

When corporations and governments seek to control the public sphere by sowing doubt, they do so as a function of the corporate-government complex in full view of the public with nothing to hide. They are not functioning as "secret cabals that successfully manipulate everything behind the scenes." It's important to make the distinction, as the author alludes to but does not say, that the corporate-government complex seeks to promote the false narrative of a so-called "secret cabal" in order to whip up conspiracy theory ideology for the express purpose of further casting aspersions on those who would think such tripe, further confusing the message: the messenger is crazy.

And now for a dose of irony:

Dexter Filkins, "The Deep State," *The New Yorker Magazine*, March 12, 2012. https://www.newyorker.com/magazine/2012/03/12/the-deep-state

Filkins explains the concept, *Deep State*, before Donald Trump ruined it four years later and destroyed its meaning and credibility like he has so many other ideas. Filkins explains that:

> Erdoğan, for his part, feared the resistance of what is commonly referred to as *derin devlet*, the "deep state." The deep state is a presumed clandestine network of military officers and their civilian allies who, for decades, suppressed and sometimes murdered dissidents, Communists, reporters, Islamists, Christian missionaries, and members of minority groups—anyone thought to pose a threat to the secular order, established in 1923 by Mustafa Kemal, or Atatürk. The deep state, historians say, has functioned as a kind of shadow government, disseminating propaganda to whip up public fear or destabilizing civilian governments not to its liking.

Interestingly, 1923 is the year Tufekci notes her grandmother was born in Turkey. She discusses how the nature of isolation and communication changed: "The new central government, born from the ashes of the crumbling

Ottoman Empire, was intent on modernizing the country and emulating European systems. It pushed to build schools and standardize education." This was Mustafa Kemal's government, controlled in part, by the *derin devlet.* Tufekci might know first hand the existence of the so-called "secret cabals" she references in her book; this suggests they are not secret at all, that the Deep State is not unknown; rather, it is simply unelected. **This point can't be emphasized enough: people confuse *unknown* with *unelected*, so they think what goes on is behind closed doors, when in fact, most of it all is simply by people who do not represent the voters' interests and therefore feels like or appears as if it's being done by some clandestine manner.**

The early-mid twentieth century in Turkey was an opening-up and democratizing era emulating European secular culture and democratic politics. This era is the birth of the modern espionage services, Edward Bernays' systematic propaganda that shaped the way the era appeared, and the manufacture of the consent of the populace first stated by Bernays' mentor, Walter Lippmann, and later made famous by Edward Herman and Noam Chomsky. All of this activity has gone on without the consent of the governed, the hired worker, nor the consumer. None of it has the force of or mandate by a vote of the populace; all of it has been done to them in the wide open. This is why it seems clandestine and done by secret cabals. The era of openness is marked not by hiding and colluding but by confusion and competition.

[7]Andy Newman, "My Frantic Life as a Cab-Dodging, Tip-Chasing Food App Deliveryman," *New York Times,* July 21, 2019, https://www.nytimes.com/2019/07/21/

nyregion/doordash-ubereats-food-app-delivery-bike.html

The author explains:

> My interactions with customers were minimal, too. In fancy new apartment buildings and airy open-plan offices, young professional-looking people opened their doors just long enough to grab the food and mouth thanks.

> This is the frictionless economy we've become reliant on: Tap your phone five times and a peanut-butter açaí bowl appears at your door. The only task left for human laborers is the physical transfer of goods.

> . . .

> In between came a lunch delivery to a Class A office building in Midtown. I was sent to a service entrance where a fellow deliveryman led me down a dumpster-lined corridor to a crammed holding pen where couriers huddled in near-silence, food packs on their backs.

> I had stumbled through a dystopian portal. I thought of what a colleague had said the day before: "You're one step above an Amazon drone." I thought of something Professor van Doorn had said, that the couriers' real value to the app companies is in the data harvested like pollen as we make our rounds, data that will allow them to eventually replace us with machines.

[8]John Stuart Mill, *On Liberty* (Oxford: Oxford University Press, 1859), pg. 23.

We're supposed to be at liberty to do as we please so long

as we do not harm others and so long as others are free from our actions if they so choose to be. Politics circles this issue of what it means to be at liberty to live free from the affects of others whenever, wherever, and however everyone chooses. Throughout history, political arguments have centered around what is harmful, and judicial decisions have always been about determining if harm has been done.

Chapter 8

[1]Written By Associated Press, Tuesday, October 2, 2012, Coquille, Ore. (AP)

From the Article:

Oregon authorities are investigating how a farmer was eaten by his hogs. Terry Vance Garner, 69, never returned after he set out to feed his animals last Wednesday on his farm near the Oregon coast, the Coos County district attorney said Monday.

A family member found Garner's dentures and pieces of his body in the hog enclosure several hours later, but most of his remains had been consumed, District Attorney Paul Frasier said. Several of the hogs weighed 700 pounds or more.

It's possible Garner had a medical emergency, such as a heart attack, or was knocked over by the animals, then killed and eaten, Frasier said, adding that at least one hog had previously bitten Garner.

The possibility of foul play is being investigated as well. "For all we know, it was a horrific accident, but it's so doggone weird that we have to look at all possibilities,"

Frasier told The Register-Guard. A pathologist was unable to identify a cause or manner of death, the newspaper reported. The remains will be examined by a forensic anthropologist at the University of Oregon.

Terry Garner was "a good-hearted guy" who cared for several huge adult sows and a boar named Teddy, said his brother, Michael Garner, 75, of Myrtle Point. Piglets were typically sold to local 4-H kids. "Those animals were his life," Michael Garner said. "He had all kinds of birds, and turkeys that ran all over the place. Everybody knew him."

Michael Garner said one of the large sows bit his brother last year when he accidentally stepped on a piglet. "He said he was going to kill it, but when I asked him about it later, he said he had changed his mind," the brother said.

Domestic hogs are not typically known to be as aggressive as their feral cousins, but "there is some degree of danger associated with any animal," John Killefer, who heads the Animal and Rangeland Sciences Department at Oregon State University in Corvallis, told the newspaper.

[2]From: http://www.agclassroom.org/gan/timeline/farmers_land.htm
Now at: https://growinganation.org/

1790 Total population: 3,929,214, farmers 90% of labor force;

1840 Total population: 17,069,453, farm population: 9,012,000 (est.), farmers 69% of labor force;

1900 Total population: 75,994,266, farm population: 29,414,000 (est.), farmers 38% of labor force, Number of farms: 5,740,000, average acres: 147;

1950 Total population: 151,132,000, farm population: 25,058,000, farmers 12.2% of labor force, Number of farms: 5,388,000, average acres: 216, irrigated acres: 25,634,869;

1990 Total population: 261,423,000, farm population: 2,987,552, farmers 2.6% of labor force, Number of farms: 2,143,150, average acres: 461; irrigated acres: 49,404,000 (1992).

The trend here is the very beginning of an arc-like shape, where from 1790 to 1840, the population quadrupled, and the number of farmers dropped by 20% of that growing population: people began to specialize in non-farm activities. The arc has continued to ascend through to the present, with no official speculation when the term "Post Agrarian Society" will signal the beginning of the slide down, although it is likely to have already happened.

Also:

Sarah Gilbert, *Daily Finance*, 07/20/08:

According to the USDA, 5,382,162 farms dotted the nation in 1950, but this number had declined to 2,121,107 by the 2003 farm census (data from the 2007 census hasn't yet been published). Ninety-one percent of the U.S. farms are small family farms, but the percentage of crop value produced by these farms is only 27%. Large-scale family farms (those with over $250,000 in annual sales) represented most of the farm value produced, but it's worth noting that commercial farms make up only 1.7% of the total but 14% of the value.

[3]Earl Butz, appointed Secretary of Agriculture by President Nixon, promoted the revision to the Farm Bill that turned a traditional food-based farming lifestyle into the monocropping industry of today, producing unlimited corn, soy, rice, and wheat into a profit center for the chemical, seed, farm machinery, processing, distribution, marketing, and feeding industries. Plant more, Butz thought, and sell more of everything else.

This is the original "Supply Side" like how you'd say "Original Gangster." Now, with pressure for unlimited commodity supply, the industry made many cheap sales all over the world, dropping prices below market capacity. The US government subsidies propped up the system to cover expenses to those selling below cost. Today, feeding humans is a huge and profitable industry, and the premise is to feed them as much as possible in the cheapest way: it's a giant hay rack for two-legged livestock.

[4]Lindsey P Smith, Shu Wen Ng, and Barry M Popkin, "Trends in US home food preparation and consumption: analysis of national nutrition surveys and time use studies from 1965–1966 to 2007–2008," *US National Library of Medicine, National Institutes of Health*, April 11, 2013, https://www.ncbi.nlm.nih.gov/pmc/articles/PMC3639863/

From the paper:

American diets have shifted towards decreased nutrient density with less than 20 percent meeting USDA guidelines for a healthy diet, including fruits, vegetables, whole grains and low-fat dairy. US consumers increasingly consume foods from away-from-home sources including fast food, cafeterias, and restaurants. In fact, one recent paper showed that for children, half of all energy from fast food is consumed at home, demonstrating that even foods consumed within the home are not necessarily home-cooked. Alongside an increase in eating out, people spend less time in food preparation, with an approximate halving of time for women and a small increase for men, a trend which continued into the 21st century. Unsurprisingly, lack of time is reported as a major barrier to preparing nutritious meals, prompting people to "buy" time through the purchase of convenience foods which are often sold ready-to-eat or requiring minimal preparation. The shift towards increased grazing and snacking also decreases time spent cooking, as people reach for portable pre-packaged snacks instead of eating meals.

[5]Eric Schlosser, *Fast Food Nation, The Dark Side of the All-American Meal* (New York: Houghton Mifflin C, 2000).

The author writes:

In 1970, Americans spent about $6 billion on fast food; in 2000, they spent more than $110 billion. Americans now spend more money on fast food than on higher education, personal computers, computer software, or new cars. They spend more on fast food than on movies, books, magazines, newspapers, videos, and recorded music - combined. And that on any given day in the United States, about one-quarter of the adult population visits a fast food restaurant.

In endnote #2, Chapter 8 above, the arc is referenced here in the way most people eat.

[6]Michael Pollan, *In Defense of Food, An Eaters Manifesto* (New York: Penguin, 2009).

Here, the author explains how the perimeter of the grocery store is where the majority of single-ingredient items are, and towards the center are where the most highly processed, multi-ingredient items are.

[7] Ibid.

"Shake the hand that feeds you." The author recommends getting to know who grows and distributes your food, recommending this as a way to ensure we eat food grown, raised, and distributed locally.

[8]"Structure and Finances of U.S. Farms: 2005 Family Farm Report" / EIB-12 -- *Economic Research Service*/ USDA;

U.S. Farms: Numbers, Size, and Ownership; USDA, *Economic Research Service*, "1989 and 1995 Farm Costs and Returns Survey and 2003 Agricultural Resource Management Survey, Phase III."

[9]James Cave, Lifestyle Staff Writer, "10 Food Things We Definitely Don't Want To See Anymore," *Huffington Post*, 12/28/2015.

For one perspective on the attitudes and behaviors that have changed, here's Jennifer Gorman from Evanston, Illinois, commenting on the article regarding the food-substitute she drinks instead of eating food-like substances:

Going to have to disagree with you on Soylent. I keep a stock around - every meal doesn't have to be a celebration, and as a single adult I don't have the desire or time to sit and make myself meals that I'll be eating as leftovers for days. I dislike prep and dislike the cleanup. So Soylent 2.0 has been a great option for me. Easily replaced my workday breakfast and all those lunches where I could only bother with Lean Pockets and chips. It might not be for you, doesn't mean it's not a useful idea for others.

Also:

Farhad Manjoo, "Personal Tech, State of the Art," "The Soylent Revolution Will Not Be Pleasurable," New York Times, May 28, 2014:

About a week and a half ago, I began drinking Soylent every day. I can't recommend that you do the same. For a purported breakthrough with such grand plans for reshaping the food industry, I found Soylent to be a punishingly boring, joyless product. From the plain white packaging to the purposefully bland, barely sweet flavor to the motel-carpet beige hue of the drink itself, everything about Soylent screams function, not fun. It may offer complete nourishment, but only at the expense of the aesthetic and emotional pleasures many of us crave in food.

...

Mr. Rhinehart [inventor of Soylent] offered a canny defense for the criticism that Soylent is leaching the joy out of food. "Obviously there's a lot more to food than nutrition," he said. "We don't expect people to live on this entirely. In fact, we think this elevates food into more of a leisure activity. You can go out with your friends or family, and if your default, staple meal is very healthy and sustainable and balanced, you can enjoy your other meals even more, because you don't have to worry about how healthy they are."

[10]   Dr. Nafeez Ahmed, "Nasa-funded Study: Industrial Civilisation Headed for 'Irreversible Collapse'," *Earth Insight*, The Guardian, March 14, 2014.

[Emphasis Added]

A new study sponsored by Nasa's Goddard Space Flight Center has highlighted the prospect that global industrial civilisation could collapse in coming decades due to unsustainable resource exploitation and increasingly unequal wealth distribution.

Noting that warnings of 'collapse' are often seen to be fringe or controversial, the study attempts to make sense of compelling historical data showing that "the process of rise-and-collapse is actually a recurrent cycle found throughout history." Cases of severe civilisational disruption due to "precipitous collapse - often lasting centuries - have been quite common.

...

It finds that according to the historical record even advanced, complex civilisations are susceptible to collapse, raising questions about the sustainability of modern civilisation:

"The fall of the Roman Empire, and the equally (if not more) advanced Han, Mauryan, and Gupta Empires, as well as so many advanced Mesopotamian Empires, are all testimony to the fact that advanced, sophisticated, complex, and creative civilizations can be both fragile and impermanent."

...

Modeling a range of different scenarios, Motesharri and his colleagues conclude that under conditions "closely reflecting the reality of the world today... we find that collapse is difficult to avoid." In the first of these scenarios, civilisation:

"...appears to be on a sustainable path for quite a long time, but even using an optimal depletion rate and starting with a very small number of Elites, **the Elites eventually consume too much, resulting in a famine among Commoners that eventually causes the collapse of society**. It is important to note that this Type-L collapse is due to an inequality-induced famine that causes a loss of workers, rather than a collapse of Nature."

Another scenario focuses on the role of continued resource exploitation, finding that "with a larger depletion rate, the decline of the Commoners occurs faster, while the Elites are still thriving, but eventually the Commoners collapse completely, followed by the Elites."

...

Applying this lesson to our contemporary predicament,

the study warns that:

"While some members of society might raise the alarm that the system is moving towards an impending collapse and therefore advocate structural changes to society in order to avoid it, Elites and their supporters, who opposed making these changes, could point to the long sustainable trajectory 'so far' in support of doing nothing."

The two key solutions are to reduce economic inequality so as to ensure fairer distribution of resources, and to dramatically reduce resource consumption by relying on less intensive renewable resources and reducing population growth:

"Collapse can be avoided and population can reach equilibrium if the per capita rate of depletion of nature is reduced to a sustainable level, and if resources are distributed in a reasonably equitable fashion."

The NASA-funded HANDY model offers a highly credible wake-up call to governments, corporations and business - and consumers - to recognize that 'business as usual' cannot be sustained, and that policy and structural changes are required immediately.

[11]   Janet McConnaughey, "Hundreds of Donkeys Abandoned In Lingering Drought," *Associated Press*, March 29, 2012. https://www.capitalpress.com/ag_sectors/hundreds-of-donkeys-abandoned-in-lingering-drought/article_b7fb314f-e515-5bd2-a5cd-1414f3bb7318.html

With pastures withered from a lingering drought,

farmers in Texas and northwest Louisiana have abandoned donkeys by the hundreds, turning them into wandering refugees that have severely tested animal rescue groups.

The nation's biggest donkey rescue group says that since March 2011, it has taken in nearly 800 donkeys abandoned in Texas, where ranchers mainly used the animals to guard their herds. Many of the cattle and goats have been sold off, largely because of the drought and the nation's economic slump, putting the donkeys out of a job.

And although the drought that began in late 2010 is over now, the flood of donkeys continues, said Mark Meyers, executive director of Peaceful Valley Donkey Rescue.

"Last week I spent two days on the road and got 20 donkeys each day," he said Wednesday. Since then, he's had a call of about 12 more in the Midlands, Texas, area.

. . .

Texas ranchers use female donkeys to guard remote herds of livestock, said Kathy Dean, CEO and founder of Longhopes Donkey Shelter in Bennett, Colo. They're docile, friendly, and don't eat like a horse, she said.

However, the animals are instinctively hostile to dogs and their cousins: wolves and coyotes. "They will bray, bare their teeth, run and chase, and attempt to bite and kick an intruder," according to a Colorado State University fact sheet. In 1989, it said, 1,000 to 1,800 of 11,000 Texas sheep and goat producers used guard donkeys.

While Peaceful Valley has about 1,850 rescued donkeys in Texas, California and Oklahoma, Longhopes has a total of about 40 at any one time. It's among a handful of donkey rescues around the country, Meyers said.

. . .

Turning Pointe Donkey Rescue in Dansville, Mich., usually has about 20 to 25 animals at a time, said president Sharon Windsor. She said she was recently asked if she could take 44 from Texas.

The number was likely to increase because none of the jacks was castrated and "they're all running around together," she said. Nor was that the only problem. To be adoptable, donkeys must be friendly and trained.

"Some of these donkeys are wilder than a March hare," Windsor said.

These donkeys hardly seem like they can't take care of themselves. The turned out donkeys are doing fine; they are tough, and similar to what Hobbes said of ancient humans, the donkey's lives are: "solitary, poor, nasty, brutish, and short." But the people can't deal with the animals' wild freedom and need to round them all up and put them back in pens. Their biggest complaint, found in the full text of the article, is not having the ability to send them to slaughterhouses.

Because these donkeys are free, roaming wild, and uncontrolled, that they are unsettling to the humans who must control everything in their environment, civilize everything, and in the case of animals, either domesticate them or hunt them down. These animals are content to be set free; it's the people who can't deal with it. The article explains how well adapted the donkeys are to the rough terrain, yet they still get picked up by rescue missions or are hunted down by authorities. It's a sign of the times that such competent and defensive and tough creatures that are like guard dogs need to be rescued.

Chapter 9

[1]Nassim Nicholas Taleb, *The Black Swan* (New York: Random House, 2010).

The author is recognized as bringing the theory of the "Black Swan" to greater popularity, although many have discussed the idea for quite some time.

[2]Based on a description found in Wikipedia.

http://en.wikipedia.org/wiki/Black_swan_theory

[3]The "Freedom Tower" has been renamed "One World Trade Center," with the emphasis put on "One World Trade," the ultimate in free trade.

It is curious to think of the notion a "Freedom Tower" is the center of free-trade when one considers that the USA, the world's superpower, wants to trade for free given that the nation is 5% of the world's population but consumes 30% of the natural resources dug up and drilled annually. The tower is a symbol of freedom to trade on America's terms. Any nation getting in the way of this freedom risks being attacked in yet another resource war. The colonial nations sent privateers to go about taking and trading however they pleased and raked in human and natural resources at the tip of a spear. Today, the U.S. garrisons troops in 150 nations to do exactly the same thing but with a slightly different process.

[4]http://en.wikipedia.org/wiki/Spiro_Agnew

The term "nattering nabobs of negativism" was written by William Safire for Vice-President Spiro Agnew to deride Vietnam War protesters and members of the media. Today, it is used to describe anyone who complains without offering up solutions and is typically quoted as "nattering nabob of negativity" when a specific person is referenced.

[5]Nancy Isenberg, *White Trash: The 400-Year Untold History of Class in America* (New York: Penguin Books Random House, LLC, 2016).

In this exhaustive look at the racist attitudes directed at poor whites from the Jamestown settlement to the present, the author depicts the ease with which poor whites have been denigrated and discriminated against. She argues they have been lambasted for being responsible for their circumstance as an inherent, congenital defect as opposed to being subject to powerful negative circumstances beyond their control.

The biggest problem the Reality Creators had with this huge population of poor whites was figuring out how to exploit them because they were seen as shiftless trash. Africans were easily capitalized on due to their enslavement, but poor whites, being "free," were useless. After the Civil War, the poor whites attacked the African-Americans because they viewed them as unworthy of the scarce resources the poor whites lacked. While this violence has only dissipated to a degree since the Civil Rights movement 100 years later, it was the end of slavery that got the Reality Creators working on how to exploit both disenfranchised groups.

[6]Rowan Williams, "A Lesson for (and From) a Dystopian World: Power is where natural and human energy meet. For better or for worse," *New York Times Opinion*, May 26, 2019. https://www.nytimes.com/2019/05/26/opinion/a-lesson-in-power-dystopian-world.html

[7]Eugene Weber, *Peasants into Frenchmen*, (Stanford: Stanford University Press, 1976).

In this ground-breaking work, the author described in the most comprehensive detail the changes from the late nineteenth to the early twentieth century, a transformation of rural France into a modern civilized era. The scope of this work cannot be overstated, and if there ever was a feeling that one cannot go back in history, go back to the way things were, then the inexorable change Weber explains about the modernization of the peasants does just that. His thesis is the ultimate proof that time flows in one direction and that culture evolves on the path of the progression of time. Any reversions back to peasantry lifestyles will only come from a total disruption of the culture and society as time continues its march forward using technology to extract natural resources and fabricate wealth. Weber makes it clear that "back to the land" is a quaint idea that is more like play than real life. When my friend said: "Chris, we just play farm," this is what he meant.

[8]Denis Hayes, "Economic Power," *Seattle Weekly*, November 10, 1993, p. 15.

This is a widely known statistic: the USA is 5% of the world's population but consumes 30% of the world's natural resources dug up and drilled annually. Globally, 20% of the world's wealthiest people consume 80% of the natural resources dug up annually, with Europe accounting for about 30% of the total, the same as the USA, but having close to 10% of the world's population, double the U.S. Annie Leonard also makes similar claims in her series, *Story of Stuff*.

[9]Active duty military personnel strengths by regional area and by country, U.S. Department of Defense. 2010.

Chapter 10

[1] Herman E. Daly, *Toward A Steady-State Economy* (San Francisco: W.H. Freeman and Company, 1973), pg. 5

The introduction to this collection of essays explains the rationale for seeking a steady-state economy, including the obvious reason being the depletion of life-supporting resources and pollution of the environment in which we live. He explains that the rate at which we burn through stuff is too fast, and the so-called "throughput" needs to slow down. He also acknowledges that people are growthmaniacs and the generalized concern throughout is that they will stop at nothing trying to accumulate wealth regardless of the consequences. At the end of his introduction, he says: "We no longer speak of "worshipping idols." Instead of "idols" we have an abomination called "GNP..." Instead of "worshipping" the idol, we "maximize" it."

[2] Ibid., pg. 21

In this note, Daly refers to Bertrand Russell's collection of essays, "In Praise of Idleness," that was published after Russell's friend, George Bernard Shaw wrote his work on the political economy, *The Intelligent Woman's Guide to Capitalism and Socialism*, in which Shaw explains how "Wealth Accumulates and Men Decay." In the chapter under that heading, Shaw discusses how the manufacture of straight pins went from a very specialized artisan craft to the mass production of pins during the Industrial Revolution, so Shaw deserves some credit in this discussion, if not more than half. I think there can be no doubt that Russell read Shaw's 400-page book on the topic: it was written for the greater populace, and Russell and Shaw share many similar views on political philosophy. And of course, we must recall Adam Smith wrote about pin manufacturing in his *Wealth of Nations*, published in 1776.

[3]Milton Friedman, "The Social Responsibility Of Business Is to Increase Its Profits," *The New York Times*, September 13, 1970.
https://www.nytimes.com/1970/09/13/archives/a-friedman-doctrine-the-social-responsibility-of-business-is-to.html

Friedman says derisively:

The businessmen believe that they are defending

free enterprise when they declaim that business is not concerned "merely" with profit but also with promoting desirable "social" ends; that business has a "social conscience" and takes seriously its responsibilities for providing employment, eliminating discrimination, avoiding pollution and whatever else may be the catchwords of the contemporary crop of reformers...Businessmen who talk this way are unwitting puppets of the intellectual forces that have been undermining the basis of a free society these past decades.

The discussions of the "social responsibilities of business" are notable for their analytical looseness and lack of rigor. What does it mean to say that "business" has responsibilities? Only people can have responsibilities. A corporation is an artificial person and in this sense may have artificial responsibilities, but "business" as a whole cannot be said to have responsibilities, even in this vague sense. The first step toward clarity in examining the doctrine of the social responsibility of business is to ask precisely what it implies for whom.

Friedman cherry-picks the bits of the narrative found in the legal fiction that is a corporate person, and in so doing, he contradicts a century of corporate law that ensconced the notion that businesses, in fact, do have such social responsibilities. His critique in this article is "notable for [its] analytical looseness and lack of rigor."

Friedman excoriates executives for " undermining the basis of a free society these past decades" when they act not just for pure profit but for public benefit as well. Friedman refuses to accept the value of public benefit activities conducted to mitigate the negative impacts profit-driven corporations impose on society.

Friedman states:

> The political principle that under lies the market mechanism is unanimity. In an ideal free market resting on private property, no individual can coerce any other, all cooperation is voluntary, all parties to such cooperation benefit or they need not participate. There are no "social" values, no "social" responsibilities in any sense other than the shared values and responsibilities of individuals. Society is a collection of individuals and of the various groups they voluntarily form.

Following his logic, an executive could choose to act with social responsibility and let the free market decide if it is going to keep him employed: will the board and shareholders fire the executive because the public is unwilling to work for or shop from the corporation due to the imposition of empathy? But Friedman's logic is that of a fairytale, what with all the pap he dribbles about there even being a free market. There is socialism for the rich and rugged individual capitalism for the rest of us. Friedman espouses socialism by ignoring that plutocrats and their hirelings bend the market to their will and desire: this control makes them fabulously wealthy and powerful. It is their power that enables such control over market forces. By denying the existence of the market manipulation by the Reality Creators while lecturing to the middle-class the market must be free from their expectations is deceitful. The greatest socialist agenda the world has ever seen is the plutocratic control of the government to suit their wealth accumulating needs. Friedman knew this and he blatantly lied for years in his capacity as the prince of right-wing economics to cover it up.

Friedman's article from 1970 inspired individuals to run corporations in as rapacious a way possible, shirking all notions of social responsibility. It was this watershed moment that spawned the "Greed is Good" motto and kicked off the $50 trillion transfer of wealth from the middle and lower classes to the upper class that the recent RAND Corporation study demonstrated that's noted in these endnotes.

[4]This quote is a paraphrase of what an extended family member heard while traveling abroad in the late 1990s. While in Tuscany, he came upon an elderly mushroom collector along a rural road and struck up a brief conversation.

Afterword

[1]Mathias Döpfner, "Elon Musk reveals Tesla's plan to be at the forefront of a self-driving-car revolution — and why he wants to be buried on Mars," *Business Insider*, Dec 5, 2020. https://www.businessinsider.com/elon-musk-interview-axel-springer-tesla-accelerate-advent-of-sustainable-energy

These are excerpts from a meandering and long, indulgent interview that sets the standard for all time what a "Puff Piece" is. *[My interspersed commentary is in italics and brackets.]*

"Going back to what I was saying earlier, I think it is important for humanity to become a spacefaring civilization and a multiplanet species. And it's going to take a lot of resources to build a city on Mars. I want to be able to contribute as much as possible to the city on Mars. That means just a lot of capital.

[We cannot afford to spend such enormous amounts of capital trying to make Mars habitable when we have so many pressing needs on Earth. Exporting capital in this way, which is always derived (and too often exploited) from human and ecological resources, is maniacal and diabolical.]

...

And I'm like, man, how are we going to keep humanity going if you don't have kids? A lot of countries have a negative replacement rate. You can't just solve it with immigration — that's not possible. So, if you believe in humanity at all, you've got to say, we need to make sure we have humans in the future. They don't come from nowhere. A lot of people would say they have the impression that the Earth is overpopulated. This is totally false. And they're just basing this on their immediate impressions because they live in a dense city. Have you gone to the countryside or looked down from an airplane? What percentage of the time, if you dropped a cannonball, would it drop on somebody? Basically zero percent.

[The claim, that the Earth is not overpopulated because one person could drop a cannonball from an airplane and not hit someone else, misses the most basic fact of overpopulation: the

carrying capacity of the Earth to absorb waste and continue producing natural resources is limited and possibly close to its limit. Furthermore, the vast expanses of "flyover country" could never support continuous sprawling suburbs and cities due to a lack of freshwater and the need to locate waste disposal. Food production, energy use, job creation, and healthcare for the billions that could fit in the center mass of the U.S., much less Canada, is utterly impossible and mad. What, on Earth, would all those people do living on the wheat and corn fields, and why would we need them there anyway?]

…

What are the right questions to ask about the universe? And the conclusion I came to is that the more we can expand the scope and scale of consciousness, so that we're better able to ask questions about the answer, that is the universe. This is the right thing to do, I think. This is the thing to help understand what the hell is it all about. Why are we here? I mean, just step back for a second, what's the meaning of life? And that's not even the right question to ask. It's like, how did we get here? Where's it going? You know, all these things. So, we want to increase the scope and scale of consciousness so that we can try to figure out how to answer these questions, and what questions to ask.

[This inquiry is so clichéd and facile, it cannot be the basis for exporting exploited human and natural resources off the planet. This kind of thinking is what stoned teenagers do. As stated in the Afterword to which this endnote attaches: Some say human consciousness and the expansion of it into the universe is the real purpose, the real mission for humanity; however, there are possibly 40 billion earth-like planets in the universe. Frankly,

there's enough consciousness out there not for us to be driven by pride to think ours is needed when we can't even care enough for the consciousness of our grand-babies and their children on this planet.]

…

I'm trying to use technology to maximize the probability that the future is good. And, at a foundational level, that means ensuring we have a future, which is why sustainable energy is so important for the future of Earth. And then becoming a spacefaring civilization and a multiplanet species is important for the future beyond Earth, to ensure, that in a worst-case situation, if there's a World War III or something like that, or global thermonuclear warfare, and maybe all civilization is destroyed on Earth, that at least it continues to exist somewhere else. And, the civilization on Mars that could end up being a stabilizing influence on Earth. But that, just fundamentally like the probability of consciousness as we know it, and life as we know it, lasting for a long time will be dramatically improved if we're a multiplanet species as a spacefaring civilization.

[So, if we nuke ourselves, we enact Plan B to live somewhere else because we're so damn important to…ourselves. That's a big Hell No. *Like the Earth, the universe doesn't give a damn about us. This pontificating is obscene because the humans of the past two centuries have trashed the planet, and the wealthy plutocrats who dream of living on Pluto (or, failing that and Mars, or a bunker on New Zealand) have known in the modern era how destructive they have been and are today. Ask yourself, who are these Plutocrats thinking will journey to live and escape to space? It would be the wealthiest people on Earth, and they*

would use our sweat and human resources, extracting massive amounts of the earth's stored energy to make their holiday to the stars possible. All their money comes from us already doing all the work humanity cranks out every day of the year; now they want us to launch them into space after leading the way trashing the earth? Such pride will never get them to thread the eye of the needle.]

...

The biggest thing is that we are getting to a stage where perhaps our reach extends our grasp. We have all this super-advanced technology, but can we really handle it? This will be the test. This will be a filter for more human civilization: Can we handle the technology and not destroy ourselves? With all these advanced technologies, is it like giving a toddler a shotgun? We've got to make sure we handle this technology in a way that's good for the future. We're going to make sure we have kids so that they as humans continue to exist. We have to think what sort of actions we must take so that the future is good.

[We have not handled the technology well, so there is little reason to believe that we will control the newer, more powerful technology of artificial intelligence and robotics any better. We made nuclear weapons that are always standing by to wipe out the flora and fauna of the Earth; we're poisoning the atmosphere, oceans, and terrestrial ecosystems that we need to survive; we already have over seven billion humans on Earth not to be clamoring for "just a little more," and we, the people, live in a global political economy we do not control and yet rely upon for everything to survive.]

ABOUT THE AUTHOR

Christopher Hall

Christopher Hall's experience in farming and the performing arts combine to create his worldview we're livestock living in a fabricated reality that fences us in.

In boarding school, he learned how the ruling class rear their young. In college, he learned how to make a difference; a few years later, his life mission to cultivate compassionate social action took form. In grad school, he learned how to pursue his mission.

Mr. Hall has worked professionally in the performing arts, fought corruption and subterfuge in redevelopment and regional politics, lived in a big city and in rurally isolated areas, farmed, worked in the nonprofit sector, and extensively researched the machinations of our political economy.

PRAISE FOR AUTHOR

"Hall discusses the imbalance of power in the world with an unsettling, sharp clarity and a brilliant sense of humor...

The book is written with stark honesty and provides a solution to break from the shackles: creating our reality based on facts and compassion for the people. Readers who are curious and who read the current political situation in the US will appreciate this brilliantly written book.

"The Reality Creators" is deeply researched and presented in a way that is both entertaining and thought-provoking, inviting readers to engage in conversations that are frank and that empowers them to take control of the social and political realities. It is written in a voice that is confident and compelling and littered with dread truths that wake readers up, at times brutally."

- KIM CALDERON, THE BOOK COMMENTARY

"Wow. This is well done. The author's intent for writing this piece is clear. The set-up of the book is easy to follow, and the introduction does a good job of telling the reader how to read the material...Reality Creators is an easy read because of how well it is written, yet it is an intense read because of the subject."

- MICHELLE DWYER, BAR CODE GRAPHICS, INC.

"Chris writes in an incredibly, just incredibly intellectual style, not like anyone out there. And to make the writing beautiful too, at the same time, is really an art in itself. At over 300 pages, this is a really condensed book, which could easily have been 10x as long if it was by an average writer. I like writing epics (poems) and varying and imitating styles, but I could never write like this guy - he's one of a kind.

- RHIANNON KIRIN, REVIEWED ON GOODREADS